The Coloured Counties

The Coloured Counties

Literary Landscapes
of the Heart of England

Anthony Gibson

foreword by Peter Benson

FAIRFIELD BOOKS

Fairfield Books
17 George's Road, Bath BA1 6EY
tel 01225-335813

First published 2017

ISBN: 978 0 9568511 8 5

Printed and bound in Great Britain by
CPI Group, Croydon, Surrey

Contents

Here of a Sunday morning
My love and I would lie,
And see the coloured counties,
And hear the larks so high
About us in the sky.

AE Housman

Foreword

Scratch a great writer and you'll discover a landscape. From William Wordsworth's lakes to the Cornwall of Daphne du Maurier, and from Tove Jansson's Finland to George Mackay Brown's Orkney, when you read their work, the words have the power to conjure the sights, sounds, smells and tastes of the places their characters inhabit. Even those writers who, you might think, abhor the idea of being welded to a particular locale (think Proust and his cork-lined room) struggle to avoid the inevitable.

With Magic in My Eyes, Anthony Gibson's book about the literary landscapes of the West Country, established him as a superb chronicler of the relationship between writers and the landscapes that inspired them. This new volume focuses on the counties of the Heart of England, and as he explores Wiltshire, Oxfordshire, Warwickshire and the shires of the Marches, we gain fresh insights and discover new things about some of our country's – and the world's – greatest writers.

As a meld of biography, philosophical tract, fireside travel guide and walking companion, the book is a gem of insight and discernment, but I believe its greatest strength is the author's refusal to be prescriptive. For example, when writing about Edward Thomas's classic poem *Adlestrop*, he writes that 'one of the station signs was salvaged … and is now in the bus shelter in Adlestrop village, but whether that is enough to merit a pilgrimage, only the reader will know.' This reader knows that it definitely is worth the pilgrimage, and would have said so, but Anthony Gibson allows you to make up your own mind.

He's also more than happy to play detective for you, and do the tough leg work. The description of the weather-beaten farms that inspired Bruce Chatwin's masterpiece *On The Black Hill* is precise and definitive, and prompts the reader (this one at least) to return to the original text with new, rekindled interest. And when he states that Shakespeare was 'fundamentally of the country, rather than the town', he places this in historical as well as literary context, stating – for example – that Oberon's brawls in *A Midsummer Night's Dream* are most likely to be blamed on the disastrous harvests the farmers of Warwickshire suffered in the 1590s.

The Coloured Counties inspires the reader to head for the hills (or vales, woods, forests and lanes) that inspired these writers, while at the same encouraging the rediscovery (or discovery for the first time) of some of our country's finest novelists, poets and playwrights. Reading the book from cover to cover is a journey in itself, but if you let it lead you on a real, tramping journey, you are sure to be rewarded with the sights, sounds, smells and tastes that inspired some of England's finest writers. And who knows, maybe be inspired to take up a pen yourself …

Peter Benson
June 2017

SHROPSHIRE

Owen
Housman

Webb

Eliot

Tolkien

WORCESTER-
SHIRE

WARWICK-

Shakespeare

SHIRE

HEREFORD-
SHIRE

Auden

Quiller-
Couch

Wordsworth

Langland

Moore
Archer

Chatwin Masefield

Barrett-Browning

Abercrombie
Gibson
Drinkwater
Brooke Frost Thomas Potter
Foley

Gurney
Harvey

OXFORDSHIRE

Thompson

GLOUCESTERSHIRE

Lee
Mansell

Arnold
Bridges
Graves
Blunden

Scott
Hughes
Chesterton
Betjeman
Hardy

Jerome

Jefferies

Kilvert

WILTSHIRE

8

Introduction

This book is an exploration of how the landscapes of the Heart of England have inspired great literature and a guide as to how we can bring the links between writers and landscapes alive for ourselves on the ground. It is the natural successor to *With Magic in my Eyes – West Country Literary Landscapes*, which focused on the four south-western counties and was published in 2012. This time our canvas is Wiltshire, Gloucestershire, Oxfordshire, Worcestershire, Herefordshire, Warwickshire and Shropshire.

So what is a 'literary landscape'? To me, it is a stretch of countryside that was a powerful inspiration to a creative writer – poet, novelist, playwright or what we might call 'imaginative autobiographer' – and is not just somewhere he or she happened to be born or to have lived. The landscape needs to be integral to the writer's vision, either in itself, or as allegory, or as a prompter of thoughts on themes deeper and wider than the fabric of the countryside in itself. In the context of the seven counties which make up my 'heart of England', it might mean Laurie Lee describing the Slad Valley of his childhood, or AE Housman's 'blue remembered hills', or William Langland standing on the Malvern Hills looking out over seemingly half of England and reflecting on everything that was happening just under the skin of what he could see. By and large, the landscapes we are talking about are rural rather than urban; the natural world, as opposed to the man-made, although the relationship between the two can have a magic of its own, as with the view of Oxford from Boars Hill.

A landscape is much more than the sum of its constituent parts. Yes, trees and fields and hills and valleys are nice to look at, but it is when the memories, the associations and then the imagination get to work that they come to life. To John Masefield, the gap in the copse on top of May Hill caused by a lightning strike made it look for all the world like a ploughman and his team of horses – an image of honest toil in a good cause which is central to his redemptive poem *The Everlasting Mercy*. The trees have been replanted since and the copse has lost its kink, but when we look at it, we can still think of the symbolism of ploughing, or of Christian redemption, or of Masefield himself, or even, for that matter, of Edward Thomas, who wrote his beautiful poem *Words* sitting on the slopes of May Hill, and who would be killed in the First World War less than two years later.

Motorways are a distinctly mixed blessing for a lover of the countryside, but at least those that run through our stretch of country take us past some of the most evocative landscape features. May Hill, ever present to the west of the M5 as you drive north through Gloucestershire, we have already mentioned. On the other side, there are the Cotswolds, the country of the Gloucestershire poets: Laurie Lee, Ivor Gurney, Frank Mansell and Will Harvey. Further on, there is the great bulk of Bredon Hill, with its memories of Housman, John Moore and Fred Archer on your right, and the magnificent Malverns, erupting from the plain like a range of mountains, on your left, bringing to mind Langland, Masefield, Auden and Sir Edward Elgar. If you branch off down the M50, the road takes you right through perhaps the most concentrated (and maybe least likely) literary landscape of them all, the Leadon Valley, which was home to the six 'Dymock poets' for a few magical weeks in the summer of 1914.

Back on the M5, look out for Worm's Ash Hill, with its tall communications mast, on the left, just before the junction with the M42. It was from that hill that AE Housman looked out as a boy to the distant Shropshire Hills; it was that view that inspired *A Shropshire Lad*. If you take the M42, you will soon, as you climb the hill between junctions 1 and 2, be in the Lickey Hills, where JRR Tolkien walked as a boy. Was this country the original for The Shire, juxtaposed with the Mordor of Birmingham? It is an intriguing thought. The M6 north of Birmingham has little to offer, I'm afraid, other than a first glimpse of the Shropshire Hills, in the shape of the grand gateway formed by the Clee Hills to the west. But take the M50 towards Shrewsbury and, once you are past Telford, the landscape is dominated by what looks like the extinct volcano of the Wrekin, with its associations with Housman and the 'fleece' of trees around its summit, which may or may not be heaving.

Nor does our other motorway, the M4, wind its way through North Wiltshire without offering food for literary thought. At the junction for Chippenham, you are in Kilvert country, his rectory of Langley Burrell a few miles south. Further on, beyond Swindon, where a footbridge crosses the motorway, you are a field away from Coate Water, home of and inspiration to Richard Jefferies. And just beyond the junction travelling east, there is the northern flank of the Wiltshire Downs, topped by Liddington Castle where Jefferies would soak up his 'ancient sunlight' and the clump of beech trees which is Liddington Tump.

In every case, it is the associations that bring the landscape to life; that give depth and meaning to the physical appearance. But to understand and appreciate fully a literary landscape, you need to walk through it. With this book, rather than mapping out suggested walks for literary pilgrims to follow, I have instead offered general guidance at the end of each chapter. With most of the landscapes, there are plenty of footpaths and viewpoints from which to choose, and they are not hard to find, if one arms oneself with the relevant OS Explorer map. The more visited any particular landscape may be, the better signposted and the more accessible the footpaths are likely to be, and many of the writers now have their own 'paths', 'ways' and 'trails' which you can find on the relevant websites, as listed at the end of each chapter.

One thing which strikes you immediately about the landscapes is that there are many more hills amongst them than vales. I suppose that was inevitable, given that we are dealing with a relatively heavily populated and intensively farmed – not just now, but historically – chunk of England. The Severn Vale was an inspiration to the Gloucestershire poets, Ivor Gurney and Will Harvey, as was the Leadon Vale, further north, to the Dymock poetic brotherhood. But it is the hills that fire the imagination, both in their own often wild and remote beauty, and in the perspective which they offer of the world at their feet. What could be more obvious to a poet seeking inspiration than to head to the top of the nearest hill?

With our cast of writers, the novelists are heavily outnumbered by the poets and the autobiographers. Shropshire's Mary Webb and Herefordshire's Bruce Chatwin are really the only 'regional' novelists in the Hardy tradition. But you could argue that Laurie Lee's *Cider with Rosie* or Flora Thompson's *Lark Rise to Candleford* are as much works of imagination as they are factual accounts of the writers' early lives, and I make no apology for stretching my definition of a 'creative writer' to include them. Within those parameters I have tried to include every writer of genuine merit to whom real countryside, as opposed to imagined, was a central theme or inspiration. That does mean that there may be what some readers might regard as serious omissions: many of the writers who spent time at Oxford, for example, including Lewis Carroll. Jane Austen hasn't made it, despite her stay at Stoneleigh Abbey, because her landscapes, such as they are, have no great 'genius loci' or sense of place. But I have had to draw the line somewhere, or this would have been a very long book!

What stands out about the poets is how many of them were close contemporaries, producing their best work in what might be called a 20-year radius of the First World War: John Masefield, Ivor Gurney, Will Harvey, Laurie Lee, Robert Graves, Edmund Blunden and all six of the Dymock poets. Partly that was down to the war and the intensity of the emotions which that inspired, not least nostalgia for a seemingly lost rural world. But it might also be argued that that period was a sort of golden age for the English countryside, when the worst of the rural poverty so brilliantly described by Flora Thompson was beginning to recede, yet before mechanisation changed the face of the farmed countryside. As the twentieth century went on, it became harder and harder for poets to wax lyrical about the beauties of England's lowland landscape, as hedges and orchards were grubbed up, farm animals (sheep always excepted) disappeared into big sheds and arable cropping became more and more intensive. It is sad but true that anyone walking through the Leadon Valley these days would struggle to understand what it was, other than their friendship, which drew so many poets to live there or visit in the years running up to the First World War. There are daffodils still in the woods, but the orchards of plums, cherries, pears and apples which were then such a feature of the landscape are long gone, and in the summer months the farm-scape seems to consist of nothing but wall-to-wall oilseed rape and wheat. One can't help feeling that it would break Edward Thomas's heart to see this precious stretch of countryside as it is now.

The plum orchards that used to turn the Vale of Evesham white with their blossom every spring are a shadow of their former selves, and much of the richest land in Herefordshire is now covered in plastic for at least six months of the year. But against that, many of our landscapes are instantly recognisable as the places that the writers described, decades or even centuries ago. The Shropshire hills still look blue from a distance and wild and forbidding close up; the Cotswolds are as golden in summer and bleak in winter as ever; the turf on top of the Malverns is as crisp and springy as it was when John Masefield first walked there in the 1890s; even the walk up to Compass Hill at Hope End, which inspired Elizabeth Barrett Browning to write *The Lost Bower* almost two centuries ago is exactly as she describes it. Some of this continuity is by happy chance, some the result of very conscious conservation, either by purchase or by designation.

In this context, I do have one small protest to register and that concerns the loss of some of the views which inspired our writers, not through development or agricultural intensification, but through a sort of benign neglect. It seems that,

The Long Mynd on a January morning

A view of the Malverns from Banbury Tower

in twenty-first-century Britain, no-one dares to cut down a single tree, and even hedge-laying seems to be frowned upon, for fear of incurring the wrath of the local green lobby. The result is that our conserved landscapes are becoming increasingly overgrown, to the point where you often cannot fully appreciate the landscape features which accounted for their protected status in the first place. The classic example is Laurie Lee's Slad Valley, where the trees now entirely block out the view from the road running up through the valley; and Bull's Cross, which Laurie Lee describes as 'a sort of island of nothing set high above the crowded valleys', has become almost completely overgrown with scrub. The entire valley could do with a jolly good trim, and that goes for several other of our landscapes as well, like Wenlock Edge and the eastern and northern slopes of May Hill. Laurie Lee's Uncle Charlie, the forester, understood the need to manage the countryside to achieve the outcomes you want and that leaving nature to itself, as the re-wilders would like, produces a countryside choked with brambles, bracken, over-grown gappy hedges and scrubby trees.

I am a Westcountryman, born in Devon and living now and for many years past in Somerset. I do know Wiltshire and Gloucestershire reasonably well, from my time with the NFU, and for the last two years of my career I was based at Stoneleigh, just up the road from Stratford-upon-Avon, and spent many an evening cycling or walking through the country of Shakespeare. But Herefordshire and Shropshire were almost entirely undiscovered country to me, and I had only once before walked on either the Malverns or Bredon Hill. The Shropshire Hills were a revelation; so near to the industrial heart of England, yet so wild and remote. The Devil's Chair, on the Stiperstones, does seem to have precisely that air of ominous foreboding that Mary Webb ascribes to it, and in all the exploring that I have done in the course of researching the book, no walk was more exhilarating than tramping across the Long Mynd on a brilliantly sunny, brilliantly snowy January morning. Herefordshire was magical as well, particularly in the contrasts which it offers between some of the richest farming country in all England in the centre of the county and the lowering hills and scattered farmsteads of the border country. Climbing the Cat's Back on Black Hill and looking out, on one side of that precipitous ridge to the Black Mountains of Wales and on the other towards Herefordshire's Golden Valley, was an experience I will never forget. And what could be more uplifting than striding along the Ridgeway on the top of the Wiltshire Downs, in the footsteps of Richard Jefferies, towards the White Horse and Uffington, with lark-song in the skies?

The seven very English counties which are our canvas may not be as celebrated for their natural beauty as the far South-West, nor have they attracted quite so many novelists and poets. But as I discovered in my travels, there are more than enough beautiful places, and more than enough great writers associated with them, to make a literary pilgrimage through the Heart of England a memorable and moving experience.

This book has no pretensions of being an academic study of the relationship between writers and their landscapes. It is born, not of analysis, but of enthusiasm and of love – for the landscapes which make up the beautiful Heart of England, for the writers who have been inspired by those landscapes and for the magic which is created when glorious landscapes and wonderful words come together.

Chapter One
Wiltshire
Richard Jefferies, Francis Kilvert

In the embrace of the sunlight
Richard Jefferies

Richard Jefferies was a countryside writer of quite remarkable influence, and many contradictions. Edward Thomas, Henry Williamson, Walter Besant and William Morris figure among his many disciples and admirers, as have, more recently, John Fowles, Brian Aldiss and Queenie Leavis. Yet he was a strange and rather lonely man, who died young and whose stock-in-trade was agricultural journalism, albeit outstandingly good agricultural journalism. His great ambition was to become a successful novelist, but only the *Bevis* books and, to a lesser extent, *After London* and *Amaryllis at the Fair* have left any mark in that department.

Richard Jefferies
(1848-1887)
The mouthpiece of Nature herself

What sets him apart is his mysticism – his belief that communing with nature could open the door to a different level of existence, which he called the 'soul life' – and his sheer depth of knowledge about the countryside he grew up in and the creatures that inhabited it. His writing could be vivid, precise – or almost incomprehensible; his philosophy by turns inspiring and bizarre; his characters sometimes compelling, often hackneyed. But of his significance to countryside literature overall, there can be no question.

He was born in 1848, on his parents' small farm at Coate, about two miles east of Swindon, and he died of tuberculosis and related conditions in 1887, at the age of just 39. He started his writing life as a journalist, moved on to becoming a celebrated essayist on countryside subjects, wrote two books for boys, one of which, *Bevis, the Story of a Boy*, has become a classic, and dabbled with novels, none of them very good. His magnum opus, certainly as he saw it, was a quasi-autobiography, *The Story of My Heart*, in which he explains at considerable length and with more passion than clarity how by communing with nature he came to know his soul.

As a man and as a writer, he divides opinion. Henry Williamson was one of his greatest admirers:

> *He was a genius, a visionary whose thought and feeling were wide as the human world, prophet of an age not yet come into being – the age of sun, of harmony.*

In a selection of Jefferies' works, with biographical notes published in 1937, Williamson compares his hero with Jesus Christ and, rather less happily, Adolph Hitler!

> *The affinity of Jefferies with Jesus of Nazareth is patent in nearly all his work. If Francis of Assisi is a little brother of the birds, Jefferies of Wiltshire is a little brother of Jesus, of the sun, of clarity, of all things fine and natural and designed and efficient. Jefferies saw with paradise-clearness.*

The reference to Hitler comes in Williamson's introduction to extracts from *The Story of My Heart*:

> *'Probably', wrote Jefferies, 'the whole mode of the thought of nations must be altered before physical progress is possible' – a sentence which (except for the word 'probably') might have come from the autobiography of Adolph Hitler. In this connection, literary criticism of a future age will discover many similarities in these two men. Both grew up solitaries, unaffected by schooling, learning only from the natural self. One withered away; the other acted, and fulfilled himself.*

Jefferies does indeed, in *The Story*, hanker for some modern day 'Caesar or Augustus': 'some far-seeing master-mind, some giant intellect, [who] should arise and sketch out in bold, unmistakeable outlines the grand and noble future that the human race should labour for.' Nonetheless, this particular literary critic would suggest that the comparison says more about Henry Williamson than it does about Richard Jefferies!

The poet Edward Thomas was another who fell under Jefferies' spell, to the extent of writing a biography which at times strays across the boundary into hagiography. 'The words of Jefferies are laced through and through with sunlight and air,' he writes. 'And they have the power of wings. What other mystics have claimed seems true of him – that he is a mouthpiece of Nature herself.'

Not everyone was quite so convinced. Another fine writer about the countryside, John Moore, is particularly dismissive:

> *Jefferies was not a very good writer, though he was sometimes a good journalist; and in his wretched last days when he became preoccupied with his sickness and his soul, he was a very bad writer indeed.*

He also seems to have been a hard man to love. Although it was his father, James, who first introduced the young Richard to the joys of fishing in Coate Reservoir and shooting rabbits, he never really got on with his parents, his mother especially. As a teenager, mooching about in the woods and downs with a notebook and a gun, he cut a lonely, curious figure, much mocked by the locals, who regarded him (and his father James for that matter) as 'nowt of a farmer'. 'Looney Dick' or 'Lazy Loppet', they called him.

'The Jefferies' household, so strange and so unsociable in his habits, was regarded by the neighbours with genuine, if not altogether friendly, amazement,' writes Jefferies' earliest biographer Henry Stephens Salt. 'Not the least surprising figure to the simple village folk was that of Richard Jefferies himself, as he grew up into the tall, lank, shambling youth, indifferent to all the considerations of dress and appearance.'

He did have two younger brothers, Harry and Charlie, and a sister, Sarah, but notwithstanding the fact that Harry features in *Bevis* as the hero's bosom pal, Mark, he doesn't seem to have been particularly close to his siblings. There were friendships – with his cousin James Cox, with whom he embarked on an ill-fated teenage expedition to Russia which got no further than France and, later, with young Mr Frampton, the reporter on the *North Wilts Herald* who got him his start in journalism – but he certainly had no soul mates, in any sense. There is more than a little truth in Salt's suggestion that perhaps the only real friendship he ever had was with the Iron Age 'warrior in the tumulus' with whom he liked to imagine himself communing, high up on Liddington Castle.

Jefferies' marriage to Jessie Baden, a neighbouring farmer's daughter, produced two children, Harold and Phyllis (another son died in infancy), and appears to have been perfectly happy, without ever being central to his largely self-absorbed existence. He was, essentially, a solitary man, never happier than when poking about in the woods, or striding across the North Wiltshire Downs, or even jostling his way through the crowded streets of London, with nothing but his thoughts – and Nature, of course – for company.

But whatever his flaws as a writer or human being, Richard Jefferies cannot be ignored in any discussion of writers, landscapes and the natural world. Much of his output was fundamentally journalistic: the lengthy letters to *The Times* on the condition of farm workers in Wiltshire which first got him noticed; his accounts of life on the Burderop estate, written for the *Pall Mall Gazette* and published as *The Gamekeeper at Home*, *Wild Life in a Southern County*, *The Amateur Poacher* and *Round About a Great Estate*, which established his reputation; and the later, more introspective essays published as *The Life of the Fields* and *Field and Hedgerow* – mostly dictated to his wife – in which, sick and far from home, he pours out his nostalgia for his beloved North Wiltshire countryside. What he really wanted to be, though, was a successful novelist. Even Edward Thomas was forced to accept that his early attempts, with such titles as *The Scarlet Shawl* and *Restless Human Hearts* were embarrassingly bad. 'The adventures of these people are very unreal, and are ill-chosen for the bringing out of their several unremarkable characters,' he laments.

There was, however, this consolation: 'His attempts, however vain, to describe human action and passion led him to search deeps of his own nature that might otherwise have been unsounded; and, almost without value as a whole, his novels were thus an exercise which he could ill have done without.'

It was when Jefferies was drawing on his own experiences that he was at his best as a novelist. The two books for which he will most widely be remembered – to the extent that his Wikipedia profile describes his 'genre' as 'children's literature' – *Wood Magic* and *Bevis, the Story of a Boy*, are both based on his own childhood and his feelings for the natural world. Similarly, the best of his later novels, *Amaryllis at the Fair*, is essentially an account of relationships within his own family – and in particular his father's fecklessness as a farmer and his mother's discontents with country life – when he was growing up.

And then there was *The Story of My Heart*, which wasn't so much written as poured out onto the page in 1883, when he was already seriously ill. It is not an easy read. I confess to feeling some sympathy for the commercial traveller encountered by Reginald Arkell – whose book, *Richard Jefferies and his Countryside* is, for my money, much the best and most balanced appraisal of the man – in a hotel in Penzance. He had been reading Jefferies' thoughts on 'the psyche'; of it being 'the mind of the mind', capable of building and constructing and looking beyond and penetrating space – and much more in similar, high-flown vein.

> *"What's the fellow driving at?" asked the commercial traveller. "What is a psyche anyway?"*
>
> *"Well," I said, "I suppose it's the only word he could find for the inner consciousness that aspires to something better."*
>
> *The commercial traveller was unconvinced. "I like the country bits," he continued, "but after that I'm stumped."*

So what, in essence, was Jefferies driving at in *The Story of My Heart*? If I can have a stab at summarising that, it would be that through contact with nature at its purest – the earth, the sea, the sun and the sky – Jefferies had been given a glimpse of a new dimension to existence, a dimension which he calls the 'soul life'. This transcends the physical world, is higher even than deity and, if only it could be fully grasped and understood, would send the human spirit soaring away on wings of immortality. Except that, somehow, it can't be grasped, not even by Jefferies himself. As Reginald Arkell concludes, *The Story of My Heart* is a remarkable but curiously unsatisfying book: 'It keeps you hovering on the verge of a great discovery which, by its very nature, can never be made.' Still, it does include some remarkably vivid passages in what the commercial traveller in Penzance called 'the country bits'.

Jefferies included the beauty of the human form in the natural qualities which could open the gateway to his soul life, and in particular the human female form. Whilst there is no suggestion of anything improper about his way of life, he certainly liked a pretty girl. In the essay *Golden Brown* he expatiates almost lubriciously on the charms of two gypsy girls, 'hips swelling at the side in lines like the full bust, though longer drawn; busts well-filled and shapely, despite the rags and jags and the washed out gaudiness of the shawl.' It was a theme he returned to in his novel, *The Dewy Morn*, written at roughly the same time as *The Story of my Heart*. It is a tale of love and rivalry, the central character being the beautiful but pure Felise:

> *Felise was lying on the flowers and grass, extended under the sun, steeped in their sweetness. She visibly sat on the oak-trunk – invisibly, her nature was reclining, as the swimmer in the sun-warmed sea … Her strong heart beating, the pulses throbbing, her bosom rising and regularly sinking with the rich waves of life; her supple limbs and roundness filled with the plenty of ripe youth …*

There is much more in similar vein.

Then finally there was *After London*, published just two years before his death, in which he describes the descent into medieval savagery after England has been devastated and London left abandoned, in the wake of some unspecified natural catastrophe. It is an early example of allegorical science fiction, showing what might happen to mankind if it continues to abuse and exploit the natural world and is thus very much in keeping with Jefferies' underlying philosophy, even if it does on the face of it appear to be quite unlike anything else he wrote.

So there, very briefly, you have the Jefferies' canon. To bring it to life and to start to understand why his impact on the literary world was so disproportionate to both the volume and, if we're being honest, the quality of his output, we need to see it in its proper context, which is the countryside in which he grew up. Which stretch of countryside in particular? It is mostly the North Wiltshire Downs, bounded by the downland escarpment between Wanborough and Uffington to the north, and the valley of the River Kennett on both sides of Marlborough to the south.

But the heart of Jefferies' country – even if, geographically, it may be at its north-western corner – is the village of Coate. It was here, on his parents' small farm, that John Richard Jefferies was born in 1848. Here he spent most of his childhood and youth. In Coate, and in the fields and woods around it, he came to know and understand, not only nature, but the relationship between nature and man. It was in escaping from Coate to the downs, to the high, silent, sunlit, ancient uplands, that he felt the first awakenings of a deeper consciousness, which he would come to call the 'soul life'. If nurture is as important as nature in shaping a man's life, then it was

Coate Farm, Jefferies' childhood home

Coate as much as anything that made Richard Jefferies the naturalist, essayist, poet and philosopher that he became.

In Jefferies' time, Coate was a quiet, out-of-the-way sort of place which straggled along the Marlborough road a few miles east of Swindon. There was a pub, *The Sun* (still there), a few cottages, a blacksmith's forge and a milestone, showing 79 miles to London. The Jefferies' farm, Coate Farm, was set back just slightly from the main road, behind a high wall:

> *Lime-tree branches overhung the corner of the garden-wall, whence a view was easy of the silent and dusty road, till overarching oaks concealed it. The white dust heated by the sunshine, the green hedges, and the heavily massed trees, white clouds rolled together in the sky, a footpath opposite lost in the fields, as you might thrust a stick into the grass, tender lime leaves caressing the cheek, and silence. That is, the silence of the fields.*
>
> ['Meadow Thoughts' in 'The Life of the Fields']

The contrast with Coate as it is today could hardly be more jarring. The village has been all but swallowed up by the great splurge of Swindon. The Jefferies' farmhouse stands alongside a busy dual carriageway. Opposite, where Jefferies' footpath lost itself in the silent fields, stands a large petrol station. Just up the road, a massive new housing development and the Great Western Hospital. In the background, the dull roar of the M4, a mile or so away to the south.

Yet it is still possible to feel something of the sense of being cut off from the hustle and bustle of the world – of being separated from London and all it stood for by 79 miles of solace and solitude – which was such a factor in Jefferies' early life. The 'great walls of the garden' provide blessed sanctuary from the surrounding noise and bustle. If anything, the feeling is even stronger, for the contrast between the tranquillity of house and garden and the clamour of the world outside.

The farmhouse is in two parts: the original slightly tumbledown thatched smallholder's cottage, dating back probably to the late seventeenth century, and – grafted on without much subtlety – a plain-fronted two storey extension, built by Richard Jefferies' grandfather, John Jefferies, as a powerful statement of agricultural success, in around 1820. Behind it, the garden is much as it was when young Dick Jefferies was growing up, complete with mulberry tree, limes and a ha-ha, beyond which a footpath leads across a small field to the stretch of water which played such a key role in Jefferies' boyhood and writings, Coate Water.

Both farmhouse and lake have been fortunate in their history. Coate Water was originally a reservoir, created by damming both ends of what was then a shallow valley, to keep the leak-prone Wiltshire and Berkshire Canal topped up. This was still its role in Jefferies' time, but as traffic on the canal declined, so it fell out of use and by the turn of the century, with the canal company bankrupt, it had become an unofficial pleasure-ground for the growing population of Swindon. In 1914, that relationship was formalised, when the lake was bought by Swindon Corporation, although it wasn't until 1925 that the Swindon Watch and Pleasure Ground Committee set about turning it into 'the Coate of our civic dreams'. This would

Coate Water

involve concerts, sailing boats, a rowing club and a swimming area, complete with (in 1935) a magnificent art-deco diving platform, which survives, even though swimming has long since been proscribed.

A superintendent was installed to oversee all of this and when he objected to the dampness of the lakeside property he'd been given to live in, the Corporation bought Coate farmhouse for that purpose, thus linking reservoir and farm in the same ownership for the first time. It has turned out to be a benevolent stewardship. Despite all of the recreational activities provided by the lake, the temptation to prettify or over-formalise it has largely been resisted so that, once you leave the main visitor facilities behind, it is very much as Jefferies would have known it. As for the farmhouse, that has passed into the care of the Richard Jefferies Museum Trust and is now the Richard Jefferies Museum.

So the heart of Richard Jefferies' life and inspiration survives virtually intact, even if it has been enveloped by roads and houses. At the time of writing, the museum was open on the second Wednesday of each month throughout the year, and on Sunday afternoons in summer. In it, you will find all manner of Jefferies' family memorabilia and imagine the young Jefferies looking out from his bedroom window through the branches of the pear tree on the world around him.

One is conscious of car parks and people and traffic noise as one makes one's way – as Richard Jefferies would have done on countless occasions – from the gate at the back of the house, across a field of pasture and so to the path around Coate Water. But what a fine sight is then revealed: a dark lake, stretching into the distance, fringed by alder, poplar and some magnificent oaks. That flotilla of Canada Geese wouldn't have been there in Jefferies' day, and I suspect that the ducks would have scarpered pretty quickly, whether or not Dick Jefferies was carrying his gun. But for the rest, the scene is very much that in which Jefferies set his two books for boys, *Wood Magic* and *Bevis*.

Wood Magic was the first to be written, in 1881. It is built around the imaginary conversations between an eight-year-old Bevis and not only the wildlife in the fields around Coate Farm, but everything he encounters in the natural world. The birds are given onomatopoeic names, like Tchink the chaffinch and Choo Hoo the wood pigeon, which certainly adds to the educational value of the book, in helping young readers to learn more about birds and their songs. It was also the inspiration for the anthropomorphism which Henry Williamson deployed so successfully in *Tarka the Otter*, a book which was inspired mainly by Jefferies' vivid account of the battles between otter and otter-hounds in his essay *By the Exe*, published in *The Life of the Fields*.

If the allegory in *Wood Magic* is rather stretched to breaking point, and sometimes beyond, then the picture that the book paints of the countryside around Coate Farm is a charming one and, in the context of the development of Jefferies' belief in the 'soul life', a revealing one, not least in the final chapter, where the young Bevis is told by the wind about the Iron Age warrior in his tumulus.

> *"He died about a minute ago, dear, just before you came up the hill ... Now this man, and all his people, used to love me and drink me as much as they ever could all day long and a great part of the night, and when they died they still wanted to be with me, and so they were all buried on the tops of hills, and you will find these curious little mounds everywhere on the ridges, dear, where I blow along. There I come to them still, and sing through the long dry grass, and rush over the turf, and I bring the scent of the clover from the plain, and the bees come humming along with me ..."*
>
> *"There never was a yesterday", whispered the wind presently, "and there never will be a tomorrow. It is all one long today."*

For recognisable locations, we need to turn to *Bevis*. Even though its central character is the same, it is not really a sequel. The book relates the adventures of Bevis, by now 12 or 13, and his friend Mark, who is less of a dreamer, more of an action man, much as Harry Jefferies was in real life to his older brother. Together they build a raft, discover the New Sea, fight a great battle, grapple with crocodiles and explore the exotic island of New Formosa. All of the locations in the book have their originals on or around Coate Water – although sadly New Formosa disappeared below the waves when Swindon Corporation raised the water level back in the '20s!

Let us start at the north-eastern corner of the lake, nearest to the farm house, and let Reginald Arkell be our guide:

> *Here is the spot where the two boys learned to swim and there is the quarry into which Caesar fell. Just behind lies the battlefield of Pharsalia, with all its memories of that bloody fight, and into Fir Tree Gulf the river Nile still runs, feeding the reservoir with water brought from Chiseldon and the*

hills beyond. Working back into the main sea, your further progress will be interrupted by the road to Hodson, which separates the main sheet of water from what is now a bird sanctuary, so back you come, past the forest, over the shallows and your tour of the Bevis country is at an end.

One location surprisingly missed by Arkell is the 'Council Oak', where Bevis, Mark and a whole gang of other boys, led by Bevis's chief rival, Ted, plan a great battle, to be fought on the neighbouring field. They gather under an old oak, just a few yards from the lake.

On higher ground beyond, a herd of cows grazed in perfect peace, while the swallows threaded a maze in and out between them, but just above the grass. The New Sea was calm and smooth as glass, the sun shone in a cloudless sky, so that the shadow of the oak was pleasant; but the swallows had come down from the upper air, and Bevis, as he stood a little apart listening in an abstracted manner to the uproar, watched them gliding swiftly in and out. He had convened a council of all those who wanted to join the war in the fields, because it seemed best to keep the matter secret, which could not be done if they came to the house, else the battle might be interfered with. The oak was chosen as it was known to everyone.

And there it still stands: truncated by great age, having lost most of its limbs, but what a wonderful spot at which to pause, sit down on the grass and read a few pages of *Bevis*.

The Council Oak

Coate Reservoir 'ranks in juvenile literature with Robinson Crusoe's island,' according to Reginald Arkell. That is a bold claim, and it is one that has not been betrayed by the lake's municipal owners over the years. The reservoir is as alive with fish and waterfowl as it was in Arkell's day or Jefferies' before him. Yes, there are paths and nature trails around the lake and on a fine week-end in summer it does get very crowded. But it is still a haven of peace and natural beauty which hasn't been prettified or tarted up. It is much more a piece of countryside than it is a glorified garden. Richard Jefferies, who believed that 'there never was a garden like the meadow' would, in spite of all the traffic and the people, have approved.

The logical next step in any exploration of Jefferies' country would be to head for the hillls, and specifically to Liddington Castle on the top of the downs, three miles away to the south-east, a landmark for miles around. It was where Jefferies would go to seek solitude, both as a boy and as a young man, to be nearer to the sun and the stars, to lie on the close-cropped turf and feel himself transported into another world where time and space had lost their meaning and all that mattered was the soul.

Sadly, it is no longer possible to follow in his footsteps, or not at least all the way. The most direct route, which he probably took more often than not, would have taken him along Day House Lane (past the farm where his wife was born) to the outskirts of Badbury, along a footpath across the broad arable fields at the foot of the escarpment, and so up the steep hill to Liddington Castle on the summit. But that was before they built the M4 and the other major roads that converge at junction 15. You can still reach Badbury village via Day House Lane and Medbourne Lane, by going over or under various big roads, and the footpath that Jefferies would probably have followed from Badbury southwards to the Chiseldon road (which is technically 'The Ridgeway' as it passes under Liddington Hill, as opposed to the path signposted as Ridgeway on the top of the downs). But there is no way from that road up the hill to the Castle at the top. The choice is either to walk for over a mile along a busy road with no pavement and fast traffic, or to make a long detour via Folly Farm to pick up the bridleway referred to as 'Ridgeway' on the OS Explorer map a good two miles south of Liddington Castle. The best bet, I am sorry to say, is to abandon the idea of walking and, instead, to drive to where the unofficial Ridgeway track crosses the Liddington to Aldbourne road (although parking space is limited), and walk up the hill from there, of which more anon.

But there is a walk from Coate Water which can illuminate another aspect of Jefferies' life and writings, and to which the M4 presents no barrier (other than the roar of the traffic, of course). If you walk south along the eastern side of Coate Water, past the Council Oak, and across the little bridge which separates Fir Tree Gulf from the main body of water, you will eventually come to a footbridge carried over the motorway on two rather splendid concrete spiral staircases. On the far side, cut off from the motorway by a barrier of trees, is a countryside of small fields, deep hedges and big trees. It has a secret, almost claustrophobic, feel to it, yet every so often you catch a glimpse of the open downland to the south. I wonder if that contrast between the enclosed, tree-darkened countryside of his home, and the wide open spaces of the sunlit downs that he could see from his bedroom window – a contrast almost as between darkness and light – didn't play a part in shaping Jefferies' thinking.

Once across the motorway, you'll be on the edge of Burderop Woods, where Jefferies learned the poacher's trade from keeper Haylock, who lived in Hodson Bottom. To get there, you'll need to follow the path as it makes its way up the hill and across the fields towards Chiseldon, turning off right when you reach Pincombe Wood and then following the edge of the wood westwards past Oaken Ground Copse until you reach the lane from Hodson back towards Coate Water. You are now in the heart of the country of *The Gamekeeper at Home*, *The Amateur Poacher* and *Round About a Great Estate*, which many good judges consider to have been Jefferies' finest work.

Edward Thomas paints the picture:

> *The keeper lived in the cottage with the thrice-scalloped thatch in Hodson Bottom, sweet chestnut behind it and birch and spruce at each side: date 1741. The other houses in the Bottom are all thatched but one. 'Spring guns set here' is the landowner's jocose invitation to the wayfarer. But Jefferies knew the woods through and through. Here were the fir trees and primroses that his mind would not separate. Here was the fray with the poachers when the squire (JJ Calley, I think) was knocked on the head; of which, and many more things, Jefferies heard much from Mrs Rawlings, widow of an old Burderop keeper. Here, on Ladder Hill, the wind is full of the scent of yellow bed-straw, and the meadow crane's-bill grows by the dogwood and hazel, beneath the oaks. Here were the rooks and wood-pigeons of "Wood Magic". Burderop Park – its beech and oak and ash and fir; its clouds (like a small earthly dawn) of purple loosestrife; its avenues of limes and wych-elms; its grassy spaces, strewn with sarsens, stately and undisturbed; its large, dull, sufficient-looking homely house, suggesting the Okebourne Chace of "Round About a Great Estate".*

I quote this at length because it describes far better than any words that I could summon the scene at Hodson Bottom today. As for Burderop Park, we have Jefferies' own description, from *Round About a Great Estate*:

> *The great house at Okebourne Chace stands in the midst of the park, and from the southern windows no dwellings are visible. Near at hand the trees appear isolated, and above them rises the distant Down crowned with four tumuli.*
>
> *In the enclosed portion of the park at Okebourne the boughs of the trees descended and swept the sward. Nothing but sheep being permitted to graze there, the trees grew in their natural form, the lower limbs drooping downwards to the ground. In that part of the park no cattle had fed in memory of man; so that the lower limbs, drooping by their own weight, came arching to the turf. Each tree thus made a perfect bower.*

Burderop House is now in the hands of a development company. But the estate of which it was once the hub is still very much alive and thriving, extending now to some

Swindon from Liddington Castle

1800 acres of woodland, pasture and arable, and still in the same family as in Jefferies' time. It is worth a visit. The woods, pastures, cottages, trees and lanes at Burderop and Hodson Bottom bring all of Jefferies' game-keeping and poaching essays to life.

If you carry on down the lane from Hodson Bottom towards Swindon, you'll cross the now silted-up and overgrown neck of Coate Water, with the bird sanctuary on your left, and be able to pick up the footpath which runs around the western side of the lake shortly thereafter.

But it is time to head for the hills, or rather for the downs. The difficulties of reaching Liddingtom Castle from Coate have already been discussed. But any sufficiently determined Jefferies disciple will certainly find some way of reaching the Ridgeway that runs along the top of the downs, and so to Liddington Castle. They might also take in a visit to Liddington Folly, the clump of beech trees which stands half a mile or so east of the Iron Age fort, and which is a landmark for miles around. It is a slightly eerie place. On the south side of the copse (which is fenced in, but not fiercely) is a concrete bunker, presumably used as an observation post during World War Two. In the copse itself are memorials to some of the, presumably, many people whose ashes have been scattered here; scattered here possibly because they loved Liddington Hill, or maybe just because it is such a prominent landmark. I daresay there must be hundreds of people who raise a hand in salutation and say a silent prayer for someone they have loved, lifting their eyes to Liddington Folly as they drive by along the motorway.

But if the copse has a feel of darkness, death and mortality about it, then the great green ramparts just along the escarpment speak of light, and life and, in Jefferies' mind at least, of immortality:

> *Moving up the sweet, short turf, at every step my heart seemed to obtain a wider horizon of feeling; with every inhalation of rich, pure air, a deeper desire. The very light of the sun was whiter and more brilliant here. By the time I had reached the summit I had entirely forgotten the petty circumstances and the annoyances of existence. I felt myself, myself. There was an entrenchment on the summit, and going down into the fosse, I walked around it slowly to recover breath. On the south-western side there was a spot where the outer bank had partially slipped, leaving a gap. There the view was over a broad plain, beautiful with wheat, and enclosed by a perfect amphitheatre of green hills. Through these hills there was one narrow groove or pass, southwards, where the white clouds seemed to close in the horizon. Woods hid the scattered hamlets and farmhouses, so that I was quite alone.*

I can't say that I enjoyed quite the ecstasy that Jefferies experienced on Liddington Hill, but to be up there on a fine summer's day, larks singing in the wide blue heaven, the ageless downs beneath one's feet and the sprawl of Swindon seemingly so small and unimportant to the north, does give one just an inkling of what he was driving at. Edward Thomas reminds us that Jefferies often thought of the sea on these hills:

> *The eye sometimes expects it. There is something oceanic in their magnitude, their ease, their solitude – above all, in their liquid forms, that combine apparent mobility with placidity, and in the vast playground that they provide for the shadows of the clouds. They are never abrupt, but, flowing on and on, make a type of infinity.*

There are any number of splendid walks to be had across these downs. One of the finest, which takes in many of the places that Jefferies liked to visit on his ramblings in these parts, is the so-called 'Aldbourne circular route' (as it appears on the OS Explorer map) or the 'Ridgeway circular route' (as it is signposted).

As its name suggests, this starts and finishes at Aldbourne, although you can pick it up at several other points along the route. Aldbourne may seem a long way from Coate, but the route takes in Liddington Hill, and Aldbourne has the great advantage over any other potential starting point of having two good pubs and plenty of parking.

Aldbourne is a pretty downland village of flint and thatch, with a handsome church, a duck-pond and the two aforementioned pubs, the Blue Boar by the Green and the rather more down-home Crown in the Square. If you walk the circular route clockwise, then the first half mile or so is along the busy Swindon road, although there is a wide verge to provide refuge from the traffic. The route then follows a signposted 'by-road' off to the left, up the slope of the downs, passing Giant's Grave, an impressive, tree-grown tumulus, fenced-off in its copse, on the right as you go up the hill.

Aldbourne

The aptly named Upper Upham is like an island of domesticity in a sea of rolling downland: an ancient, grey-stoned house, a group of (presumably) estate-workers' houses and a biggish farm, all perched on the highest point in this stretch of countryside. It struck me that this is a liberating landscape, freeing the mind to roam wherever it may. As Edward Thomas observed, the cloud-shadows racing across the slopes of the downs make one ever-conscious of the sky. It is easy to see why Jefferies spent so much time looking heavenwards on his walks up here. As I reached the field where the track from Upham joins the Ridgeway, a lark burst suddenly into song – in mid-February!

The way turns almost due north from here, climbing towards Liddington Hill. There is a short-cut which you can take, down across the valley to rejoin the circular route at Sugar Hill, but if you yield to the temptation, you'll miss out on Liddington Castle, which was Jefferies' favourite spot of all. Reaching the ramparts does require a short detour along a well-signposted permissive path, but is well worth it. Cutting into the flank at around this point of the walk are two steep valleys, either one of which might be the 'deep, narrow valley in the hills, silent and solitary' which Jefferies loved to frequent, where 'the sky crossed from side to side, like a roof supported on two walls of green.'

The return journey starts from where the Ridgeway crosses the road from Swindon to Aldbourne, and you don't have to brave the road itself, as a bridleway runs parallel to it for the first mile or so, on the field side of the hedge. The going is easier on the homeward stretch, even if the farmer has ploughed as close as he possibly could to the edge of the path. Behind you, Liddington Folly; on the right, the woods and copses of Upper Upham; on the left, the M4 winding its way up to Membury Services;

'Clouds across the slopes of the downs'

and ahead, the distant Hampshire Downs and beyond them – as Jefferies must have imagined – the sea!

Just as Jefferies was 'quite alone' when he walked here, so was I. I passed not a living soul in the course of my 12-mile trek. I daresay it's rather busier in the summer months. Even so, it does make for a perfect downland walk, especially the last few miles, along a broad, firm, grassy trackway, unmarked by the ruts left by off-roaders of various descriptions, which do so scar the Ridgeway. You pass a line of four tumuli – the Four Barrows – just as you begin the final descent into Aldbourne. It reminds one that this is an ancient as well as a beautiful landscape.

As I sank my first pint in the comfort of the Crown, I felt that I understood a great deal more about what it was about this stretch of countryside that had so fired Richard Jefferies' imagination than I had when I'd set off, four hours earlier.

Richard Jefferies was acutely aware of the way in which his Wiltshire countryside had shaped his writing and his thinking. 'There have been few things I have read of or studied, which in some manner or other I have not seen illustrated in this county whilst out in the fields,' he wrote in the essay *Sport and Science*. In terms of his writing, we can identify four key locations: Coate Farm, for his best novel, *Amaryllis at the Fair*; Coate Water, that gave us *Bevis*; it was in the cloistered country of Burderop Woods where he gathered the material for the best of his essays; and it was, of course, to Liddington Hill and the North Wiltshire Downs that Richard Jefferies owed not just *The Story of My Heart* but the entire system of belief which underpinned his life and work.

The Reverend Francis Kilvert

As a diarist, Francis Kilvert strictly falls outside the scope of this book. But he cannot possibly be denied at least a cameo, given that very few people have written as lyrically and lovingly of the countryside and its people as he did, in any format.

Despite being most closely associated with the Radnorshire countryside around Clyro, where he served as curate from 1865 to 1872, Kilvert was a Wiltshireman. He was born at his father Robert's rectory at Langley Burrell, two miles north of Chippenham, in 1840. The family were comfortably off and, after a private education in Bath and a degree from Wadham College, Oxford, Francis followed his father into the church, as curate first at Langley Burrell, then at Clyro, then back to Langley Burrell from 1872 to 1876 and then as a vicar in his own right, at St Harmon in Radnorshire and finally at Bredwardine in Herefordshire, before his sadly early death from peritonitis in 1879.

*Francis Kilvert
(1840-1879)
From Wiltshire to the Wye*

He started writing his diary on 1 January, 1870. By the time of his death it ran to 29 volumes of notebooks and over a million words. Thanks to a whole chapter of accidents, only about a third of what he wrote survives. First, his widow Caroline got out her scissors and removed anything relating to her or anything else she deemed too sensitive to see the light of day. Then, after the diaries had been discovered, transcribed, and extracts published in 1938 in three volumes by William Plomer, a reader for Jonathan Cape, the transcript was lost during the war. The final misfortune came when Kilvert's niece, Essex Hope, who had inherited the surviving 22 notebooks, took it upon herself to destroy all but three of them, in a misplaced desire to, as she put it, 'preserve the family's good name'.

However, more than enough of the diaries survive to provide us with a wonderful picture of Kilvert himself, the communities to which he ministered, the people he met and the countryside in which he loved to walk. Clyro being marginally the wrong side of the Welsh border, we will focus on what he wrote about Langley Burrell and also Bredwardine in Herefordshire, where he and his wife are buried. One could choose any number of passages to illustrate the perception of his gaze and the vividness of his outlook, but the two places where he most liked to walk near Langley Burrell were Langley Common, just south of the village, and what he called 'Happy Valley', to the west, running from below Langley ridge to the village of Kington St Michael.

This is how he saw the common on a sunny June morning in 1873:

> *A beautiful peaceful summer morn such as Robert Burns would have loved.
> Perfect peace and rest. The sun and the golden buttercup meadows had it*

Langley Common

'Happy Valley'

*almost all to themselves. A few soft fleecy clouds were rising out of the west
but the gentle warm air scarcely stirred even the leaves on the lofty tops of
the great poplars. One or two people were crossing the common early by
the several paths through the golden sea of buttercups which will soon be
the silver sea of ox-eyes. The birds were singing quietly. The cuckoo's notes
tolled clear and sweet as a silver bell and a dove was pleading in the elm
and 'making intercession for us with groanings which cannot be uttered'.*

Langley Common had lost its official 'common' status even at the time that Kilvert
was writing, but the big grass fields in question are still criss-crossed by footpaths and
it still a fine place for a walk, even if it does now border a noisy industrial estate!

'Happy Valley' is more secluded:

*This afternoon I went down out of the heat and glare of the summer day
into the cool green shades of the Happy Valley. Thence I went on through the
opposite side of the slope through the beautiful meadows of Langley Fitzurse.
As I mounted the slope there were lovely glimpses of the far blue hills and
chalk downs seen through the tops of the luxuriant elms of the Happy Valley,
a sea of rich, bright green foliage. To me this was all enchanted ground, for
Ettie's dear sake. I came into a long narrow meadow sloping down from
Langley Ridge at its head to the Happy Valley at its foot. In this meadow,
about halfway down the slope grew three beautiful elms all a-row and lower
still a solitary tree in the midst of the meadow. In a sweet day-dream I
seemed to see the white frocks of three girls sitting on the grass and nestling
under the shadow of the elms in the sultry midsummer afternoon.*

Langley Fitzurse is the original name of the parish of Kington Langley, taking its name
from Reginald Fitzurse, who was one of the knights who murdered Thomas à Becket,
and is remembered today thanks mainly to Langley Fitzurse primary school. 'Dear Ettie'
was the love of Kilvert's life, Ettie Meredith Brown, with whom he had fallen in love in
1876, only for her parents to put an end to the relationship, to Kilvert's huge distress.

Francis Kilvert's final posting was as vicar of the parish of Bredwardine in north-
west Herefordshire, not far from his beloved Clyro. He spent two years there, up to
his death in August 1879, and they included the bitter winter of 1878-9, the coldest,
according to Kilvert, for 100 years.

*As I went up the snowy hill to Bethel I pursued the fast retreating and
ascending wan sunshine of the still winter afternoon. I overtook the sunshine
just as I got to the lone house on the bleak windy hill top. All the valley and
plain lay bathed in a frosty rosy, golden glow, and just as I got to Cae
Perthan the sun was setting behind the lone level snowy blue-white line
of the Black Mountains and the last rays were reddening the walls and
chimney stack of the solitary cottage.*

As that beautiful description suggests, Kilvert was a poet as well as a diarist. We can
but wonder what he might have achieved had he been spared, and be thankful that at
least some of what he wrote has survived.

Richard Jefferies – where to experience his 'ancient sunlight'

Walks

Around **Coate Water Country Park**. Large free car park.

From Coate Water, take footbridge over motorway to Chiseldon and back via Hodson.

You can walk to **Liddington Castle**, where Jefferies liked to bask in his ancient sunlight, from Coate Water but it involves a motorway junction, main roads or a long detour via the Ridgeway. The best thing to do is to park just south of where the B4192 crosses the B4507 and walk up the Ridgeway, with Liddington Tump on your right. A permissive path leads off right to Liddington Castle.

For a longer Jefferies walk: Take the Ridgeway (path not road) to **White Horse Hill** (see chapter 2), returning via the villages of Knighton, Ashbury, Idstone, Bishopstone and Hinton Parva.

The **Aldbourne Circular Route** is described in the text.

Viewpoints

Any view of Coate Water.
Liddington Castle, or White Horse Hill looking back towards Liddington.

Pubs

The Sun, virtually next door to Jefferies home/museum. Much altered from Jefferies' day but the same pub! Real ale and decent food.
The Patriot's Arms, Chiseldon; Real ale and good food.
The Calley Arms, Hodon: Cosy country pub with real ale and food.
The Blue Boar, Aldbourne: Smartly refurbished village pub overlooking village green with excellent choice of real ale and good food.

Birthplace and museum

Richard Jefferies Museum, Coate Water, Swindon SN3 6AA.
Museum open Sunday afternoons in summer and second Wednesday of each month.
Contact info@richardjefferies.org for full details.

Richard Jefferies Society

richardjefferiessociety.co.uk
07768 917466

Select Bibliography

Autobiography
The Story of My Heart (1883)

Novels
Wood Magic (1881)
Bevis, the Story of a Boy (1882)
Amaryllis at the Fair (1887)

Essays
The Gamekeeper at Home (1878)
Wildlife in a Southern County (1879)
The Amateur Poacher (1879)
Hodge and his Masters (1880)
Round About a Great Estate (1880)
The Life of the Fields (1884)
Field and Hedgerow – Being the Last Essays of Richard Jefferies (1889)
The Toilers in the Field (1892)
Landscape with Figures – Selected Prose Writings (Penguin, 2013)

Biography
Henry Stephens Salt: *Richard Jefferies – His Life and His Ideals* (1906)
Edward Thomas: *Richard Jefferies, His Life and Works* (1909)
Henry Williamson: *Richard Jefferies* (1937)
Reginald Arkell: *Richard Jefferies and his Countryside* (1946)

Chapter Two

The Vale of the White Horse

Walter Scott, Thomas Hughes, GK Chesterton, John Betjeman, Thomas Hardy

Before the gods that made the gods
Had seen their sunrise pass,
The White Horse of the White Horse Vale
Was cut out of the grass.
GK Chesterton

There must be something quintessentially English about the Uffington White Horse and its Vale, if only for the fact that it has been either a home or an inspiration or both to four of the most intensely 'English' writers who ever put pen to paper: Richard Jefferies, Thomas Hughes, GK Chesterton and John Betjeman, not to mention Thomas Hardy, who set a crucial passage in *Jude the Obscure* a little further east along the downland ridge.

Let us start with Jefferies, or rather with his first biographer, Edward Thomas, another deeply English writer who knew and loved this stretch of countryside.

The Ridgeway

Jefferies must often have walked east along the northern escarpment of the Wiltshire Downs from Liddington Castle to Uffington, looking north across the broad acres stretching away to the Cotswolds in the distance. The obvious route would have been the Ridgeway, which these days is most easily picked up where it crosses the B4192.

From there to Uffington Castle is about seven miles. I'll leave Edward Thomas to describe the walk:

> For Jefferies at Coate, the summer sun rose over Whitehorse Hill, eight miles off in Berkshire, with the ancient entrenchment above and the westward-ramping white horse below; and to reach the hill meant a long, lonely walk on the Ridgeway through the high corn-land and past Wayland Smith's cave, or along the more frequented parallel road below, through Wanborough, Little Hinton, Bishopston, Ashbury and Compton Beauchamp ... North of this road is the flat land, which has so many elms bordering so many small fields that from a distance it seems one wood. South, and close at hand, are the Downs – the solitary arable slopes, the solid beech clumps, the coursing and racing turf of Ashdown and Lambourn.

Alas, the elms are no more, many of the fields have been greatly enlarged by hedge removal and a wind farm blights the panorama looking north. But the description of the downs still holds good, and a fine, sweeping sight they make, rolling away towards the southern horizon. It is not hard to see why they put Jefferies in mind of the billowing ocean.

The Ridgeway will eventually take us to Wayland's Smithy, one of the most impressive and best preserved Neolithic barrows on these downs, which stands, alongside the old road, in its grove of trees. Four massive monoliths stand sentinel at the mouth of the burial chamber, over the entrance to which a great flat stone serves as a lintel. From there the barrow stretches back in a wedge shape for a good forty yards, with smaller standing stones on either side. And, unusually in this neck of the woods, it owes its main literary claim to fame not to an Englishman but a Scotsman, Sir Walter Scott and his novel, *Kenilworth*, published in 1821.

The novel's plot is constructed around the secret marriage of Robert Dudley, Earl of Leicester and favourite of Queen Elizabeth 1, to Amy Robsart, the pretty daughter of a Devonshire landowner. Amy's former fiancé, Tressilian, is travelling westwards from Leicester's seat of Cumnor Place near Abingdon, to inform Sir Hugh Robsart about his daughter's seduction and secret marriage and organise a petition to the Queen to secure Amy's

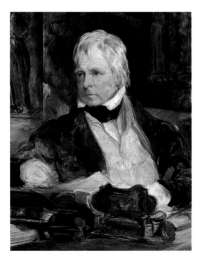

Walter Scott
(1771-1832)
Loved the Uffington legends

release. He is heading for Marlborough when his horse loses a shoe, not far from a 'miserable, muddy little village', which we may take to be Uffington. He asks an old woman, Gammer Sludge, if there is a blacksmith in the area. She introduces him to the Latin-speaking school-master Erasmus Holiday who tells Tressilian about Wayland, the blacksmith who takes no money for his work, and deputes his pupil, Dickie Sludge, to show him the way.

Up to the top of the hill they climb and along the Ridgeway, until Dickie announces that they have arrived at Wayland Smith's forge door.

> *"You jest, my little friend", said Tressilian. "Here is nothing but a bare moor, and that ring of stones, with the great one in the midst, like a Cornish barrow."*
>
> *"Ay, and that great flat stone in the midst, which lies across the top of these uprights," said the boy, "is Wayland Smith's counter that you must tell your money down upon."*

He goes on to describe the elaborate ritual to be followed:

> *"You must tie your horse to that upright stone that has the ring in't, and then you must whistle three times, and lay me down your silver groat on that flat stone, walk out of the circle, sit down on the west side of that little thicket of bushes, and take heed you look neither right nor left for ten minutes, or so long as ye shall hear the hammer clink, and whenever it ceases, say your prayers for the space you could tell a hundred, and then come into the circle, you will find your money gone and your horse shod."*

Wayland's Smithy

36

Tressilian, being a down-to earth Cornishman, is less than impressed at what he takes to be a practical joke and chases after the urchin Sludge to exact punishment – to no avail. The boy is too quick for him, and eventually an exhausted Tressilian is left with no option but to comply. Except that, instead of saying his prayers when the clink of the hammer stops, he dashes round to the back of the barrow, there to discover, not the Devil incarnate, but 'a man in a farrier's leather apron, but otherwise fantastically attired in a bear-skin dressed with the fur on, and a cap of the same, which almost hid the sooty and begrimed features of the wearer.' This, it turns out, is Wayland Smith, who has turned back to his family trade of smithing after the doctor he was previously working for had tried to blow him up as part of an experiment! Having tried and failed to obtain custom in the ordinary way, he had decided to take advantage of the 'smithy' and its legends, with Sludge, whom he calls 'Flibbertigibbet' (who also features in Wayland's Smithy legends), as his accomplice. His forge was hidden in the barrow. It turns out that Tressilian and the blacksmith have met before, and eventually all three of them set off, first for Devon and subsequently for the Earl of Leicester's castle at Kenilworth, where the denouement of the tale is played out.

How did Scott hit upon the idea of using this remote bronze-age barrow as the location for what, in the context of the story, is a key encounter, bringing together as it does his 'three musketeers'?

Well, Wayland is a corruption of Wolund, a Saxon smith-god, and the barrow has been called Wayland's Smithy since at least the tenth century, possibly earlier. There was a long-standing tradition, born of the practice of leaving votive offerings at a sacred site, and maybe influenced as well by the proximity of the Uffington White Horse, that if you left a horse there overnight and placed a silver coin on the stone, you would come back in the morning to find the horse shod and the coin gone. The inference that the invisible blacksmith was actually the Devil appears to have been a Scottian invention.

As to how Sir Walter Scott came to hear of all this, the finger points firmly to a lady called Mary Anne Watts, by whom hangs a significant literary connection. She was Uffington born and bred, her father, grandfather and great grandfather having all held the living of St Mary's parish church. She met and married Thomas Hughes, canon of St Paul's and much older than her, and persuaded him to move to Uffington. Mary long out-lived her husband and became a well-known and popular figure in literary circles, becoming friendly not only with Sir Walter Scott, but also with Robert Southey, RH Barham, of Ingoldsby Legends fame, and Harrison Ainsworth. She later settled at Kingston Lisle house, just a few miles from Uffington, breeding Dandy Dinmont terriers from dogs given her by Scott. Her son John bought himself a farmhouse in Uffington, and settled for a life as a 'scholarly dilettante'. He married a Yorkshirewoman, Margaret Wilkinson, by whom he had eight children, the second of them being Thomas Hughes, who would in time seal Uffington's place in literary history.

Thomas spent most of childhood in and around Uffington. The early chapters of *Tom Brown's School Days* paint a vivid and deeply affectionate portrait of the village, the surrounding countryside, the local customs and eccentricities, and his own childhood. He was devoted to his father, an old-fashioned, paternalistic Tory, with a well-developed social conscience, who was also a talented essayist, story-teller, polyglot and mimic, whom Thomas would immortalise as Squire Brown:

> *Here, at any rate, lived and stopped at home, Squire Brown, JP for the county of Berks, in a village near the foot of the White Horse range. And here he dealt out justice and mercy in a rough way, and begat sons and daughters, and hunted the fox, and grumbled at the badness of the roads and the times. And his wife dealt out stockings, and calico shirts, and smock frocks, and comforting drinks to the old folks with the 'rheumatiz' and good counsel to all; and kept the coal and clothes clubs going, for yule-tide, when the bands of mummers came round, dressed out in ribbons and coloured paper caps, and stamped round the Squire's kitchen, repeating in true sing-song vernacular the legend of St George and his fight, and the ten-pound doctor, who plays his part at healing the saint – a relic, I believe, of the old Middle-Age mysteries.*

But Squire Brown stood for more than just Thomas Hughes' father. He and his family represented what, to Hughes, was a very special breed: the sturdy, dependable yeoman stock to which Britain owed much of its greatness:

> *For centuries, in their quiet, dogged homespun way, they have been subduing the earth in most English counties, and leaving their mark in American forests and Australian uplands. Wherever the fleets and armies of England have won renown, there stalwart sons of the Browns have done yeomen's work.*

Here then was the solid raw material to be shaped, enlightened and liberalised by Dr Matthew Arnold's 'muscular Christianity', and an appreciation of the British countryside and the influences which had helped shape it was an important part of the mix.

If that suggests that Thomas Hughes looks at 'Olde England' and his family's part in it through rose-tinted spectacles, then, as I'm sure he would say, so be it. He was proud of being a Saxon, proud of being a 'Vale-man', proud of the local customs and pastimes, like Uffington's regular 'Veasts' and the violent and often bloody 'back-sword play', which was such a feature of them, proud even of the local legends, revolving as they do around Dragon Hill, King Alfred and the White Horse itself. He would, in time, devote an entire book, *The Scouring of the White Horse*, to recounting

*Thomas Hughes
(1822-1896)
Muscular Christian*

and celebrating them, in the context of an extended holiday spent at Uffington by an imaginary young lawyer. (The book was effectively commissioned, shortly after the overnight sensation which *Tom Brown's School Days* created, by the organising committee of a revived Scouring Veast, held in 1857.)

This is a stretch of country which is quite remarkably rich in history, legend and interest, a neighbourhood in which – and we can agree with Thomas Hughes on this – 'there is enough of interest and beauty to last any reasonable man his life.'

To explore it, let us return to the top of the downs and to the Ridgeway. Walking east from Wayland's Smithy, in front of us is White Horse Hill, topped by the Iron Age fort of Uffington Camp, known to Thomas Hughes as the Roman Camp, from the period when it was commandeered by the legions. The best way to reach the summit plateau is to take the stile leading off the Ridgeway signposted 'Whitehorse Hill' and so up a short but steep stretch of the proper crisp downland turf, so beloved of Jefferies as well as Hughes. And what sight will greet you as you reach the top? Well, Thomas Hughes' description will serve well enough, even if it was written 160 years ago:

> *And then what a hill is White Horse Hill! There it stands, right above all the rest, nine hundred feet above the sea, and the boldest, bravest shape for a chalk hill that you ever saw ... Yes, it's a magnificent Roman camp, and no mistake, with gates and ditch and mounds, all as complete as it was 20 years after the strong old rogues left it. Here, right up on the highest point, from which they say you can see eleven counties, they trenched round all the table-land ... The ground falls away rapidly on all sides. Was there ever such turf in the world? You sink up to your ankles at every step, and yet the spring of it is delicious ... It is altogether a place that you won't forget – a place to open a man's soul and make him prophesy, as he looks down on that great Vale spread out as the garden of the Lord before him, and wave after wave of the mysterious downs behind, and to the right and left the chalk hills running away into the distance, along which he can trace for miles the old Roman road 'the Ridgeway' keeping straight along the highest back of the hills; – such a place as Balak brought Balaam to prophesy against the people in the valley beneath. And he could not, neither shall you, for they are a people of the Lord who abide there.*

Stirring stuff, which exposes the strong Christian faith which was such a vital component of Hughes' life and work.

The White Horse itself is carved into the hillside just below the northern edge of the escarpment. And for all Hughes' admiration of its 'Saxon' qualities, it has always seemed to me to speak of an earlier Celtic culture, with its sweeping curves. It is a galloping white horse as imagined by an impressionist painter, and all the more striking and beautiful for it. Thomas Hughes repeats the old myth that the figure was cut in the hillside on the orders of King Alfred the Great, to commemorate his defeat of the Danes on the battlefield of Ashdown, which Hughes places on, or just to the west of, Uffington Camp. This seems implausible, to put it mildly. An

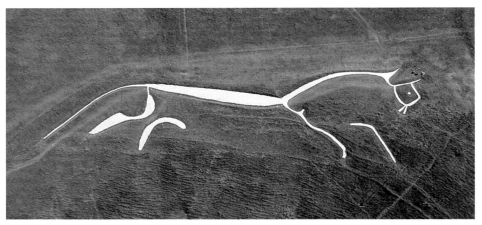

The Uffington White Horse

archaeological process known as 'optical stimulated luminescence' suggests that the Uffington White Horse is at least 3,000 years old, whilst the most likely location for the Battle of Ashdown is further east, towards Newbury and Reading. (In *The Scouring of the White Horse* Hughes does concede that the actual site of the battle is uncertain, whilst insisting, probably correctly, that it must have been 'somewhere in the western part of Berkshire' rather than at any of the other Ashdowns in the south and east of England.)

Immediately beneath the White Horse is the steep-sided gully known, for fairly obvious reasons, as the Manger, into one side of which the hills fall with a series of the most lovely sweeping curves known as 'the Giant's Stairs'. One of the most popular – and dangerous – events of the 'Veasts' held to accompany the seven-yearly 'scouring' of the White Horse, was the race from the top of the hill to the bottom of the manger, in pursuit of a 'Berkshire Five', a cylindrical cheese set rolling by the umpire at the top. It must have been very similar to, and probably even more hazardous than, the cheese-rolling held at Cooper's Hill in the Cotswolds every Whitsun.

The eastern side of the Manger is formed by the conical hillock known as Dragon Hill. Or at least it would be a cone, had someone not removed its apex, to leave a small plateau as its summit, with a bare patch of chalk at its centre. Opinions have differed down the years as to whether it is a natural feature or, like Silbury Hill, on the other side of the downs, man-made, with the balance favouring the former. But, whatever its origins, so unusual a feature, so close to the ancient and famous White Horse could hardly not have attracted its share of legends. Thomas Hughes relates, with a wry smile, the legend that it was on this hill that St George, or possibly King George, killed the dragon. Hence the name, of course, and hence also the fact that grass has never grown on that bare patch on the summit, or in the two channels down one side, where the dragon's blood was spilt (and which just happen to be the two easiest paths to the top!). An alternative theory is that the hill may have had something to do with Uther Pendragon, father of King Arthur. Or, if indeed man-made, it could have been a Celtic burial mound guarded by a dragon, in accordance with Celtic tradition.

But for all the attractions of the Manger and Dragon Hill, unless you particularly want to explore either or both, it is probably best to admire them from the top of the hill, up by the White Horse, as the best way to reach our next *Tom Brown's School Days*-celebrated port of call is along the Ridgeway, rather than braving the busy B4507 which winds its way along the bottom of the ridge. A mile or so east of the White Horse, having passed Ram's Hill on your right, the Ridgeway crosses a lane at Kingstonhill Barn. Turn left down the steep and narrow lane, and just before it reaches the main road at the bottom you will find, crouching modestly in a small enclosure, alongside a cottage garden, the famous Blowing Stone.

It is, as Thomas Hughes describes it, 'a square lump of stone, some three and a half feet high, perforated with two or three queer holes, like petrified antediluvian rat-holes'. By applying your mouth to one of the holes, and blowing with all your might, you are supposed to be able to produce, in Hughes' words, 'a grewsome sound between a moan and a roar (which) spreads itself away over the valley, and up the hillside, and into the woods at the back of the house, a ghost-like awful voice.' I say supposed, because I tried – Lord knows I tried – with every breath in my body to get the stone to roar, and produced not a squeak. At any event, legend has it that in the old days, the stone would be blown to warn the local population of an impending attack. It is even suggested that King Alfred himself may have blown it to summon his forces on the eve of the Battle of Ashdown. It is just a pity that the cottage alongside the stone is now just a cottage, and no longer the Blowing Stone Inn. (There is a

The Blowing Stone

41

Blowing Stone Inn about half a mile away in the village of Kingstone Lisle, but it is not the one described in *Tom Brown's School Days*.)

Thomas Hughes wrote what very quickly became not just a hugely popular but also highly influential account of Tom Brown's days at Rugby in 1856, 15 years or so after he had left Uffington, first for Oriel College, Oxford, later to be called to the bar. He himself was perhaps more of an East than a Tom Brown – a boy of whom it could be said that 'if he's got nothing odd about him and answers straightforward and holds his head up, he gets on.' Rough and tough though life even at the most enlightened public school could be in those days, Hughes loved it, just as he revered his headmaster, the great Dr Arnold. As he said later of his time at Rugby: 'I passed all of those years under the spell of this place and Arnold and for half a century have never ceased to thank God for it.' Hughes, more so than Arnold even, was the archetypical 'muscular Christian'. At school he captained the eleven at cricket, and Bigside at rugby, known for the ferocity of his tackling, which earned him the nickname of 'the executioner'! He won his cricket blue at Oxford, and was a keen organiser of and participant in boxing matches long into his adult life.

As for the other part of that tag, he joined the Christian Socialists in 1848 and became a leading light in the formation and development of the co-operative movement. In 1854, he helped found the Working Men's College and served as Liberal MP for Lambeth (1865-68) and for Frome (1868-74). One of his closest friends was Charles Kingsley, sharing his concern for social justice and opportunity for all, if not his jingoism. In 1847 he married Frances Ford, a vicar's daughter, who bore him nine children, five boys and four girls. They lived in suburban Wimbledon, far away from the Vale of the White Horse, although his connections with Uffington remained strong, not least through his brother John, the rector of Longcot, just three miles from White Horse Hill.

It cannot seriously be argued that Hughes' lovingly detailed descriptions of the landscape and legends of the countryside in which he grew up are integral to the story, or even the message, of *Tom Brown's School Days*. Yes, they help us to understand where Tom Brown is coming from, and Thomas Hughes would doubtless argue that a proper understanding and respect for our landscape, history and customs is an essential characteristic of the true Englishman. But my sense is that they were essentially self-indulgent: evidence of how much relish Hughes took from having had the good fortune to be brought up at Uffington in the Vale of the White Horse. As for ourselves, it seems to me that re-reading those early chapters of *Tom Brown's School Days* is not only a joy in itself, but helps us to understand just what a very special landscape this is.

GK Chesterton had no family connection with the Vale of the White Horse, nor was he is any sense a countryman, having been born in London and living most of his life there. Rather like Thomas Hughes, he was a great advocate for the co-operative movement and first came to know the downlands of southern England whilst canvassing for the Liberals in the run-up to the 1906 General Election. But Chesterton's politics – like his personality – were complex and many faceted, interwoven with his Catholicism, which he viewed as a shield against a pagan darkness. He was profoundly moved by his first visit to the Berkshire Downs. What he called 'that enormous area of noble hills and valleys which had seen so many struggles in the past' reminded him powerfully of 'the aboriginal struggle of the pagans and the Christians, wherein is the genesis of our history.'

What he had in mind when he wrote that was the struggle, and eventual victory, of the Christian King Alfred the Great over the pagan Danes. It was at the heart of the way he thought about England and what it meant to him, and by this stage he was already thinking about writing what he referred to as his *Epic of Alfred*. But it was a chance visit to Uffington which gave the poem not only its eventual title but its central motif:

Gilbert Keith Chesterton (1874-1936) Scourge of the Pagans

> *Such primitive things* [i.e. the struggle between Christians and pagans and Alfred's role in it] *were already working their way to the surface of my own mind: things that I afterwards attempted to throw into very inadequate but at least more elemental and universal literary form. For I remembered the faint and hazy inspiration that troubled me one evening on the road, as I looked beyond the little hamlet, patched so incongruously with a few election posters, and saw, hung upon the hills, as if it were hung upon the heavens, remote as a pale cloud and archaic as a giant hieroglyph; the White Horse.*

Chesterton wrote his own introduction to *The Ballad of the White Horse*, as his epic poem became. In it, he explains that it is based on three episodes in Alfred's life: his victory over the Danes at Ethandune; the story that, prior to the battle, he entered the Danish camp in disguise and played his harp for their king, Guthrum; and the burning of the cakes near Athelney. He is quite clear that the poem is not intended to be historical:

> *A tradition connects the ultimate victory of Alfred with the valley in Berkshire called the Vale of the White Horse. I have seen doubts of the tradition, which may be valid doubts. I do not know when or where the story started; it is enough that it started somewhere and ended with me; for I only seek to write upon a hearsay, as the old balladists did.*

The ballad is indeed a magnum opus, running to 2,684 lines in eight 'books'. The White Horse features at the start, and towards the end, when Alfred orders it to be 'scoured' of the weeds and other detritus which the Danes had allowed to spoil its pristine whiteness (which might well be true, and could explain the Alfred connection to which Thomas Hughes was so attached).

43

Before the gods that made the gods
Had seen their sunrise pass,
The White Horse of the White Horse Vale
Was cut out of the grass.

Before the gods that made the gods
Had drunk at dawn their fill,
The White Horse of the White Horse Vale
Was hoary on the hill.

Age beyond age on British land,
Aeons on aeons gone,
Was peace and war in western hills,
And the White Horse looked on.

For the White Horse knew England
When there was none to know;
He saw the first oar break or bend,
He saw heaven fall and the world end,
O God, how long ago.

The scouring was, of course, a symbolic act: it was the cleansing of England from the corruption of the pagan, and it needed to be done, not once, but regularly, for ever, to keep England pure and white.

And it fell in the days of Alfred,
In the days of his repose,
That as old customs in his sight
Were a straight road and a steady light,
He bade them keep the White Horse white
As the first plume of the snows.

And right to the red torchlight,
From the trouble of morning grey,
They stripped the White Horse of the grass
As they strip it to this day.

The magnificent *Lepanto* apart, *The Ballad of the White Horse* was probably Chesterton's most popular work of poetry, certainly at the time. As Chesterton had fully intended, it stood for an English hero defending English values against a barbarian foe. As such it became particularly popular with English troops in the trenches in World War One, many of whom must have carried it with them to their deaths. In World War Two it was quoted in *Times* editorials when things were going badly: 'I tell you naught for your comfort' for the fall of Crete; and when things were going well: '"The high tide!" King Alfred cried, "The high tide and the turn"' after the Battle of El Alamein and Churchill's 'end of the beginning' speech. The ballad may be over-long and patchy, but it cements the Uffington White Horse at the very heart of what it means to be English.

And so to Uffington itself, no longer Sir Walter Scott's 'miserable, muddy little village' but a thriving, prosperous place, complete with well-populated school, handsome church, decent pub and a museum dedicated mostly to Thomas Hughes, in the old schoolroom, outside which the privately tutored Tom would wait impatiently for the village boys with whom he loved to play.

The old farmhouse in which the Hughes family lived until Thomas was 11 has long since been pulled down. But Garrards Farm, where another great English writer lived for 12 years almost exactly a century later is still there, on the left-hand side of the High Street as you head out of the village towards the Fox and Hounds, with White Horse Hill ahead of you. It is a solid, stone-built, white-washed farmhouse, with red brick lintels over the windows, and from 1933 to 1945 it was home to John Betjeman and his wife, Penelope Chetwode.

John Betjeman
(1906-1984)
Happy at Uffington

Betjeman had been to school at Marlborough, on the other side of the downs, and, as an enthusiast for all things English, would have known all about the White Horse. But none of that played any real part in the Betjemans choosing Uffington for their first home together. The house had been found for them by JB's editor at the *Architectural Review*, Christian Barman, who lived in the village. Its attraction to Betjeman was twofold: first it got him out of 'noisy smelly London', which he hated; but secondly, as he later explained, the Vale of the White Horse was just about as far outside London as one could live, and still be able to commute in and out every day.

The Betjemans' was a turbulent marriage. They quarrelled constantly. I particularly like the story related by AN Wilson in his excellent biography of JB, about the Betjemans' German cook, who spoke no English, and who for the first year of her employment thought that John's name was 'Shut up' because Penelope said it to him so often!

Nor did Penelope's insistence on moving in her beloved Indian-bred grey horse Moti do anything to build harmony in the household. But for all that, they were probably as happy at Uffington as they ever were, and threw themselves into village life with a vengeance. John became the 'people's warden' at St Mary's parish church, while Penelope started the Uffington Parochial Youth Fellowship. They were great organisers, as well: of dances, whist drives, concerts, tennis matches. And John in particular was a regular at the local pub, then known as the Craven Arms, where he would amuse the clientele by playing darts underarm.

But for all his enthusiasm for village life, Uffington never became a poetic inspiration for him in the way that Cornwall was. Only two of his poems mention the village directly, both written long after he had left. The first, entitled simply *Uffington*, is so short we can include it in full:

Tonight we feel the muffled peal
  Hang on the village like a pall;
It overwhelms the towering elms –
  That death-reminding dying fall;
The very sky no longer high
  Comes down within the reach of all.
Imprisoned in a cage of sound
Even the trivial seems profound.

It was written in 1966, possibly when Betjeman was going through one of his regular crises of faith. Maybe he was thinking back to the death of his father, which had occurred not long after the move to Uffington in 1934. Perhaps hearing a muffled peal had reminded him of the bells of St Mary's, for there is a nostalgic undertone to the lines.

At any rate, as an architectural critic he had a proper and profound appreciation of the handsome beauty of the 'Cathedral of the Vale', as the church was inevitably known. He confirms this in the second of his Uffington poem, written in 1975 as a 65th birthday tribute to his friend, the archaeologist Stuart Piggott (whose many Wessex Downs excavations included Wayland's Smithy).

It begins:

Stuart, I sit here in a grateful haze
Recalling those spontaneous Berkshire days
In straw-thatched,
        chalk built,
                pre-War
                    Uffington

And concludes, joyfully, with this perfect picture of the centrality of the church to village life in the 1930s:

Under great elms which rustled overhead
By stile and foot-bridge village pathways led
To cottage gardens heavy with the flower
Of fruit and vegetables towards your tower,
St Mary, Uffington, famed now as then
The perfect Parker's Glossary specimen
Of purest Early English, tall and pale,
– To tourists the Cathedral of the Vale,
To us the church. I'm glad that I survive
To greet you Stuart, now you're sixty five.

John and Penelope left Uffington in 1945, when their landlord, John Wheeler, decided he wanted Garrards Farm for his son. The obligatory blue plaque remembers their time there. Their daughter, Candida Lycett Green, who loved this stretch of country, would return to live at Uffington, and before her death donated copies of all her father's correspondence that she had amassed, to the museum, for public access.

We have one further stop to make along this stretch of downland, and that is at Letcombe Bassett, about six miles east of Uffington, not far from Wantage. It is a pretty little village, tucked into a fold in the downs and has an air of quiet prosperity about it. The old cottages have all been smartly renovated; the handful of newer properties manifestly expensive. It seems extraordinary that, only 70 or so years ago, Berkshire County Council tried to close the village down, and move its inhabitants elsewhere, because they believed the village was too small and too poor to be sustainable. For Letcombe Bassett's renaissance, we have the horse-racing industry to thank. It is firmly within the orbit of Lambourn and the big racing stables. I would guess that at least half of the people living now in the village are connected with horses in some way or other, with the balance being either retired or long-distance commuters.

It is all very different from when Thomas Hardy chose Letcombe Bassett as a key location for his final novel, *Jude the Obscure*, when he was looking for settings which epitomised the crudeness and poverty of rural life in the second half of the nineteenth century. It was actually a different village – Fawley, now just over the border into Berkshire, a couple of miles south of Letcombe Bassett – which first focused his attention on this corner of the downs. It was at Fawley that his maternal grandmother, Betty, had struggled to bring up her family, having been disowned by her relatively wealthy father for marrying a 'sturdy yeoman', who promptly died on her. The fact that many of its old cottages had been pulled down, the trees on the green cut down, and its original 'hump-backed, wood-turreted and quaintly-hipped' church torn down

Thomas Hardy
(1840-1928)
Painful memories

to make way for a 'German-Gothic' monstrosity underlined his profound dislike for the village, and its surrounding countryside: 'At Great Fawley, Berks,' he wrote in his diary. 'Entered a ploughed vale which might be called the Valley of Brown Melancholy. The silence is remarkable. Though I am alive with the living I can only see the dead here, and am scarcely conscious of the happy children at play.' He decided to give the tragic anti-hero of his most controversial novel a name of ill-omen. What better then than Jude Fawley?

Equally, if he wanted to underline the coarse, animal spirit of the girl who first ensnares the unfortunate Jude, where better to place her than at Letcombe Bassett? In those days, the village was known for two things: its watercress (the beds are still there, although no longer commercially exploited) and its pigs. The young Jude, dreaming of studying at Christminster (Oxford), is wandering through the village one day when – splat!! He's hit on the head by a piece of flesh which turns out to be a pig's pizzle.

More than somewhat surprised, he looks over the hedge to see three girls, kneeling by the stream, in which they are cleaning pigs' chitterlings – intestines – for use as sausage and black-pudding casings. It turns out that the full-lipped, prominently bosomed Arabella Donn is the guilty party, and her distinctly unusual – and significantly coarse – opening salvo does indeed have the desired effect. She and Jude arrange to meet the following day, a Sunday, for a walk on the downs.

Arabella's cottage – 'a small homestead, having a garden and pigsties attached' – is still very much there, down a bank on the left as you enter the village on the Letcombe Regis road. It has been enlarged since Hardy's day, but it is as pretty as a picture, with its smartly thatched roof, deep-set windows and beautifully tended garden. The only sadness is that the Yew Tree Inn, almost opposite, where the villagers organised their campaign to stop the county council uprooting them in the 1940s, is a pub no longer.

Arabella's cottage

There is really only one way to go if you are setting off on a walk from Letcombe Bassett, and that is up the hill to the top of the downs. That was certainly the direction that Jude and Arabella took, not only on the day after their unconventional introduction, but several times subsequently, and there is now – thanks to the creation of permissive footpaths, as well as the established rights of way – a delightful circular route, taking in most of the key *Jude* locations. We start by heading up Gant's Hill, taking the second of the two footpaths leading off it to the left. The path leads through (inevitably, in these parts) a horse field, then down a slope into a little dell (don't take the path signed left into the woods) and so up the steep hill to the top. This is perfect downland country: crisp, rabbit- and sheep-cropped turf, buzzards, kites and larks overhead and, at the summit when I was there in late spring, what seemed like an entire field of cowslips. It is an oasis of 'proper countryside' in what is otherwise a sea of arable and racing gallops and has, I suspect, been funded under one of the Countryside Stewardship programmes, together with the permissive footpaths. If so, it is public money well spent.

Right at the top, we are back on the Ridgeway. If you turn left and follow it for half a mile or so, you will come to the point where it crosses the road from Wantage to Hungerford. This is where 'Browns Barn' once stood, where Jude climbed the ladder propped up against the barn and saw, far away across the Oxfordshire countryside at twilight, the 'points of light like the topaz ... the spires, domes, freestone-work and varied outlines', and vowed, then and there, that that would be his destiny.

The barn is long gone and, even were it still there, I doubt one could see anything of Oxford from its roof. But the views from here are magnificent nonetheless, and one can still experience 'the absolute solitude – the most apparent of all solitudes, that of empty surrounding space', which Jude enjoyed after he and Arabella had chased up the hillside in pursuit of an escaped pig. The cottage where Jude and Arabella lived after she'd tricked him into marriage, and where she forced him to kill the pig, was once up here as well, but burned down many moons ago, which was probably just as well.

Segsbury Camp, yet another of the Iron Age forts with which the Wessex Downs are populated, lies between the top of the footpath and the crossroads. It is a broad green platform, surrounded by a single rampart and ditch, which you can now walk all the way round. Jude and Arabella walked here as well, 'Jude thinking of the great age of the trackway *[The Ridgeway]* and of the drovers who had frequented it, probably before the Romans knew them.' It is a magical place.

The best way down is via the new permissive footpath, which takes you across more pristine downland, and offers, at the foot of the hill, two alternative ways back into little Letcombe Bassett, where Jude the Obscure fell victim to fate and a pig's pizzle.

Exploring the literary connections of the Vale of the White Horse

Walks

Uffington: You can walk from Uffington to White Horse Hill, perhaps ideally taking in Kingston Lisle and the Blowing Stone on the way either there or back. The **Blowing Stone** can be found in its own little enclosure just south of the junction between the B4507 and Blowingstone Lane. The cottage next door was once the *Blowing Stone Inn*, the modern incarnation of which is to be found not far away in Kingston Lisle.

Alternatively, drive to the large car park on the hill above Woolstone (it is signposted White Horse Hill) and walk from there to the **Ridgeway**. Here you can either turn right for **Wayland's Smithy**, about a mile away, or turn left up the hill to **Uffington Castle**, and then down on the far side of the White Horse, joining the lane at the foot of **Dragon Hill**, and so back up the lane to the car park.

Garrards Farm, where the **Betjemans** lived, is on the left as you head southwards down the High Street, about 100 yards before you reach the *Fox and Hounds*. It now has a blue plaque.

For more information on walks, visit: **www.museum.uffington.net**

Letcombe Bassett: Arabella's cottage is down a bank on the left as you enter the village from the Uffington/Wantage direction. To repeat the walk taken by Arabella and Jude on their first excursion together, park in the village and walk up the hill, taking the footpath which branches off left. Do not turn left after you have crossed the next field but keep straight on, down into the valley and up the steep hill on the other side until you reach the Ridgeway at the top. Turn left and follow the Ridgeway until you reach Segsbury Castle (or continue to the junction with the A338, which is where the barn was, from where Jude first laid eyes on Oxford, and then re-trace). From Segsbury Castle a splendid new permissive footpath takes you back down to the village.

Viewpoints

White Horse Hill for Uffington, the Ridgway and the Downs.
Segsbury Castle for Letcombe Bassett and the country around (on right hand side)

Pubs

The Fox and Hounds, Uffington: smart village pub with rooms, serving real ale and good food.
The Blowing Stone, Kingstone Lisle: substantial village pub, described in Good Beer Guide 2016 as 'large, friendly and relaxed', although it has since changed hands.

Museum

Tom Brown's School Museum – **www.museum.uffington.net** – is housed in the Old Schoolroom, next to the church, dedicated to preserving artefacts and records of life in Uffington and the other local villages and, of course, to the memory of Thomas Hughes. At the time of writing, it was open on Saturday, Sunday and Bank Holiday Monday afternoons from Easter until the end of October.

Tom Brown's School Museum

Select Bibliography

Sir Walter Scott   www.walterscottclub.com
Kenilworth (1821)
Eileen Dunlop: *Sir Walter Scott – A Life in Story* (2016)

Thomas Hughes
Tom Brown's School Days (1857)
The Scouring of the White Horse (1859)
Edward Mack: *Thomas Hughes – The Life of the Author of Tom Brown's Schooldays* (1952)

John Betjeman   www.betjemansociety.com
Uffington and *To Stuart Piggott 1975* in *Collected Poems*
AN Wilson: *Betjeman* (2007)

GK Chesterton
Autobiography (1936)
The Ballad of the White Horse (1911)
Ian Ker: *GK Chesterton – A Biography* (2011)

Thomas Hardy   www.hardysociety.org
Jude the Obscure (1895)
Robert Gittings: *The Young Thomas Hardy* (1975)
Claire Tomalin: *Thomas Hardy – The Time-Torn Man* (2006)
Tony Fincham: *Hardy's Landscape Revisited* (2010)

Chapter Three

Oxfordshire

Matthew Arnold, Robert Bridges, John Masefield, Robert Graves, Edmund Blunden, Jerome K Jerome, Flora Thompson

I know these slopes; who knows them if not I?
Matthew Arnold

Oxford's literary connections are, of course, virtually limitless. But our concern is with writers linked with landscapes, and they are rather thinner on the ground, given that of the many and varied literary inspirations that the city and university of Oxford have provided over the centuries, its surrounding countryside would not feature particularly prominently.

There is, however, one place, just outside the city, which is as rich in literary landscape associations as any in England, and that is Boars Hill. For many centuries it was in Berkshire, rather than Oxfordshire, an outlier of the Berkshire Downs, in fact: high, bare, sandy, gorsy heathland, with just a few red-brick cottages by way of habitation, looking down on the city from the west. That is how Matthew Arnold would have found it when he was introduced to Boars Hill by his friend, fellow Rugbeian and, as he became, fellow poet Arthur Hugh ('Say not the struggle naught availeth') Clough, when he arrived at Oxford in 1841.

Matthew Arnold was the son of the great Dr Thomas Arnold of Rugby. He began writing poetry at Oxford and was soon winning prizes for it. In some estimations, he became the third most important Victorian poet, after Tennyson and Browning.

Matthew Arnold
(1822-1888)
A signal poet

He and Clough loved walking through the countryside or boating on the river, watching the country people at work, revelling in the clear air, birdsong, wild flowers and all-encompassing beauty of a still unspoilt England. Eynsham, Sandford, Fyfield (with its famous elm tree, now, sadly, no more) and Cumnor Hill were among their favourite destinations, but the spot that meant most to them – around which Arnold would build his pastoral lament for his friend when Clough died young in 1861 – was the single tree which stood – and stands still – at the crest of the ridge on Boars Hill. The poem is entitled *Thyrsis*, the name that Arnold gives to Clough as a Virgilian reference to the shepherd who loses a singing contest with his rival Corydon.

The Signal Tree on Boar's Hill

Runs it not here, the track by Childsworth Farm,
　Up past the wood, to where the elm-tree crowns
　　The hill behind whose ridge the sunset flames?
The signal-elm, that looks on Ilsley Downs,
　The Vale, the three lone weirs, the youthful Thames?—
　　This winter-eve is warm,
Humid the air; leafless, yet soft as spring,
　The tender purple spray on copse and briers;
　And that sweet City with her dreaming spires,
She needs not June for beauty's heightening.

- -

Well! wind-dispers'd and vain the words will be,
　Yet, Thyrsis, let me give my grief its hour
　　In the old haunt, and find our tree-topp'd hill!
Who, if not I, for questing here hath power?
　I know the wood which hides the daffodil,
　　I know the Fyfield tree,
I know what white, what purple fritillaries
　The grassy harvest of the river-fields,
　Above by Ensham, down by Sandford, yields,
And what sedg'd brooks are Thames's tributaries;

53

I know these slopes; who knows them if not I?—
But many a dingle on the loved hill-side,
With thorns once studded, old, white-blossom'd trees,
Where thick the cowslips grew, and, far descried,
High tower'd the spikes of purple orchises,
Hath since our day put by
The coronals of that forgotten time.
Down each green bank hath gone the ploughboy's team,
And only in the hidden brookside gleam
Primroses, orphans of the flowery prime

If *Thyrsis* is Matthew Arnold most passionate poem, his best-known is probably *The Scholar Gipsy*, and that too draws heavily on his visits to Boars Hill and the surrounding countryside. It tells the apparently true story of an Oxford undergraduate who, long before, had taken himself off with a troupe of Romany gipsies

And roamed the world with that wild brotherhood,
And came, as most men deem'd, to little good,
But came to Oxford and his friends no more.

The poet writes on Cumnor Hill – Boars Hill's poor relation – a mile or so north, not far from the old road to Faringdon and Swindon. He has beside him an account by Glanvill of how the scholar had abandoned his studies to join the gipsies and was never seen again. But in the mind of the poet, the gipsy-scholar's fame renders him immortal, and he imagines him still frequenting his old haunts, unrecognised in his gipsy scruffiness.

This said, he left them, and return'd no more.—
But rumours hung about the country-side,
That the lost Scholar long was seen to stray,
Seen by rare glimpses, pensive and tongue-tied,
In hat of antique shape, and cloak of grey,
The same the gipsies wore.
Shepherds had met him on the Hurst in spring;
At some lone alehouse in the Berkshire moors,
On the warm ingle-bench, the smock-frock'd boors
Had found him seated at their entering,

But, 'mid their drink and clatter, he would fly.
And I myself seem half to know thy looks,
And put the shepherds, wanderer! on thy trace;
And boys who in lone wheatfields scare the rooks
I ask if thou hast pass'd their quiet place;
Or in my boat I lie
Moor'd to the cool bank in the summer-heats,
'Mid wide grass meadows which the sunshine fills,
And watch the warm, green-muffled Cumner hills,
And wonder if thou haunt'st their shy retreats.

For most, I know, thou lov'st retired ground!
  Thee at the ferry Oxford riders blithe,
    Returning home on summer-nights, have met
Crossing the stripling Thames at Bab-lock-hithe,
  Trailing in the cool stream thy fingers wet,
    As the punt's rope chops round;
And leaning backward in a pensive dream,
  And fostering in thy lap a heap of flowers
    Pluck'd in shy fields and distant Wychwood bowers,
And thine eyes resting on the moonlit stream.

One suspects that all of the places where the scholar-gipsy may have been seen, and probably his experiences as well – like lying in a boat on the Thames and looking up to the Cumnor hills, or leaning back, pensively dreaming, in a punt – were Arnold's favourites, and that he himself must once have climbed Cumnor Hill, on a winter's night, and

Turn'd once to watch, while thick the snowflakes fall,
The line of festal light in Christ-Church hall —

Arnold's pastoral Latin style as a poet can be distinctly long-winded to modern tastes, but he does paint beautiful pictures of the countryside around Oxford in the mid-nineteenth century. And besides being a first-rate poet, he was also a highly influential educational reformer. He died of a heart attack brought on by running for a tram in 1888.

The peaceful rural settlement of Boars Hill began to be colonised in the second half of the nineteenth century, mostly by academics looking to put a bit of distance and perspective between themselves and the university. One of the first to arrive was the poet Robert Bridges, now almost forgotten, but a remarkable man in his way. He had always wanted to be a doctor and, after a gilded education at Eton and Corpus Christi College,

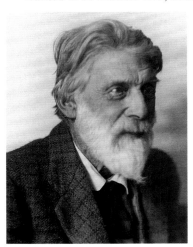

Robert Bridges
(1844-1930)
A pure aesthete

Oxford, he duly took a post at St Batholomew's Hospital in London. But he had been writing poetry since his Oxford days and, when his own ill-health forced an early retirement from medicine in 1882, he took to poetry and literary research full-time, first at Yattendon near Newbury and, from 1907 until his death in 1930, at Boars Hill.

He was married by now, to Monica Waterhouse, daughter of the architect Arthur Waterhouse, and neither his nor her family were short of money. Boars Hill was chosen for the healthiness of its climate, high up above swampy old Oxford, and Bridges designed Chilswell House, on the hill above Chilswell Farm, himself. It is now, much altered and extended, a Carmelite priory. Bridges was something of an aesthete. AL Rowse, in *Q*, his biography of Sir Arthur Quiller-Couch, describes him as 'a very superior person, a pure aesthete, dedicated to poetry and music, of an absolute integrity, aloof and hard to know. People found him rather formidable ...'

His poetry now has a distinctly old-fashioned, Victorian ring to it, especially when compared with Masefield and the Georgians. His favourite themes were religion and love, in all its manifestations. But he was very far from being oblivious to the natural world. *The Hill Pines Were Sighing* was actually written before he moved to Boars Hill, but I daresay Bridges recalled it many times, as the development of that hilltop proceeded:

> *The hill pines were sighing,*
> *O'ercast and chill was the day:*
> *A mist in the valley lying*
> *Blotted the pleasant May.*
>
> *But deep in the glen's bosom*
> *Summer slept in the fire*
> *Of the odorous gorse-blossom*
> *And the hot scent of the brier.*
>
> *A ribald cuckoo clamoured,*
> *And out of the copse the stroke*
> *Of the iron axe that hammered*
> *The iron heart of the oak.*
>
> *Anon a sound appalling,*
> *As a hundred years of pride*
> *Crashed, in the silence falling;*
> *And the shadowy pine-trees sighed.*

There are, in truth, rather too many tall pines – or at least tall firs – on Boars Hill these days, shutting out the views to south and west. Even Jarn Mound, the viewpoint which the archaeologist Sir Arthur Evans had built precisely so as to preserve at least one view from Boars Hill, now only offers a limited prospect to the Berkshire Downs, with nothing of Oxford visible at all. Most of the trees were planted by the wealthy academic colonists, to beautify their gardens and protect their privacy, among them John Masefield and his wife, who moved to Hill Crest, just a few hundred yards from the Bridges at Chilswell, in 1917. He and his wife Constance had been living in a beautiful old moated manor house at Lollingdon under the Berkshire Downs. They both loved walking on the downs, and John wrote several very good poems whilst he was living there, including *Up on the Downs, No Man Takes the Farm* and *Lollingdon Downs*. But it was a damp house, their son Lewis's health was suffering in consequence and, with John away on war duties, Constance was lonely.

The house they moved into, Hill Crest, was a solid red-brick late Victorian villa with, in those days, splendid views both south to the Berkshire Downs and west to Oxford. 'The air is delightful, and although we haven't the dear walk up Lollingdon Hill, we have very pure fresh air, and a jolly scent of gorse and bracken,' wrote Constance. John had a study in the attic and a shed in the garden in which to write, and throughout his time at Boars Hill he maintained a prodigious output, of plays, essays, articles, speeches, children's stories, novels and, of course, poetry. The relatively rural location of his new home re-kindled his rural interests. The first poem he completed there was *Reynard the Fox*, a slightly unlikely extended paean to the joys of hunting for someone who wouldn't have been seen dead riding to hounds himself. The poem offers as rollicking a ride as the hunt itself, which is seen through the eyes of both hunter and hunted, and ends with a delicious twist. The country over which they gallop is, I think, imaginary, but clearly owes something to the Berkshire Downs, judging by this delightful description of Reynard's lair:

> *On old Cold Crendon's windy tops*
> *Grows wintrily Blown Hilcote Copse,*
> *Wind-bitten beech with badger barrows,*
> *Where brocks eat wasp-grubs with their marrows,*
> *And foxes lie on short-grassed turf,*
> *Nose between paws, to hear the surf*
> *Of wind in the beeches drowsily.*
> *There was our fox bred lustily*
> *Three years before, and there he berthed,*
> *Under the beech-roots snugly earthed,*
> *With a roof of flint and a floor of chalk*
> *And ten bitten hens' heads each on its stalk,*
> *Some rabbits' paws, some fur from scuts,*
> *A badger's corpse and a smell of guts.*
> *And there on the night before my tale*
> *He trotted out for a point in the vale.*
>
> *He saw, from the cover edge, the valley*
> *Go trooping down with its droops of sally*
> *To the brimming river's lipping bend,*
> *And a light in the inn at Water's End.*
> *He heard the owl go hunting by*
> *And the shriek of the mouse the owl made die,*
> *And the purr of the owl as he tore the red*
> *Strings from between his claws and fed;*
> *The smack of joy of the horny lips*
> *Marbled green with the blob by strips.*
> *He saw the farms where the dogs were barking,*
> *Cold Crendon Court and Copsecote Larking;*
> *The fault with the spring as bright as gleed,*
> *Green-slash-laced with water-weed.*
> *A glare in the sky still marked the town,*
> *Though all folk slept and the blinds were down,*
> *The street lamps watched the empty square,*
> *The night-cat sang his evil there.*

Great stuff!

Having thus got the bit between his teeth, as it were, Masefield followed up with two more long poems featuring horses: *Right Royal*, a drama of the steeplechase, and *King Cole*, the story of a travelling circus. Both are worth a read, without owing anything in particular to Boars Hill, other than the fact that living there had clearly reinvigorated Masefield's creative juices.

Unlike Robert Bridges and his wife, who lived a reclusive life just along the way, John and Constance Masefield were a sociable couple, who liked entertaining literary-minded undergraduates to tea on a Sunday afternoon and organising amateur productions of John's own plays. He didn't spend much time in Oxford itself, although he was awarded an honorary doctorate by the university in 1922 and spent much time organising a verse-speaking competition which he devised called the 'Oxford Recitations' – spoken verse being one of his great enthusiasms.

When Robert Bridges died in April 1930, Masefield was one of several obvious candidates to succeed him as Poet Laureate, alongside Kipling, Yeats, Housman, Henry Newbolt and even that former Dymock poet, John Drinkwater. But Masefield was reputed to be King George V's favourite poet and, more to the point, he had the Prime Minister, Ramsay MacDonald, on his side. Within less than three weeks from Bridges' death, Masefield's appointment was announced. It was well received, even by those who had been passed over. AE Housman wondered jokingly from Cambridge whether, if Boars Hill were to win the Laureateship for a third time, they would get to keep it, while Yeats suggested that his long-time friend would 'touch hearts nobody else could have touched.' In the event, he proved to be a conscientious, if not particularly inspired, Laureate for the ensuing 37 years.

But most of those years would not be spent at Boars Hill. As early as 1929 he had suggested in a letter to Laurence Binyon that continuing development meant that the place was 'no longer pleasant country here, but thrusting suburb' and that he and Constance wold probably leave in three or four years' time. In the event, they left in April 1933, with Constance still recovering from a brain tumour, and moved to the Cotswolds. It was the end of a particularly happy and productive chapter in John Masefield's life.

In the meantime, yet another poet had added further lustre to the reputation of 'that Helicon of Boars Hill, so hallowed by poetic associations' as Masefield's doctoral citation had put it, one Robert Graves. Graves had won an exhibition to read English at St John's shortly before the outbreak of war, but had enlisted instead and been commissioned in the Royal Welch Fusiliers, where he fought alongside Siegfried Sassoon and Frank Richards. By the time he was able to resume his academic studies he had been badly wounded at the Somme (so badly that he was actually declared dead and was able, subsequently, to read his own obituary in *The Times*), published a well-received volume of poetry and married Nancy Nicholson. As a married man, he couldn't live in college and digs were hard to come by. Fortunately, John Masefield, who had read and liked Graves' war poems, heard of the couple's plight and came to their rescue, offering them the lease of a cottage at the bottom of his extensive garden.

*Robert Graves
(1895-1985)
Poet and shopkeeper*

In *Goodbye to All That*, Graves describes Boars Hill as, by now, 'almost a tourist centre, dominated by Robert Bridges, the poet laureate, with his bright eye, abrupt challenging manner, and a flower in his buttonhole, one of the first men of letters to sign the Oxford recantation of war-time hatred against the Germans.'

He also provides a striking vignette of Masefield: 'a nervous, generous, correct man, very sensitive to criticism, who seemed to have suffered greatly in the war as an orderly to a Red Cross unit; he was now working on Reynard the Fox. He wrote in a hut in his garden, surrounded by tall gorse bushes, and only appeared at mealtimes. In the evening he used to read his day's work over to Mrs Masefield and they corrected it together.'

Mrs Masefield wasn't quite sure what to make of the distinctly Bohemian Robert and Nancy, especially when they decided to set up and run a village shop for the settlement. This was initially a great success:

'Another caricature scene,' wrote Graves in his autobiography. 'Myself, wearing a green-baize apron, selling a packet of Bird's Eye tobacco to the Poet Laureate with one hand, and with the other, weighing out half a pound of brown sugar for Sir Arthur Evans' gardener's wife.'

But the couple (Graves especially) were not great business-people – over-charging their wealthier customers so as to subsidise the poorer ones, for example – and when post-war deflation set in, the shop quickly went downhill. After six months, they were forced to sell up at a heavy loss, which was covered in the end by gifts from Nancy's father and Graves' friend TE Lawrence, who at this stage was a Fellow of All Souls. The experience also rather turned them against Boars Hill, and in June 1921, after less than two years in the Masefields' cottage, they left to live on the other side of Oxford, in World's End cottage at Islip, down by the river.

Two other poets spent time at Boars Hill just after the war, both best known for their war poetry: Robert Nichols and Edmund Blunden. Nichols turned out to be something of a shooting star in the literary firmament, burning brightly one moment, gone the next. But Blunden would go on to become a brilliant and prolific writer, academic and critic; not only a poet himself, but instrumental in bringing other poets to public prominence, including his hero, the 'farm-worker poet' John Clare, and Gloucestershire's Ivor Gurney. He had enlisted in 1915, somehow surviving two years in the front line in France and winning the MC and, like Graves, he was a married man who had arrived at Oxford to take up the place he had won back in 1914. In fact, the two men were on the same course and became friends.

Blunden was given permission to live on Boars Hill because the clear air up on the hill was better for his gas-damaged lungs than the low-lying vaporous city. He wasn't there for very long, being forced by financial necessity to abandon his studies in 1920 to go and work for John Middleton Murry on the *Athenaeum* magazine. He wrote any number of lovely poems about the English countryside, English villages and English country life, *Forefathers* being perhaps the best-known. The one I have chosen to illustrate his work is *Village Sketch*, partly because it was inspired by Bampton-in-the-Bush, just a few miles from where Blunden lived at Boars Hill, and partly because it combines three of Blunden's greatest loves: landscape, village life and, last but by no means least, cricket!

Edmund Blunden
(1896-1974)
Conflict, countryside and cricket

> *Horses, their heads together under a tree;*
> *Elm trees and oaks, mantled in glistening green;*
> *Streams silver-brimmed, the stream-divided lea,*
> *Wide-rising ground with barley thronged or bean:*
> *A town-end of good houses, something grave,*
> *Gray, square and windowing far; cypress and yew*
> *Topping a longer gray wall; five poplars wave*
> *Above the dark-plumed wall; against high blue*
> *Spear-flashing white the spire, and windcock new*
> *Aloft the spire, proud plaything of these gales*
> *Which bring more violent wreaths of cloud and swirl*
> *Of whistling rain; the storm's great ghost assails*
> *The boys with bat and ball, the blue-capped girl*
> *Who leans with her young love against the pales;*
> *While over the level the terrier speeds and springs,*
> *Hoping to catch the swallows in their low swift rings.*

Edmund Blunden would follow his fellow Boars Hillian, Robert Nichols, as Professor of English at the University of Tokyo. His account of his wartime experiences, *Undertones of War* is every bit as compelling as Graves' *Goodbye to All That* or his great friend Seigfried Sassoon's *Memoirs of an Infantry Officer*. After a long and distinguished career, tinged with some controversy over his 'peace at all costs' attitude to the rise of Nazi Germany, he was honoured with the Professorship of Poetry by his old university in 1966, and died at his home in Long Melford in Suffolk in 1974.

Boars Hill would probably by now have been completely obliterated by development were it not for the sterling work of the Oxford Preservation Trust. The Trust was set up in 1927, specifically to buy the Old Berkeley Golf Course from the Estate of Lord Berkeley which would otherwise have been sold for housing. Since then, the Trust has acquired further land on the slopes below Boars Hill, at Chilswell Farm and, most recently, the field in which Matthew Arnold's 'signal-elm', or possibly 'signal-oak', either stood or stands. All of which has meant that the magnificent views of Oxford offered from the road which runs along the top of the old golf course – the views which inspired Arnold and many others – have been protected. Not only that, but the Trust has used its land holdings to provide what it calls a 'dreaming spires walk' which takes in all the most important Boars Hill literary locations. There is no better way of exploring the area, and a modest extension to the north will take in Cumnor Hill where, in *The Scholar-Gipsy*, Matthew Arnold imagined himself lying on the grass, looking down on Oxford, 'in all the live murmur of a summer's day'.

The starting point is any one of the kissing gates that give access to the old golf course from Berkeley Road. The way runs down across the lovely old turf of the golf course, the dreaming spires in full, glorious, view. As you come back on yourself, and reach the brow of the hill, there in front of you is a single oak tree, probably at least 200 years old, its great trunk pitted with an ancient wound. Is this really Matthew Arnold's 'signal elm' as some have suggested? Might he have been either unable to tell the difference between an oak and an elm (unlikely) or preferred the sound of elm to oak in the context of his poem? Possibly. At any rate it is in exactly the right spot, and stands proudly, fenced off from the rest of its field, protected for as long as it survives.

The dreaming spires of Oxford

61

On the Dreaming Spires walk

The way back to Boars Hill runs along a bridleway, through beech woodland, the vegetation getting heathier the nearer you get to the houses. There is a high brick wall to the left of the final slope up to the Ridgeway and, on the other side of it, a cottage. Walk a little further and you realise immediately whose cottage this would have been. For at the point where the bridleway reaches the Ridgeway, there on the left is Masefield House, as it is now called, home of the Masefields, and the cottage you have just passed, at the bottom of its gardens, must have been where the Graves lived. A little way further on along the Ridgeway is the entrance to Jarn Wild Gardens and Mound, with their memorial to Sir Arthur Evans, excavator of Knossos, 'who loved antiquity, nature, freedom and youth (and who) created this viewpoint and wild garden for all to enjoy.' I'm sure he would approve of the 'dreaming spires walk'.

From the slopes of Boars Hill, you can tell where the River Thames runs through its flood plain west of Oxford, even if you can't actually see the river itself, and the River Thames brings immediately to mind Jerome K Jerome and his *Three Men in a Boat*. No-one would claim that this is a work of great literature, but it has always been hugely popular and, at the time it was published, in 1889, gave a massive boost to water-borne tourism on the river, which was more or less what Jerome had intended. His account of a boat trip from London to Oxford and back by himself and his two friends George and Harris – not forgetting Montmorency, the fox terrier – was meant to be part-humorous, part-travelogue, inspired as it had been by his own honeymoon, spent on 'a little boat on the Thames' with his beloved Ettie. Most of the journey is through Middlesex and Berkshire, and so outside our compass. But when they reached Dorchester-on-Thames, they reached Oxfordshire, stopping for the night not long afterwards at the Barley Mow, Clifton Hampden:

> *Round Clifton Hampden, itself a wonderfully pretty village, old-fashioned, peaceful and dainty with flowers, the river scenery is rich and beautiful. If you stay the night on land at Clifton, you cannot do better than to put up at "The Barley Mow". It is, without exception, I should say, the quaintest, most old-world inn on the river. It stands on the right of the bridge, quite away from the village. Its low pitched gables and thatched roof and latticed windows give it quite a story-book appearance, while inside it is even still more once-upon-a-timeyfied.*

Alack and alas! Whilst the exterior of the Barley Mow is as quaint as Jerome describes, the inside has been transformed, and not in a good way. A serious fire in the 1960s is partly to blame, but this is now a 'Chef and Brewer', more a rather tacky restaurant than a pub, all horse brasses and 'Farrow and Ball'. You have to 'Wait to be Seated', having a drink without a meal is discouraged, the food is pricey and unexciting and the beer ordinary. It is all very disappointing, especially as the setting by the old bridge over the Thames is so lovely.

But if the Barley Mow has changed for the worse, the river itself is still very much as Jerome describes it, in the purple prose which sits slightly uncomfortably alongside the jokes and anecdotes. This is how he saw it as the trio start off on what turned out to be a rain-soaked return journey:

The Barley Mow at Clifton Hampden

But the river – chill and weary, with the ceaseless raindrops falling on its brown and sluggish waters, with the sound as of a woman, weeping low in some dark chamber; while the woods, all dark and silent, shrouded in their mists of vapour, stand like ghosts upon the margin; silent ghosts with eyes reproachful, like the ghosts of evil actions, like the ghosts of friends neglected – is a spirit-haunted water through the land of vain regrets.

The critical reception for *Three Men in a Boat* may have been distinctly mixed, but there was never any doubt about what the public thought. Millions of copies have been sold down the years, the book has never been out of print, and there is still no better way of exploring the Thames between London and Oxford than in a camping skiff, with a copy of the book to hand.

And so to our final stop in Oxfordshire: Juniper Hill, in the far north of the county, almost on the Northamptonshire border. It is better known, of course, as Lark Rise, the name that Flora Thompson gave to the hamlet in which she grew up. Do not expect anything very uplifting in the way of scenery. It is very much as she describes it in *Lark Rise*, the first of the trilogy which makes up her *Lark Rise to Candleford*:

All around, from every quarter, the stiff clayey soil of the arable fields crept up; bare, brown and windswept for eight months out of the twelve. Spring brought a flush of green wheat and there were violets under the hedges and pussy-willows out beside the brook at the bottom of the 'Hundred Acres'; but only for a few weeks in later summer had the landscape real beauty. Then the ripened cornfields rippled up to the doorsteps of the cottages and the hamlet became an island in a sea of dark gold.

Flora Thompson
(1876-1947)
An Oxfordshire Laurie Lee

These days, with wheat generally being sown in the autumn, the arable fields surrounding the cottage will only be brown for maybe a month or so. By the time winter arrives, they will be green with the shoots of the new crop, turning gold in July. Most of the old thatched cottages that were there in Flora Thompson's day have also gone, being replaced by larger, smarter properties. It is now a slightly forlorn hamlet, especially since the pub, the Fox Inn, closed back in the 1990s. Twenty years or so before that, I had stopped at the pub on my way to visit the in-laws in Cambridgeshire, and remember being disappointed then by how little it resembled Flora's 'Wagon and Horses', with its 'roaring fire, red window curtains and well-scoured pewter'.

Flora Thompson's End House today

End House, where Flora lived with her father Albert, mother Emma and brother Edwin, is still there, looking out over the cornfields which now occupy what was once Cottisford Heath at the end of an unmade road leading off to the right as you enter the village from the main road, although it is better to park somewhere near the park bench donated by the Juniper and Cottisford Wives Group and walk. The surrounding countryside is, well, as functional now as it was 130 years ago. I heard plenty of chaffinches and blackbirds but no larks, and the noise from the busy A43 dual carriageway less than half a mile away is ever-present. Even when Flora Thompson was writing her trilogy in the late 1930s, it had become a much busier road than the one on which nothing came or went for hours at a time. You wonder what she would make of it now.

Perhaps the best way of exploring this bit of 'Flora Thompson country' is to take the same footpath that Flora and her brother Edwin took when he first started school. It runs south from the lane through the hamlet across the field via Cuckoo Clump to Lower Heath Farm, and so into the 'mother village' of Cottisford (Fordlow in the book). This too is instantly recognisable from Flora's description:

> The little squat church, without spire or tower, crouched back in a tiny churchyard that centuries of use had raised many feet above the road, and the whole was surrounded by tall windy elms in which a colony of rooks kept up a perpetual cawing.

The approach to Juniper Hill

The trees now are limes, but Cottisford House, with its 'pleasure grounds', where the school-children would be taken once a year for tea, is instantly recognisable, as are the old rectory and the two farms. It remains the sort of place of which the story could be told of how 'a stranger had once asked the way to Fordlow after he had walked right through it.' A footpath opposite Manor Farm, and its attendant barn conversions, offers an alternative route back to Cuckoo Clump and Juniper Hill, running as it does alongside 'a tiny trickling stream'.

Rather like *Cider with Rosie, Lark Rise to Candleford* is what you might call 'embellished autobiography'. Given that the events it covers occurred in the 1880s and '90s, and that Flora Thompson didn't start putting her memories down on paper – originally as a series of essays – until almost 50 years later, she must have been blessed, as Laurie Lee was, with a remarkable memory. Not all of the locations are real. 'Candleford', for example, is more or less where Bicester is on the map and has that town's market place, but there are elements of Banbury and Buckingham in there as well, and Fringford, the original for Candleford Green, where Laura/ Flora worked in the post office, is in no danger yet of being absorbed into the nearest market town.

This again has all the features which Flora describes in the third book of her trilogy, *Candleford Green*: its green with the 'spreading oak', the long thatched cottage on the edge of the green – distinguishable for its old AA yellow distance sign – which, in Flora's time had the post office, where she worked, at one end and the village forge in the single-storey thatched building at the other, the Old Rectory and the Old School. Curiously, though, she gives St Michael and All Angels Parish Church a spire, whereas it has in fact a rather dumpy tower. Anyway, Fringford is well worth a visit and, unlike either Juniper Hill or Cottisford, it does have a pub, the excellent Butchers Arms, where you can sit and watch cricket on the green. It is only two miles or so from Cottisford to Fringford – an easy drive or an interesting walk through Shelswell Park, home to 'Sir Timothy' in *Candleford Green* (in reality Edward Slater-Harrison) with whom Flora's cousin Dorcas Lane probably didn't have an affair. The house was pulled down in the 1970s, but a stable block survives.

Flora Thompson's great skill as a writer was to be able to describe the lives of poor people in the countryside towards the end of the nineteenth century, just before mechanisation on the land and the motor car changed everything. She evokes not just countryside but country living, beautifully, vividly, personally but without self-pity. The stretch of countryside around Juniper Hill and Cottisford may be very far from being the most beautiful and striking in the Heart of England, but it produced a writer who was able to bring that countryside to life in a way that few others have managed, in any era.

She wrote her trilogy whilst living at Dartmouth. It was her only real success. Neither the sequel, *Heatherly*, nor her only genuine novel, *Still Glides the Stream*, touched similar heights. She died of a heart attack at Brixham in 1947 at the age of 70.

The post office and the forge at Fringford

Boars Hill and beyond – putting places to words

Walks

Boars Hill and Cumnor Hill: The Dreaming Spires Walk, created by the Oxford Preservation Trust (**www.oxfordpreservation.org**), clearly way-marked from Berkeley Rd and described in the text, is as good a way of exploring Boars Hill's literary heritage as any, although there are plenty of variations available on that basic theme.

You can walk to **Cumnor Hill**, from where Matthew Arnold saw the lights shining in the Christ Church hall one snowy winter's evening, from Boars Hill. Otherwise, park where Hurst Lane, off the old Botley to Cumnor road, comes to a dead end, and take the bridleway across Cumnor Hill. The first footpath on the right will take you up to Cumnor Folly on the hill-top.

Juniper Hill, Cottisford and Fringford: There is a pleasant circular walk, as described in the text, from Juniper Hill (Lark Rise) to Cottisford (Fordlow) and an extension can also be made to Fringford (Candleford Green), which has the added attraction of *The Butchers Arms*. Take the footpath which runs south off the main road just to the east of the village, and head for Cuckoo Clump and Lower Heath Farm, which is on the edge of Cottisford. After walking through the village past the church and Cottisford House, take the first footpath you come to on the left, which takes you back along a stream to Cuckoo Clump and so back to Juniper Hill. A long straight lane will take you on to Fringford, although a more interesting (if slightly tortuous) route will take you along footpaths through Shelswell Park and past the site of the medieval village of Willaston.

Viewpoints

The best vantage point on Boars Hill is the obvious one: the Ridgeway at the top of the old golf course. The views from the Signal Oak are also very fine.

The countryside of Flora Thompson is rather flat, so doesn't offer striking views, although the road into the village from the A43 provides a view of Juniper Hill much as Flora would have seen it.

Pubs

For Boars Hill, *The Fox*, which is just over the hill on the road to Wantage, is the only pub close at hand. It is fairly typical of the modern country pub – smart, comfortable and offering real ale but much more interested in eaters than drinkers. Not a poet in sight when I visited!

By contrast, *The Butchers Arms* at Fringford is everything a village pub should be, with excellent beer, good value pub food, a warm welcome for all-comers and a garden which leads directly onto the village cricket ground. Well worth the three-mile walk from Juniper Hill!

I can't honestly recommend *The Barley Mow* at Clifton Hampden, but no Jerome K Jerome enthusiast would want to miss it, and it does serve draught Bass.

The Butchers Arms at Fringford

Select Bibliography

Matthew Arnold
Thyrsis and *The Scholar Gypsy* in *The Complete Poetical Works of Matthew Arnold*
Nicholas Murray: *A Life of Matthew Arnold (1997)*

Robert Bridges
The hill pines were sighing and other poems written at Boars Hill can be found in
The Complete Poetical Works of Robert Bridges
Catherine Phillips: *Robert Bridges – A Biography* (1992)

John Masefield   see page 139

Robert Graves   www.robertgraves.org
Goodbye to All That (1929)

Edmund Blunden   www.edmundblunden.org
Village Sketches in *Elegy and Other Poems* (1937)
Barry Webb: *Edmund Blunden – A Biography* (1990)

Flora Thompson   www.florathompson.co.uk
Lark Rise to Candleford trilogy (1939-1943)
Gillian Lindsay: *Flora Thompson – The Story of the Lark Rise Writer* (1991)
Martin Greenwood: *In Flora's Footsteps* (2009)

Chapter Four

Shakespeare's County

William Shakespeare, George Eliot, JRR Tolkien

When daffodils begin to peer,
With heigh! The doxy, over the dale,
Why, then comes in the sweet o' the year;
For the blood-red reigns in the winter's pale.
William Shakespeare

Warwickshire means Shakespeare. He dominates the county's literary landscape just as he remains the dominating figure of English literature. And although he will forever be associated most closely with Stratford-upon-Avon, he was fundamentally of the country, rather than the town.

His father's family were farmers, at Snitterfield, some three miles north of Stratford. His mother's family were Ardens, taking their name from the 'forest' which had once stretched north and west from Stratford towards Birmingham and beyond. Even by Shakespeare's time, most of it had gone, cut down to build houses and ships. From what we can gather from contemporary sources, the land north and west of Stratford was a mixture of woodland, small farms and arable, the so-called Wealden; to the south, the country was much more open, a mixture of crops, pasture and open heath, the Fielden. Both William Camden and John Speed looked out across this country from the top of Edgehill at around the time that Shakespeare was writing. Camden described it as 'plain champaign country and being rich in corn and green grass yieldeth a right goodly and pleasant prospect'. To Speed,

William Shakespeare
(1564-1616)
A countryman at heart

it was 'the medowing pastures with their green mantles so imbrodered with flowers' that most impressed. As Peter Ackroyd, to whom I am indebted for those last two references, observes in his *Shakespeare – The Biography*, it is the quintessential picture of rural England.

To an extent, that is still the case. The elms may have gone, and the forest been reduced to just a few woods and copses. But there is still plenty of old pasture to be seen, much of it bearing the tell-tale marks of ridge and furrow, which is how it would have been farmed in Shakespeare's day, and still relatively few trees. But it would be fair to say that there is nothing particularly distinctive about this landscape: no high hills, deep vales, impenetrable forests or blasted heaths. It is, in the best sense, just typical English countryside; the sort of countryside you might picture in your mind's eye if you were thinking of the Heart of England; the perfect setting, in fact, for the most English of writers.

Not that Shakespeare consciously set any of his plays in the landscapes of his home county, or used them to any extent in his poetry. Leaving aside the history plays, of the 27 plays which Shakespeare wrote in whole or in part, only two – *The Merry Wives of Windsor* and *As You Like It* – are ostensibly set in England, and even in that latter instance the playwright may very well have had the Forest of the Ardennes in mind rather than the Forest of Arden. The fact that when Charles says of the Old Duke, 'They say he is already in the forest of Arden, and a many merry men with him; and there they live like the old Robin Hood of England' does rather suggest a location overseas. Yet for all what looks like a conscious attempt to add a touch of glamour and romance to his dramas by placing them in exotic, faraway places, like Venice, Illyria, Verona and Navarre, the English countryside keeps breaking through.

When Oberon paints his lovely picture of Titania's bower in *A Midsummer Night's Dream*, it sounds like the sort of place you would be much more likely to find in a secluded spot just up the road from Stratford, than on some stony hillside near Athens:

> *I know a bank where the wild thyme blows,*
> *Where oxlips and the nodding violet grows,*
> *Quite over-canopied with luscious woodbine,*
> *With sweet musk roses and with eglantine*

As that quotation serves to demonstrate, Shakespeare knew his botany: weeds as well as flowers. The late sixteenth century was a difficult time for farming in England. A series of bad harvests forced many people off the land. Shakespeare's distinctly choleric uncle Richard, still farming at Snitterfield, would doubtless have told his nephew precisely what he thought about all of this perfectly good farmland being allowed to go to rack and ruin. Then, as now, it made for the perfect metaphor for the sort of neglect and decay that the Duke of Burgundy bemoans when reflecting on the state of war-torn France in *Henry V*:

> *Her fallow leas*
> *The darnel, hemlock and rank fumitory*
> *Doth root upon, while that the coulter rusts*
> *That should deracinate such savagery;*
> *The even mead that erst brought sweetly forth*
> *The freckled cowslip, burnet and green clover,*
> *Wanting the scythe, all uncorrected, rank,*
> *Conceives by idleness, and nothing teems*
> *But hateful docks, rough thistles, kecksies, burs,*
> *Losing both beauty and utility.*

Only a countryman could have written that, although only a poet would have talked about the simple act of ploughing in terms of deracinating the savagery!

Shakespeare may have long since gone to London by the time that he wrote *A Midsummer Night's Dream* in the 1590s, but he was well aware of the impact which one wet summer after another was having on his friends and family back in Warwickshire. The four harvests from 1594 onwards were disastrous, not just for England but for all Europe. The 'Great Famine', as it was called, lasted for three years, with stories abounding of people being forced to eat rats, cats and dogs, snakes and even their own children (in Hungary that was – allegedly!) to keep themselves alive. In England, there were food riots in Oxfordshire and the government was forced to restore the Act for the maintenance of husbandry and tillage, whose repeal had been a big factor in the abandonment of land to which we have already referred.

So, when Shakespeare has Titania blaming Oberon's 'brawls' for all manner of evils, it was the state of the English countryside that the playwright had very much in mind:

> *As in revenge, have suck'd up from the sea*
> *Contagious fogs; which falling in the land*
> *Have every pelting river made so proud*
> *That they have overborne their continents:*
> *The ox hath therefore stretch'd his yoke in vain,*
> *The ploughman lost his sweat, and the green corn*
> *Hath rotted ere his youth attain'd a beard;*
> *The fold stands empty in the drowned field,*
> *And crows are fatted with the murrion flock;*
> *The nine men's morris is fill'd up with mud,*
> *And the quaint mazes in the wanton green*
> *For lack of tread are undistinguishable:*
> *The human mortals want their winter here;*
> *No night is now with hymn or carol blest:*
> *Therefore the moon, the governess of floods,*
> *Pale in her anger, washes all the air,*
> *That rheumatic diseases do abound:*
> *And thorough this distemperature we see*
> *The seasons alter*

Of the English place-names in Shakespeare's plays, the vast majority are in the history plays, and in no case does the context shed any real light on what the place was like, other than its having been the site of a battle, a crucial meeting or some other important event. The Gloucestershire connection is an interesting one, which is dealt with in the Gloucestershire chapter, and Barton-in-the-Vale, where Shakespeare's aunt lived, gets a mention in *The Tempest*. But for the most part, if you want to find Shakespeare, you are much better off going to Shakespeare's birthplace in Henley Street in Stratford, or maybe to Mary Arden's House at Wilmcote, or the Globe Theatre in London, rather than making a pilgrimage to, say, Kenilworth (*Henry VI pt 2*), or Bosworth Field (*Richard III*) or Shrewsbury (*Henry IV pt 1*). If you want to feel yourself in Shakespeare's countryside, then a climb to the top of the Welcombe Hills Country Park is as good a bet as any, although almost any vantage point within a few miles of Stratford will suffice.

If specific, as opposed to generalised, literary landscapes are distinctly thin on the ground in Shakespeare's plays, then I'm afraid that the same goes for his poems. The sonnets are essentially stylised love poetry, addressed either to a handsome young man, urging him to marry, or an unnamed woman or, with the final 27, the infamous 'Dark Lady'. Sonnet 73 makes telling use of the seasons as a visual metaphor for ageing:

> *That time of year thou mayst in me behold*
> *When yellow leaves, or none, or few, do hang*
> *Upon those boughs which shake against the cold,*
> *Bare ruined choirs, where late the sweet birds sang.*

And, as I suggest in the Gloucestershire chapter, Sonnet 33 reads very much as if it might have been written on a high hill, looking westwards. But that's about it for rural references in the sonnets, unless one counts the first four lines of the *Sonnet to sundry notes of Music*, in which, with more than a nod to Christopher Marlowe, Shakespeare seems to confirm his affection for the English countryside:

> *Live with me and be my love,*
> *And we will all the pleasures prove*
> *That hills and valleys, dales and fields*
> *And all the craggy mountains yields*

However, I cannot leave Shakespeare without recalling Autolycus's song in *The Winter's Tale* which, for all its setting in 'Bohemia', captures so joyously the spirit of spring in England:

> *When daffodils begin to peer,*
> > *With heigh! the doxy over the dale,*
> *Why, then comes in the sweet o' the year;*
> > *For the red blood reigns in the winter's pale.*
>
> *The white sheet bleaching on the hedge,*
> > *With heigh! the sweet birds, O, how they sing!*
> *Doth set my pugging tooth on edge,*
> > *For a quart of ale is a dish for a king.*
>
> *The lark, that tirra-lirra chants*
> > *With heigh! with heigh! the thrush and the jay,*
> *Are summer songs for me and my aunts,*
> > *While we lie tumbling in the hay.*

George Eliot is Warwickshire's next great literary figure. She was born Mary Ann Evans at South Farm, on the Arbury Hall Estate not far from Nuneaton in north Warwickshire in 1819, to Robert Evans, manager of the 7,000-acre estate and his wife Christiana, the daughter of a local farmer.

George Eliot
(1819-1880)
Roots in North Warwickshire

The family were comfortably off and Robert was thought highly of by his coal-owner employers, the Newdigate family, both for his devotion to duty and his high standards of behaviour, both characteristics inherited by Mary Ann. She spent most of her childhood at Griff House, an imposing property complete with farmyard and out-buildings on the main road from Nuneaton to Coventry. Happily (I suppose) it is now a pub, a Whitbread-owned Beefeater with Premier Inn attached. Despite the garishness of the signage, it isn't so much the use to which the old house has been put that jars, as its situation. It stands at one side of one of the biggest and busiest roundabouts in the Midlands, hemmed in on every side by commercialised clutter. A less evocative situation for a building which stands for one of our greatest and most socially aware novelists could hardly be imagined.

Inside, the building has been comprehensively 'Beefeater-ised'. An inconspicuous plaque by the entrance to the bars represents the only acknowledgement of Griff House's literary heritage. Loud music is piped into every public space, the toilets not excepted. This is sadly not the place in which to attempt to call forth the spirit of George Eliot. (In fairness, one should add that at the time of writing Whitbread were in discussion with the George Eliot Fellowship about a proposal to open a visitor centre in one of the out-buildings.)

It is a pity, because upbringing was a powerful influence in shaping George Eliot the novelist. From her father's job, looking after the estate's tenants and managing its large staff, and the keen interest which she came to take in it, she learned about the finer points of farming, as well as gaining a keen appreciation of – and uneasiness about – the great gulf between the rich man in his castle and the poor man at its gate. From her walks through the countryside with her brother and sister, she learned all about the flowers, wildlife, woods and hedgerows of the pastoral north Warwickshire countryside. And whilst all of her novels are given fictional settings, most of them away from her home, scenes which can only have been taken from her country childhood do frequently appear.

Mary Ann's mother, with whom she was never particularly close, died of cancer in 1836 and five years later, her father retired and the family moved to Foleshill, just outside Coventry, where she acted as his housekeeper and towards the end of his life, carer. Here, the highly intelligent, well-read, deeply serious Mary Ann came under the influence of Charles Bray, a progressive philanthropist and successful businessman, who introduced her to a wide circle of like-minded intellectuals and gave her her first job, on the *Coventry Evening Telegraph and Observer*. By now, she was questioning her Christian faith, which caused her father unhappiness and created a rift with her brother and sister. Her father died in 1849; she was taken to the continent by the Brays to recover from her shock and grief and, when she got back, she decided that her future lay in London.

But if that was the end of Mary Ann Evans' direct Warwickshire connection, it lived on in her novels. Her first job was with the radical-leaning *Westminster Review*, under its distinctly unconventional editor John Chapman, who embarked on an affair with Marian, as she was now calling herself, at the same time as living in a ménage à trois with his wife Susannah and mistress! After that unhappy episode, she fell in with the highly talented polymath, George Henry Lewes – also already married, but semi-separated from his wife and children – and it was he who persuaded her to try her hand at writing novels.

Mary Ann Evans was the archetypal blue-stocking, combining a deep seriousness and a high moral tone with a disdain for conventionality which allowed her, without any apparent qualms, to take off with her lover Lewes for what the pair of them called a 'honeymoon' on the continent, even though he was still married. She decided to use a male pseudonym partly because she did not want to be associated with the female novelists of the day and their soppy romances, and maybe partly as well to avoid the tittle-tattle that would have accompanied her being known as Lewes' common law wife.

Besides her writing, she also took a keen interest in landscape and landscape painting. One of her most influential articles as editor of the *Westminster Review* was a review of John Ruskin's book *Modern Painters*.

'The truth of the infinite value that it teaches us', she wrote, 'is that of realism – the doctrine that all truth and honesty are to be obtained by a humble and faithful study of nature, and not by substituting vague forms, bred by imagination on the mists of feeling, in place of definite, substantial reality.'

It was a lesson that she carried with her, into her novels. That is not to say that she does not appreciate the romanticism of Wordsworth, whom she greatly admired, and his feeling for the emotional impact of landscape, but she is closest to Ruskin's realism, in that she paints a scene, with figures on it, very much as a landscape artist would do.

There are beautiful descriptions of landscape in all of her novels. The first of them, *Scenes of Clerical Life*, her trilogy of short stories, is set closest to home. The town of 'Milby' is recognisably Nuneaton; Shepperton Church in *Amos Barton* is All Saints, Chilvers Coton, where her parents are buried, now subsumed by the suburbs of Nuneaton; Cheverel Manor in *Mr Gilfil's Love Story* – 'the castellated house of grey-tinted stone, with the flickering sunbeams sending dashes of golden light across the many-shaped panes in the mullion windows' – is the Arbury Hall of reality, home to Mary Ann's father's employers, the Newdigate family; and Paddiford Common in the third of the short stories, *Janet's Repentence*, which was barely even a common in the book, was at Stockingford, also now swallowed up by Nuneaton.

The Mill on the Floss is probably her most autobiographical novel, even though – disappointingly, from our perspective – it is set in Lincolnshire.

The Coventry Canal

However, there is a walk which you can follow which does take you past at least one recognisable location from the book. It is promoted on the website of the excellent George Eliot Fellowship, and sets off from Griff House, taking in first the canal towpath and then an important setting in the novel for a fateful encounter between Maggie Tulliver and Philip Waken:

> *Just where this line of bank sloped down again to the level, a by-road turned off and left to the other side of the rise, where it was broken into very capricious hollows and mounds of an exhausted stone-quarry – so long exhausted that both mounds and hollows were now clothed with brambles and trees, and here and there by a stretch of grass which a few sheep kept close-nibbled. In her childish days, Maggie held this place, called the Red Deeps, in very great awe ... But now it had the charm for her which any broken ground, any mimic rock and ravine, have for the eyes that rest habitually on the level; especially in summer, when she could rest on a grassy hollow under the shadow of a branching ash, stooping aslant from the steep above her, and listen to the hum of insects, like tiniest bells on the garment of Silence, or see the sunlight piercing the distant boughs, as if to chase and drive home the truant blue of the wild hyacinths. In this June time too, the dog roses were in their glory ...*

The Red Deeps of the novel are the Griff Hollows of reality. Together with the canal, they provide an enclave of peace and quiet in a ferment of motorised activity. You can see why Mary Ann liked to walk here; and wonder whether the junction of two canals – the main Coventry Canal and its spur, branching off to the Arbury coal mines – might have sowed the seed for the setting of the main river Floss and its tributary the Ripple in *The Mill on the Floss*. This is unlikely, however, given that the Floss is tidal and the vessels on it are sailing-boats with red-brown sails, as opposed to flat-bottomed coal barges.

The only problem is reaching them from Griff House. Mary Ann would have strolled up narrow, muddy Gipsy Lane from her home and dropped down onto the tow-path at Gipsy Lane Bridge. But Gipsy Lane is now a busy single carriageway road with no footway on either side and halfway between the hotel and the bridge is a big quarry from which enormous lorries issue at regular intervals. I attempted the walk, gave up, and drove, parking in a one-car layby just beyond the bridge.

But once you've reached the canal, the walk along it is a blessed relief after the hustle and bustle of Nuneaton. You have to go carefully after you've used the little brick-built Turn Bridge about half a mile north of Gipsy Lane Bridge to cross from the towpath to the other side. The path may be part of the Centenary Way, but it is narrow and slippery and the dark waters of the canal are very close.

A notice board, where you reach the point where the Griff Hollows Canal once branched off towards the Arbury coal mines, informs us that Griff Hollows is now one of Nuneaton and Bedworth Council's 'Wild Spaces', and wild it certainly is. The word 'hollows' describes it very well. It is as if some giant hand has scooped up fistfuls of earth to leave a cratered, mounded, moonscape of a surface to be colonised by the bushes, trees, brambles and old man's beard – exactly as described in *The Mill on the Floss*. It is a secret, slightly sinister place, which has no doubt seen plenty of romantic

Griff Hollows

encounters over the years, and must have struck Mary Ann as the perfect setting for the initiation of a pivotal love affair. A circular path takes you up one side of the Hollows to the main road at the top and then back down the other side.

There are some lovely descriptions of landscape as well in *Adam Bede*, notably in the contrasts between rough, tough Stonyshire to the north and what a farmer would call the 'boy's land' of fertile Loamshire to the south, as well as the setting of the village in which most of the action takes place, Hayslope. But the consensus of opinion seems to place the original for the village beyond our bounds, namely Ellastone on the River Dove near the Staffordshire/Derbyshire border, where the novelist's father had worked as a carpenter many years before.

If George Eliot's themes as a novelist were mostly social and political (usually with a dash of romance thrown in) and her settings mostly urban, she remained a country girl at heart. Nothing provides better evidence for that than the introduction to her fifth full-scale novel *Felix Holt the Radical*, published in 1866. It was inspired by the political ferment produced by the Second Reform Act of 1867, although its chronological setting is the aftermath of the first such Act, the so-called Great Reform Act of 1832. Both acts extended the franchise, only to a fairly limited extent in 1832; much more widely, to take in ordinary working men, in 1867, but both produced considerable unease and upheaval. The country was changing. Olde (rural and agricultural) England was giving way to new (urban and industrial) England, something about which George Eliot evidently had mixed feelings. She had no love at all for the old order, yet she clearly cherished the countryside it had created. In the introduction to *Felix Holt*, she imagines a traveller, by coach, crossing the central Midland plain, from the Avon to the Trent:

> As the morning silvered the meadows with their long lines of bushy willows marking the watercourses, or burnished the golden corn-ricks clustered near the long roofs of some midland homestead, he saw the full-uddered cows driven from their pasture to the early milking. Perhaps it was the shepherd, head-servant of the farm, who drove them, his sheep-dog following with a heedless unofficial air of a beadle in undress.

And she continues with this paean of praise to the English hedgerow:

> But everywhere the bushy hedgerows waisted the land with their straggling beauty, shrouded the grassy borders of the pastures with catkined hazels, and tossed their long blackberry branches on the cornfields. Perhaps they were white with may, or starred with pale-pink dog-roses; perhaps the urchins were already nutting amongst them, or gathering the plenteous crabs. It was worth the journey only to see those hedgerows, the liberal homes of unmarketable beauty – of the purple-blossomed ruby-berried nightshade, of the wild convolvulus climbing and spreading in tendrilled strength till it made a great curtain of pale-green hearts and white trumpets, of the many-tubed honeysuckle which, in its most delicate fragrance, hid a charm more subtle and penetrating than beauty. Even if it were winter the hedgerows showed their coral, the scarlet haws, the deep-crimson hips, with lingering brown leaves to make a resting place for the jewels of the hoar-frost.

'The liberal homes of unmarketable beauty' – what a wonderful description of the English landscape's defining feature, especially at a time when sundry academics are endeavouring, ill-advisedly and probably counter-productively, to put a monetary value on our countryside. Natural beauty is invaluable, and for the purposes of this argument, I'm classing hedges as natural! If nothing else, George Eliot's description of the Midland countryside as she knew it does show us what we have lost.

Most of the action in *Felix Holt* takes place in and around the fast-growing town of 'Treby Magna'. Its original seems to me to be an amalgam of Nuneaton, where George Eliot grew up, and Coventry, where she lived in the 1840s. Nuneaton was probably the dominant influence, thanks not least to the riot which erupted there on the occasion of the first election after the passing of the Great Reform Act, when Mary Ann was 13. It was the basis for the riot which is so central to the novel.

But Coventry, and indeed Stoneleigh, gets a look-in as well. It sounds very much as if it was Coventry from which 'Mr Sampson', George Eliot's imaginary coachman, sets out in the introduction to *Felix Holt*:

> When, leaving the town of Treby Magna behind him, he drove between the hedges for a mile or so, crossed the queer long bridge over the river Lapp, and then put his horses to a swift gallop up the hill by the low-nestled village of Little Treby, till they were on the fine level road, skirted on one side by grand larches, oaks, and wych elms, which sometimes opened so far as to let the traveller see that there was a park behind them.

If the 'queer long bridge' is, as many have suggested, the bridge over the Avon at Stoneleigh, a pretty village a few miles south of Coventry which fits very well the description of 'low-nestled' and on a hill, then Sampson would have been approaching it from the wrong side. But leaving that aside, as the coach rolls on alongside the parkland, and the passengers catch a glimpse of 'Transome Court', with its 'river winding through a finely timbered park', the setting fits Stoneleigh Abbey just perfectly. It may be taking the connection too far to point out that just as the rightful ownership of Transome Court was a central theme in *Felix Holt*, then so had the rightful ownership of Stoneleigh Abbey become something of a cause célèbre some 60 years or so before George Eliot was writing – the parties involved being members of the Leigh family – relatives on her mother's side of a certain Jane Austen! Austen stayed at Stoneleigh Abbey with her mother and sister for ten days in 1808, and used elements of the house in both *Mansfield Park* and *Northanger Abbey*.

After *Felix Holt* came George Eliot's masterpiece, *Middlemarch*, a complex tale of love, religion, politics and personalities set in a 'provincial town'. It is a great novel, but not in the least bit rural. George Lewes died in 1878. She sought solace with John Cross, whom she married in May 1880, although she too would be dead, from a kidney infection, in less than eight months.

She was not one of the 'regional novelists' in the accepted, Hardyesque sense, but both her rural and more urban novels do have a wonderfully strong spirit of place.

And so to JRR Tolkien. 'Tolkien?' I hear you say. 'What's the creator of a fantasy world doing in a book on literary landscapes? And anyway, wasn't he brought up in Birmingham and lived virtually his entire adult life in suburban Oxford and Bournemouth?'

Well, yes, dear reader, you have a point on both accounts. You will not find the original for Helms Deep in the Severn Valley near Kidderminster and the mountains of Mordor are not modelled on the Clent Hills. And apart from four years, between the ages of four and eight, Tolkien did indeed live all his life in an urban environment. But what a significant four years those were! "The longest-seeming and most formative part of my life," said Tolkien, looking back.

They were spent in a cottage in the hamlet of Sarehole, just over the border into Worcestershire and, at that time, just beyond the Birmingham urban sprawl. Ronald, as he

John Ronald Reuel Tolkien
(1892-1973)
A man of the shire

was always known to his family, lived there from 1896 to 1900 with his brother Hilary and mother Mabel, his father John, a bank manager, having succumbed to rheumatic fever shortly after the rest of the family had returned home from South Africa.

Across a meadow on the other side of the road from their house was the River Cole and Sarehole Mill. Ronald and Hilary would spend hours there, peering into the dark depths of the mill-pool, shuddering at the power of the great wheel churning, and watching fascinated as the white-dusted miller – the White Ogre, as they called him – loaded the sacks of flour onto wagons. If they weren't at the mill, they would be in a deep sandpit halfway up the hill to Moseley or maybe exploring the woods on the Lickey Hills, just to the south of where they lived.

At the time, it must have seemed a magical place, which shaped Tolkien's feelings for the English countryside for the rest of his life. But the idyll was not to last. When he was eight, in 1900, Ronald won a scholarship to King Edward's School in the centre of Birmingham, prompting a move for the family first to Moseley and then, after Mabel's conversion to Roman Catholicism, to 26 Oliver Road, alongside the Birmingham Oratory in Edgbaston. And just as Tolkien was seemingly engulfed by the city, so in time was Sarehole. When he returned to his childhood paradise in 1933, he was appalled, and described the experience in his diary:

> *I pass over the pangs to me of passing through Hall Green – become a*
> *huge tram-ridden meaningless suburb, where I actually lost my way – and*
> *eventually down what is left of beloved lanes of childhood, and past the very*
> *gate of our cottage, now in the midst of a sea of new red-brick. The old mill*

Birmingham from the Lickey Hills

*still stands and Mrs Hunt's still sticks out into the road as it turns uphill;
but the crossing beyond the now fenced-in pool, where the bluebell lane ran
down into the mill land, is now a dangerous crossing alive with motors and
red lights. The White Ogre's house … is become a petrol station, and most
of Short Avenue and the elms between it and the crossing have gone. How I
envy those whose precious early scenery has not been exposed to such violent
and peculiarly hideous change.*

However, whilst the situation now is certainly no better now than it was when Tolkien
visited, nor is it much worse. Sarehole Mill, its attendant meadow and the River Cole
remain an oasis of green in a desert of red-brick, as part of 'The Shire Country Park'.
It is true that the meadow is more of a park, and that the mill offers guided tours
and refreshments for visitors. But at least the Tolkien connection is being celebrated.
There is even a 'Hobbit Café' by the roundabout. And more than enough remains
for us to get at least some idea of what it was that so ignited young Ronald Tolkien's
imagination more than 100 years ago.

The Shire Country Park is well named. When Bilbo Baggins returns with Gandalf
from their adventures and they come in sight of the country in which he had been
born and bred 'where the shapes of the land and of the trees were as well known to
him as his hands and toes', it is Sarehole Mill in Worcestershire to which they are
returning, as much as Hobbiton in the Shire:

*And so they crossed the bridge and passed the mill and came right back to
Bilbo's front door.*

81

The Hobbit was published in September 1937 and the first edition was sold out by Christmas. It would be another 16 years before Tolkien completed its sequel, *The Lord of the Rings*. And what years of toil they were, as he struggled to complete his masterpiece, making sure that it was consistent and correct in every detail of the essentially British mythology which he had created as its context and in its own invented geography. The underlying theme – the allegory, if you like – was exactly as before: not only the struggle and eventual triumph of the good little people over the bad over-mighty ones, but the successful resistance of the countryside to the despoliation of development. I know it is an over-simplification, but essentially it was a battle between the countryside of his childhood, Sarehole and the Lickey Hills, and the dark forces of Mordor, aka Birmingham, even if the country on which it was fought out belonged entirely to Tolkien's imagination.

With one exception, the inspiration for all of this was, once again, those four years that Tolkien had lived as a child at Sarehole. One of the stranger things about him in his adult life was that, despite his passionate love for the English countryside, he very rarely visited it. Partly, this was because it upset him so much to see trees being cut down to make way for airfields and new roads, or red-brick houses spreading out into the pastures. But it was also, as his biographer Humphrey Carpenter argues, because he already had enough fuel in his mental tank to sustain even as monumental a work as *The Lord of the Rings*.

> By the time he reached middle age his imagination no longer needed to be stimulated by experience; or rather, it had received all the stimulus it required in the early years of his life, the years of event and changing landscapes; now it could nourish itself on these accumulated memories.

The exception, the rural literary inspiration which post-dates his time at Sarehole, is Tom Bombadil, a nature spirit based on his son William's Dutch doll, which he used to represent the English countryside. His poem *The Adventures of Tom Bombadil* was first published in the *Oxford Magazine* in 1934, but when his publishers turned down the idea of a volume of poems on a similar theme, he crops up again, somewhat enigmatically, at various stages in *The Lord of the Rings*, a great survivor, comforter of the Hobbits and seemingly unconcerned at the rise of Sauron. He represented, wrote Tolkien in a letter to his publishers, 'the spirit of the [vanishing] Oxfordshire and Berkshire countryside'.

The other Tolkien location to be visited in these parts is the Lickey Hills. The best view of Tolkien's front line in his battle between the encroaching town and the resisting countryside is to be obtained from the 'Topograph' on the summit of Beacon Hill, given to the people of Birmingham in 1907 by the Cadbury family and now part of the Lickey Hills Country Park. To the north-east lies Mordor – sorry, Birmingham –not nearly as smoky these days as it would have been when the young Tolkien walked here, but still a slightly threatening urban sprawl, pushing its tentacles out into the surrounding countryside like Tolkien's Shelob; to the south, through the one gap left in the trees, the Worcestershire countryside, stretching away to the Malverns. And there are other literary connections to be enjoyed as well: Worm's Ash

Sarehole Mill

Hill to the south-west and, to the north-west, the Shropshire Hills, appropriately blue in the distance.

The main body of the Lickey Hills stretch away to the east. The country reminds me of the wealthier parts of Surrey: leafy lanes, heathy woodland, ever so smart properties half-hidden in the trees. But there are some lovely walks to be had in the woodlands, walks which Tolkien might well have taken as a child. As I burst through one thicket, I came across a double line of tall Scotch pines framing a sandy track, and seeming somehow to nod their heads in recognition of my presence. They reminded me immediately of the Ents 'clean-limbed and smooth-skinned like forest trees in their prime'.

I ventured deeper into the woods, passing other 'entish' trees, this time 'bearded and gnarled like hale but ancient trees' until I came across a strange figure, carved from the living wood. Treebeard! It had to be: the very embodiment of the unconditional love which Tolkien had entertained for trees from his earliest years. He most certainly would not concur with my strictures about an overgrown countryside!

He may, as I say, have spent only four years of his life at Sarehole but, for the rest of his life, Tolkien regarded Worcestershire in general, and this place in particular, as his home.

> *Any corner of that county (however fair or squalid) is in an indefinable way 'home' to me, as no other part of the world is.*

83

Exploring Warwickshire's Literary Landscapes

Walks

Shakespeare country: There is a Shakespeare Walk around Stratford-upon-Avon (details on **www.stratfordtownwalk.co.uk**). Follow the 'Monarch's Way' long-distance footpath from Stratford town centre to the obelisk at the top of the Welcome Hills Country Park, from which there are fine views of Shakespeare's countryside.

George Eliot country: The walk described, from Griff House, along the canal, to Griff Hollows is pleasant and enjoyable, once you have navigated Gipsy Lane. It is probably easier to access the footpath that runs through Griff Hollows to the canal (the Centenary Way) from the town side, Bermuda Park station being one option.

At the time of writing, Arbury Hall, the Cheverel Park in *Mr Gilfil's Love Story*, was open to the public on the Sunday and Monday of bank holiday weekends between April and August, or you could go on one of the tours organised by the George Eliot Fellowship, which also include South Farm where Mary Ann Evans was born.

Tolkien country: Details of Sarehole Mill opening hours and special events can be found on **www.birminghammuseums.org.uk**

There is a circular walk around Lickey Hills Country Park – the details are on **www.gps-routes.co.uk** – and following the North Worcestershire Way eastwards will take you deeper into the Lickey Hills woodland.

Pubs

Stratford: Good pubs include the *Dirty Duck*, the *Yard of Ale*, the *Old Thatch* and *The Bear* at the Swan's Nest. Country pubs in the Stratford area tend to have been gastro-ised. The two nearest pubs to the Mary Arden Museum are both in Wilmcote: the *Masons Arms* and the *Mary Arden Inn*, which also does accommodation.

Nuneaton: *Griff House* is worth a visit, especially if and when a George Eliot visitor centre is established in the outbuildings. The best pub in the town itself is probably the *Felix Holt*, not far from the statue of George Eliot in Newdigate Street, which is not to be missed.

Lickey Hills: Much the best pub in the Lickey Hills area is the *Coach and Horses* at Weatheroak, which offers an impressive range of real ales, including from the on-site Weatheroak Hill Brewery, and excellent food.

However, the pub which Tolkien pilgrims will most want to visit is, of course, the *Eagle and Child*, aka the Bird and Baby, in St Giles in Oxford, where the Inklings, Tolkien and CS Lewis amongst them, would gather every Monday or Tuesday lunchtime.

Griff House

Select Bibliography

William Shakespeare   www.shakespeare.org
Peter Ackroyd: *Shakespeare – The Biography* (2005)

George Eliot   www.georgeeliot.com
Scenes of Clerical Life (1857)
The Mill on the Floss (1860)
Felix Holt (1866)
Jenny Uglow: *George Eliot* (1987)
Kathryn Hughes: *George Eliot – The Last Victorian* (1998)
Philip Davis: *The Transferred Life of George Eliot* (2017)

JRR Tolkien   www.tolkiensociety.org
Humphrey Carpenter: *J.R.R. Tolkien – A Biography* (1977)

Chapter Five

Shropshire

Mary Webb, Wilfred Owen, AE Housman

Beyond were meadows, blue distance, purple distance, smoke-coloured hills, and more hills so pale as to fade on the sky.

Mary Webb

Shropshire is a county of contrasts, more so perhaps than any other. It has something of almost everything: from the urban sprawl of Telford, through the cradle of the industrial revolution in Ironbridge gorge, to the mysterious meres of north Shropshire, the abrupt eruptions of the Wrekin and the Cley Hills and, to the south and west, long, remote, dramatic ranges of hills, which seem more like mountains, rising as they do so steeply from the surrounding plain. It is almost as if England and Wales have collided and great ridges of rock been squeezed out of the earth in the impact.

There is something else profoundly singular about the landscape, especially of south Shropshire, and that is the feeling of other-worldliness, of mystery, almost of foreboding, which those long fingers of hill country and the deep valleys in between seem somehow to inspire. I say that as someone who had visited the county only fleetingly before I came to write this book, but it is palpable. It may have something to do with the Celtic influence, which is as strong as you would expect in the border country. Clun feels as Celtic as Bridgnorth does Anglo-Saxon. Shrewsbury looks both ways.

Given all of that, it would have been remarkable had Shropshire not inspired some great literature, although to use the word 'great' is pushing it a bit. AE Housman's *A Shropshire Lad* teeters on the brink of greatness but, as we will discover, the poems were inspired more by the idea of Shropshire than by the reality.

But first there is Mary Webb, high priestess of the romantic rustic school of literature, in whose novels – *Precious Bane* being much the most famous – the Shropshire landscape is not so much a back-drop as centre stage. She was a mystic, who believed profoundly not just in the spirit of place but in the influence of place on human behaviour and emotion. Her novels live and breathe Shropshire. Put her together with Housman and his 'land of lost content' and you can begin to understand why Shropshire – on the edge of the industrial West Midlands – can sometimes feel, as Matthew Engel puts it, 'the most remote of English counties'.

Like so many of her heroines, Mary Webb cuts a fragile and slightly tragic figure. A daughter of Shropshire, who came to love and understand the countryside around her during an idyllic childhood under Wenlock Edge, she wrote passionate novels and deeply personal poetry, imbued with the very essence of her native country. She was a highly strung, mystical and rather needy woman, who half-believed the myths and folklore that feature so strongly in her writings; a turn-of-the-century hippy, who loved nothing better than to run on tiptoe through a dewy Shropshire meadow as the dawn was breaking.

Mary Webb
(1881-1927)
Her father's 'precious bane'

Her health and looks were marred by the protuberant eyes and goitred throat which are the symptoms of Graves' disease, her marriage to her beloved Henry was childless and eventually broke down, and she died at the age of just 47. For a time after that, it seemed that the gods might finally have taken pity on her, for she was hailed as a neglected genius by none other than the Prime Minister, Stanley Baldwin, and became a posthumous literary sensation. But not for long. Critical opinion soon turned decisively against her blend of the mystic with the rustic, and she became the main target of Stella Gibbons' brilliantly cruel parody of the entire 'loam and lovechild' genre, *Cold Comfort Farm*.

She does make an easy target. Her characters have strange names, like Kester Woodeaves, Hazel Woodus and Gillian Lovekin. They converse in an unlikely dialect: all 'oots' and 'tuthrees', 'gledys' and 'raughts'. Hills brood, dark woods glower, peewits call to each other across the empurpled moors, while the wind soughs in the whinberries. As Robert Lynd observes, in his foreword to *Seven for a Secret*:

> *If it is necessary to classify novelists ... Mary Webb must be put in a class that contains writers so different as Emily Bronte and Thomas Hardy, for whom the earth is predominantly a mystery-haunted landscape inhabited by mortals who suffer. To class her with these writers is not to claim that she is their equal; all we need to claim is that her work is alive with the fiery genius of sympathy, pity and awe.*

So, not a great novelist, but certainly a passionate and strangely compelling one, whose books do have an almost magnetic force about them, thanks not least to their settings. Shropshire provides the perfect moody backdrop to the goings-on of her cast of rustic characters: 'The land of betwixt and between,' as she describes it in her final novel. It may not be very many miles from the office-blocks and industrial estates of Telford to the ancient rocks and bilberries of the Stiperstones but it feels as if they are separated by a thousand years. All of this is not merely reflected in Mary Webb's novels, but magnified and brought to life. One of her greatest and most distinguished admirers, John Buchan, summed her up pretty well when he wrote: 'She is at once the offspring of this mysterious landscape and the interpretation of it.'

Each of her novels has a different Shropshire context. Taking them in the order in which they were written, the setting for *The Golden Arrow* (1916) is the Long Mynd and the Stiperstones, in particular the spectacular outcrop of quartzite rock known as 'The Devil's Chair'; for *Gone to Earth* (1917) it is Lords Hill and the lead mines around Snailbeach; with *The House in Dormer Forest* (1920) she moves south-west to the Hope Valley; *Seven for a Secret* (1922) is set in the border country around Clun; the meres of north Shropshire provide a suitably ominous backdrop for *Precious Bane* (1924); and for her final, unfinished, novel, *Armour Wherein He Trusted* we are back in the Shropshire Hills at Culverbatch.

She married Henry Webb, a teacher, in 1912. He was her first and only love, and she was utterly, hopelessly, devoted to him. They lived first at Weston-super-Mare and, according to her biographer Gladys Mary Coles, it was the feeling of separation from her native landscape that she experienced there – 'her feeling of exile intensified by the knowledge that there was now no Shropshire home to return to, [which] was the vital factor in her genesis as a novelist.'

They moved back to Shropshire in 1914, buying Rose Cottage in Pontesbury, nine miles or so south-west of Shrewsbury. For a time they operated a small market garden, Mary taking her fruit and vegetables to market at Shrewsbury on foot. They seem to have been surpassingly happy. Mary loved to climb the two hills which overlook the village, Earl's Hill and, especially, Pontesford Hill:

> *This is the hill, ringed by the misty shire,*
> *The mossy southern hill,*
> *The little hill where larches climb so high ...*

Mary had been writing since her childhood. Her mind must have been over-flowing with stories and settings. *The Golden Arrow* was knocked off in just three weeks. Henry bought her a special fountain pen, with an accelerated ink flow, to keep pace with her speed of composition. She was all the speedier for the fact that she had done her homework. A key influence on the way she approached her novels was the example of JM Synge, the Irish playwright, who had taken himself off to the Aran Islands for extended stays over the course of four years before finally putting pen to paper, to make sure that he got the language, landscape and folklore of the west of Ireland just right in *The Playboy of the Western World*. With all of her novels, Mary did much the same. If her descriptions of landscape are sometimes over-blown, there is no faulting their fundamental accuracy; likewise, so good judges attest, with her reproduction of the Shropshire dialect, as it was just after the turn of the twentieth century. It wasn't just the details of settings she was after, it was their atmosphere. The Devil's Chair looms over *The Golden Arrow*, just as Lords Hill, its chapel and its mines, infuse *Gone to Earth*, and the north Shropshire meres haunt *Precious Bane*.

The Golden Arrow is set in Deborah Arden's parents' stone cottage in Wilderhope 'in the midst of the hill plateau'; in other words, on the Long Mynd. Her father John is a shepherd, and she has a brother Joe, who is courting Lily, the daughter of an eccentric near-neighbour Eli Huntbach. A handsome young preacher turns up, much admired by both Deborah and Lily, although it is Deborah who wins his affections. The story is built around the parallel relationships between the two couples (as they become). Joe and Lily marry, not very happily; Stephen and Deb run off together to live in sin in a cottage near the lead mines (where Stephen gets a job, having given up his ministry) at the southern end of the Stiperstones, in the shadow of the Devil's Chair.

Deborah falls pregnant and persuades Stephen to marry her, but he becomes depressed, oppressed by the 'apocalyptic' nature of the landscape, and in particular by the Devil's Chair and its associations. In desperation, he makes a rather feeble effort to blow it up, but leaves scarcely a scratch on the adamantine rock. Eventually he decides to go off to America, with a farmer exporting a herd of Shorthorns. Deborah is beside herself with grief and burns their home and belongings before eventually being rescued by her father. She gives birth to a little boy, Stephen returns from America and, after a final hiatus, they all (Lily and Joe excepted presumably) live happily ever after!

The Devil's Chair dominates the book, just as it dominates the landscape:

> *In the plain this pile of rock and the rise on which it stood above the rest of the hill-tops would have constituted a hill in itself. The scattered rocks, the ragged holly-brakes on the lower slopes were like small carved lions beside the black marble steps of a stupendous throne. Nothing ever altered its look. Dawn quickened over it in pearly and emerald; summer sent the armies of heather to its very foot; snow rested there as doves nest in cliffs. It remained inviolable, taciturn, evil. It glowered darkly on the dawn; it came through the snow like jagged bones through flesh; before its hardness even the venturesome cranberries were discouraged. For miles around, in the plains, the valleys, the mountain dwellings, it was feared. It drew the thunder, people said. Storms broke around it suddenly, out of a clear sky; it seemed almost as if it created storm.*

The Devil's Chair

One cannot help but be reminded of the description of Egdon Heath in *The Return of the Native*, by Thomas Hardy, whom Mary much admired. Even so, it is a fine, passionate piece of writing, and if the Devil's Chair doesn't quite live up to its billing in reality, there is an ominous feel to the place. Clouds do indeed seem to gather above it, as the prevailing westerlies are forced suddenly skywards by the great ridge on which it stands. They hover over it like one of Tolkein's Nazgul, and when the great rock is swallowed up by the clouds ...? That, so legend has it, is when the 'devil is in his chair'!

The easiest way to the Devil's Chair is from the car park and visitor centre at The Bog, just to the south of the ridge and hard by the lead mines where Stephen Southernwood worked. There is also a lonely and rather ugly chapel nearby, which may have served as the original for the one where Lily and Deb first encountered Stephen. The cottage where Stephen and Deb lived, supposedly high on the ridge, is a Mary Webb invention (albeit one that was probably inspired by the miners' cottages a couple of miles to the north at Blakemoor Gate). There is nothing on the summit save heather and whinberries, a few stony tracks and the four tors: Cranberry Rock, Manstone Rock, Shepherd's Rock and the Devil's Chair.

The threads running through the story are those of contrast: the contrast between Deb's all-consuming, heart-and-soul love for Stephen (and which Stephen eventually comes to feel for her) and the superficial sexual attraction which Lily feels for Joe – 'the age-old feud between storm-tossed greatness and sheltered littleness'. But when it comes to the Stiperstones and the Long Mynd – their respective evil and goodness symbolised by the Devil's Chair on the one hand, and the white cross of a signpost on the other – things get much more complicated:

> She looked across at the Devil's Chair – dark and shining as a night-sapphire. It seemed to her that there was no hostility now between the two ranges, between the towering throne and the small white cross. Always before, she had superstitiously regarded the Chair as wholly evil, the Flockmaster's cross as wholly good. Now she saw good and evil mingled, and felt a slumbering terror in the protecting cross, a hidden beneficence in the inimical stronghold across the valley.

Make of that what you will. It rather reads as if Mary is trying to find a way of reconciling the two sides of her sexuality, something which is certainly a recurrent theme in her novels.

Nonetheless, it is surely Deb and Stephen who find 'the golden arrow', which courting couples are said to go looking for in this part of Shropshire at Easter-time. If they find it, it may cut them and give them pain, but the reward will be a 'vast of joy' in which 'naught could part them, neither in the flower of life nor in the brown winrow.'

The Long Mynd and the Stiperstones do, for sure, make a fascinating contrast: love and lust, good and evil, serenity and anguish – take your pick. Perhaps the best way of appreciating the starkness of their differences is to climb up the western side of the Long Mynd, more or less where Mary Webb places the Ardens' stone cottage. There is an enjoyable, not too challenging, all-weather walk which you can take from the car park at Bridges, one which has the added advantage of bringing you back to one of the best pubs in the area, the Horseshoe.

Beeches on the Long Mynd

Clouds gathering over Stiperstones

It doesn't much matter whether you start by taking the road to Ratlinghope (pronounced Ratchup), or the even narrower lane that runs up to Coates Farm. I chose the latter – by mistake! – but it turned out to be an inspired error. I had to ask the way when I reached the farm, as there seemed no way through or past it. I needn't have worried. "Just go straight through the yard and then turn left up the hill," I was advised. And sure enough, the lane did indeed run slap bang through the middle of a farmyard as busy as any I'd encountered in Shropshire. I was accompanied by a large tractor, armed with two distinctly menacing metal spikes (for lifting and carrying big bales), as I tramped through the silage and past the cow sheds. But take the old mule track up the hill, and you are soon in a different world.

If the Stiperstones ridge, crowned by its jagged tors, behind you as you go up the hill, has a savage and ominous look, the Long Mynd is almost voluptuous in its curves as the soft slopes roll away on either side. It's really not very hard to see why Mary Webb chose this place to make her point about contrast. As you follow the old track up the hill, green fields give way to heather as you climb. This is not, on a snowy day in January at least, the busiest corner of the Shropshire hills. I was struck by the emptiness, and the silence. It is magnificently wild, without being in the least bit threatening, and the views from the top, stretching from the Clee Hills in the east to the mountains of Wales all the way to Cader Idris in the west, are breathtaking.

The track from Coates Farm runs up the southern side of a heathery cleft in the hillside. For the descent (or it could be the other way round), there is either the lane back to Bridges, or a bridle path running more or less parallel to it. I preferred the path. I imagined myself with Joe and Lily, Stephen and Deb, coming back to the valley after their day out at Lammas Fair in Church Stretton, making their way down the hill to 'Slepe', as Mary Webbs calls Ratlinghope. This turned out to be a bit of a disappointment. It is barely a hamlet, let alone a village, and is mostly taken up with a large and rather scruffy farm. But there is at least the tiny church, where both the couples are married, tucked in under the hill. There is a cottage, which might be the original for Joe and Lily's, but it has been unsympathetically modernised. Still, the last half a mile or so of the walk, past Manor Farm and across the bridge over the River Onny is blissfully arcadian, made all the more enjoyable for the fact that the Horseshoe Inn is just around the corner!

We don't have to travel very far to find the setting for Mary Webb's next novel, *Gone to Earth*. It is the second best known of her novels, having been made into a film in 1950, which was re-issued by the National Film Archive in 1985 and can now be seen on YouTube. It is unashamedly melodramatic, its central character, Hazel Woodus, being torn between her spiritual love for the young preacher, Edward Marston, and her physical desire for the lustful, hard-hearted, fox-hunting local squire Jack Reddin. Written at the height of the First World War, it can be seen both as a cry of anguish on behalf of the victims of that terrible conflict and as a further exploration of Mary's own conflicted sexuality. For there is no doubt that Hazel is the embodiment, if not of the whole Mary Webb, then certainly of what Gladys Mary Coles calls 'the most ethereal and fey side ... as well as her most passionate and earth-loving.'

Hazel and her father Abel, an odd sort of cove who keeps bees, makes coffins and plays the harp, live in a tiny cottage by the hill called Bromlow Callow, a mile or so west of the village of Hope on the western side of the Hope Valley. It is still much as described in the book – 'a spinney of silver birches and larches that topped a round hill' – which is crossed by a footpath running north-east to south-west, and repays a visit, not least for the fine views both to the Welsh mountains in the west and to the hill which Hazel/Mary call God's Little Mountain, towering darkly some five miles away to the east. It was there, at an eisteddfod in the Baptist chapel, that her parents had met and it would be there, at the fulcrum of the story, that Hazel first encounters Edward.

For Lords Hill, we need to head first to Snailbeach, under the northern end of the Stiperstones ridge. There is a narrow lane which goes almost all the way to the summit, but there is no parking when you get there, so the best thing is to leave your car at Snailbeach Village Hall, and walk up the steep hill, past the remains of the lead mines, dating back to Roman times, which play such a key part in the story. Just beyond the summit, down a steep slope to the right, was and is what must be the most remote non-conformist chapel in England.

Lords Hill Chapel

The chapel and minister's house at God's Little Mountain were all in one – a long, low building of grey stone surrounded by the graveyard, where stones, flat, erect, askew, took the place of a flower garden. Away to the left, just over a rise, the hill was gashed by the grey steeps of the quarries. In front rose another curve covered with thick woods. To the right was the batch, down which a road – in winter a water-course – led into the valley. Beyond the house, God's Little Mountain sloped softly up and away, apparently to its possessor.

The scene today is virtually identical, with one exception. The chapel has been painted white and is quite a handsome building, if now slightly distressed, with the little cottage of a manse tucked up against its side. It was built in 1873, to serve the local mining community, and replaced an older chapel, but as *Gone to Earth* is set in around 1910 that can't be the explanation for the discrepancy between Mary Webb's description of the chapel, and its appearance today. Perhaps it is just that coat of paint which has made all the difference.

It is a delightful spot, and if you follow the path onwards and upwards, you will come first to a grove of holly and thorn trees, then to the two isolated Blakemoor miners cottages, and finally to the open moor, where on dark and stormy nights the 'death pack' – 'phantom hounds of a bad squire' – is supposed to scour the country, bringing death to anyone who sees them. Hazel Woodus believed in this sort of stuff implicitly, especially as she had adopted a fox cub, called, with a certain lack of originality, 'Foxy', as well as an old rabbit, a one-eyed cat and a blind bird. Mary Webb was nothing if not sentimental about animals, and had a particular hatred of fox-hunting (slightly ironically, given that one of her beloved Shropshire's most notorious sons was the great hunting squire, John 'Mad Jack' Mytton, who drank, hunted, gambled and gave away a fortune worth well over £10 million in his short life, and who is commemorated today in the long distance footpath the 'Jack Mytton Way'). The fact that Hazel's seducer and nemesis, Jack Reddin, is master of the local hunt, and evidently utterly careless of the welfare of dumb creatures, is a significant sub-text.

But the main story is really all about Hazel's sexuality. She marries the minister at Lords Hill, Edward Marston, but despite her obvious charms, he cannot bring himself to consummate the match. Meanwhile, she is being relentlessly pursued by Reddin, who had rescued her on her way back from an errand to Shrewsbury. Eventually, he has his wicked way with her, in one of Mary Webb's favourite 'little woods', but she still can't make up her mind whether to choose sexless virtue with Edward (mother-in-law living on the premises probably didn't do much to stoke the fires of passion), or yield to the pleasures of the flesh with Reddin, and I won't spoil things by revealing the outcome!

Gone to Earth had been written whilst Mary and Henry were living in rented accommodation at Lyth Hill, where their new bungalow was being built. It is the perfect spot for a poet and novelist of the Shropshire countryside, looking out as it does across the Shropshire plain, surrounded by its great horseshoe of hills. The bungalow is a modest property, threatened with demolition at the time of writing, the current owners wanting to build a much grander house on the site. But Mary loved it deeply, not just for its views but for the fact that just a few hundred yards down the lane to the west was the perfect 'little wood' of her imagination. Spring Coppice, it is called, and Mary would spend hours there, writing poetry or planning her novels, drinking in its sylvan sights and sounds:

Into the scented woods we'll go
And see the blackthorn swim in snow.
High above, in the budding leaves,
A brooding dove awakes and grieves;
The glades with mingled music stir,
And wildly laughs the woodpecker ...

As that extract from *Green Rain* serves rather to demonstrate, she was a poet of more passion than accomplishment. Two volumes of her poetry were published posthumously by Jonathan Cape, *Fifty One Poems* and *Poems and the Spring of Joy*, which includes the Jefferies-esque essays that she wrote quite early in her life on the healing power of nature.

Like Jefferies, she had an acute eye for the detail of the natural world. Also like him, she was a mystic, much influenced by Dame Julian of Norwich's *Revelations of Divine Love*. The critic, Gerald Gould, summed up her particular brand of mysticism in the *New Statesman*. 'Mary Webb is a mystic,' he wrote in his review of *Gone to Earth*, 'with that genuine mysticism which feels the essential oneness of the world and neither cares nor is able to disassociate the seen from the unseen ... the physical world (inanimate as well as animate) lives for her with a passionate intensity.'

Both her mysticism and her use of landscape as allegory are well to the fore in her next novel, *The House in Dormer Forest*. It is set in the Hope Valley, immediately to the west of the Stiperstones ridge:

Dormer Old House stood amid the remnants of primeval woodland that curtained the hills. These rose steeply on all sides of the house, which lay low by the water in the valley. This was called Oolert's Dingle, and there were plenty of owls to justify the name. On a moonlit night, passing, high up, from side to side of the cuplike valley, they looked like breeze-blown feathers. Higher still, on the very rim of the cup, the far-travelled winds shouted across to one another, all winter, news of the world ... From these heights, in fine weather, the house and its gardens lay open to view, small but clear, beside the white thread that was Dormer brook.

That striking description of the setting notwithstanding, the landscape does not play a major role in the novel, other than as an allegory, for pointing up the contrast between the reassuring permanence of nature (as the forest) as against the rottenness of society (symbolised by crumbling, rat-infested Dormer House). Once again, the central character is a version of Mary Webb herself, in this case Amber Darke, who provides us with a further insight into Mary's relationship with the natural world:

"The love of nature is a passion for those in whom once it lodges," she has Amber declare. "It can never be quenched. It cannot change. It is a furious, burning, physical greed, as well as a state of mystical exaltation."

Sadly, the book was not well received, casting Mary into deep gloom and bringing on an attack of Graves' Disease. Her depression also contributed to the decision to move, in January 1921, to London, where Henry had secured a teaching post at the ground-breaking King Alfred School in Golders Green. They lived in a flat in Bayswater, Henry happy in his new job, Mary torn between her love for her husband and homesickness for Shropshire and Lyth Hill. She had started work on a new novel – *Seven for a Secret*, which she'd researched on a short holiday with Henry the previous year to its setting on the Welsh border near Clun – but she found it difficult to achieve her characteristic flow of words without the constant inspiration of the Shropshire landscape. She returned to Lyth Hill for a short visit but could not survive long without her Henry. It wasn't a happy arrangement and not until the summer school holidays, when they could be together in Shropshire, did she find the peace of mind to make real progress with her novel.

The title *Seven for a Secret* is taken from the old magpie superstition (One for Sorrow, etc). The plot is a melodramatic one, with yet another of Mary Webb's mixed-up women at its heart: Gillian Lovekin, 'in love with passion', torn between the dependable, devoted Robert Rideout and the disreputable, dastardly sheep-dealer turned publican, Ralph Elmer. Most of the action takes place either at Gillian's farm, Dysgwlfas-on-the-Wild-Moors, or at the remote inn called The Mermaid's Rest, nearby. The latter is assuredly The Anchor, a roadside inn about seven miles west of Clun, just short of the Welsh border, which must be a contender for the title of the most remote pub in the Heart of England and certainly, in a freezing January dusk, the most forbidding. Surrounded by crumbling out-buildings, a deserted cottage hard by, with just a single light flickering in a battered window frame, it would make the perfect setting for a murder mystery or perhaps a ghost story. I am sure that on a Saturday night, with a good crowd in and a roaring blaze in the hearth, it is the very soul of homeliness and good cheer, but it is not the sort of pub in which I'd look forward to spending the night. Mary Webb describes it thus:

> Below him, the inn with its huddled roofs, its bright pale-green square
> of winter cabbage and dark blue of orchard, its small windows gleaming
> forlornly, its whole air proclaiming that within held not a revelry, not a
> bridal chamber, not a new-born child, but corruption.

At the end of the story, The Mermaid's Rest is left abandoned. 'Nobody would live there, so the moor began to flow back over it, covering its sorrow with beauty. The sign of the 'Mermaid' swung creaking in the wind, and as no one renewed her, the lady was at last obliterated.'

There is no equivalent of the 'unket (ie ill-omened) wood', which features prominently in the story, and if we are being strictly honest, there's no moorland nearby, either. The landscape is one of high, rolling, enclosed sheep pastures, interspersed with forestry plantations, although I suppose the hedges and fences could post-date Mary Webb. But for all that, the place does have an air about it of remoteness, at the very least,

Clun itself doesn't really feature in *Seven for a Secret*; curiously, given that it was to Clun that Mary and her husband Henry headed when she set out to research her story in the summer of 1921 and that the small town, laid out in a grid in the shadow of its magnificently ravaged Norman castle, would appear to have all the essentials for a Mary Webb location. The two towns which do play a part, 'Mallard's Keep' and 'Weeping Cross', are based, respectively, on Bishop's Castle to the north and

Clun

Knighton to the south-west. In this case, it was the plot that dictated the choice of location rather than the other way around, requiring as it did a railway station, from which Gillian could depart for Craven Arms junction and so on to Shrewsbury, which Clun has never had, and a big livestock fair, for the occasion of Gillian's seduction, which made Knighton the obvious place.

The depiction of the approach to Bishop's Castle is a lovely piece of writing:

> *There it shone, its clustered roofs, square church tower and miniature railway station all sloping up a hill with the inconsequence of a card house. Beyond were meadows, blue distance, purple distance, smoke-coloured hills, and more hills so pale as to fade on the sky.*

The 'miniature railway station' is worth a mention as well. For this was the terminus of, arguably, the most ill-fated line in Britain. A branch line to link Bishop's Castle with the main railway network at Craven Arms was first mooted in 1860. It took five years to complete, had to use borrowed engines and rolling stock, was never properly funded and went into receivership within two years of being opened. And there it stayed, for the remaining 69 years of its existence, until final closure in 1935. Even the museum which was eventually set up to remember the line burnt down, although I am glad to say that it has been re-established on a different site in the town.

We will return to Clun when we come to Housman. For our final Mary Webb destination we need to head north, perhaps taking in Pulverbatch and Shrewsbury en route, to the north Shropshire meres. This is the setting for her most famous, and probably her best, novel, *Precious Bane*. I am indebted to Gladys Mary Coles for the information that 'Precious Bane' (from Milton's *Paradise Lost*) was Mary's father's nickname for her as a child.

For Mary Webb as novelist, it breaks new ground: her first novel to have a historical, as opposed to contemporary, time-frame, being set at the time of the Napoleonic Wars, and the first to be written in the first person. Prue Sarn is that person, writing as an old lady, drawing upon her diaries and looking back to her life as a young woman. The story is shot through with Shropshire customs, folklore and superstition. There are 'love-spinnings' and 'sin-eating'; 'raising Venus' and 'bidding letters'. And there is, of course, Prue's 'precious bane' itself – her hare-shotten lip, the result of her mother's path having been crossed by the Devil disguised as a hare when she was pregnant with Prue, and so making Prue herself not merely disfigured but a witch into the bargain. Over-burdened with local colour as it is, and distracting as the unremitting use of dialect can certainly be, it is a powerful story of how a strong and intelligent woman comes to defeat all the forces of superstition and prejudice ranged against her, up to and including her own disability. It won the Prix Femina Vie Heureuse for 1925 and the unqualified admiration of the Prime Minister of the time, Stanley Baldwin, who praised its 'blending of human passion with the field and the skies'.

'Nature to Mary Webb was not a pattern on a screen,' he wrote, in an introduction to the 1928 edition, published after Mary's death. 'Her sensibility is so acute and her power over words so sure and swift that one who reads some passage in Whitehall has almost the physical sense of being in Shropshire cornfields.'

However, the Mary Webb pilgrim who goes in search of the original of 'Sarn Mere' will search in vain. The setting is what her biographer, Gladys Mary Coles, calls 'a distillation of Shropshire'. She wrote the book in 1923, mostly whilst living in Hampstead with Henry, but not before spending long hours sitting beside Bomere Pool, not far from her home at Lyth Hill, to get atmosphere and plot just right. That isn't to suggest that Bomere Pool is the original for Sarn Mere, any more than Ellesmere or Colemere is. You can visit any one of the meres and, depending on the season, imagine yourself with Prue, looking towards Sarn 'where the woods began and the great stretch of grey water [lay] gleaming and wincing in the sun'; or maybe, on a winter's night, watch 'the long shadows of rushes go thin and sharp across the sliding stars.' None is perhaps as ominous as Sarn, with its 'frittening' after dark, the 'troubling of its waters' and the church bells sounding 'beneath its furthest deeps'. But, with all of them, as with Sarn, 'there is summat to be felt there.'

All of the meres are fine stretches of water, mostly surrounded by woodland. You might imagine them to be well-landscaped reservoirs but they are, in fact, entirely natural. Ellesmere is the largest, stretching eastwards from the town. A footpath runs around roughly two thirds of its perimeter, before, rather irritatingly, heading off towards the village of Welshampton. Not that the countryside beyond the mere isn't attractive. It is a classically English mix of arable and grassland, studded with big oaks and ash, grazed by slow-moving, good-natured, white-faced Hereford cattle. But it is frustrating not to be able to go all the way round. Colemere, a couple of miles to the east, has much less of the feel of a municipal park about it, and the North Shropshire Way, on the banks of the Llangollen Canal, passes close by, on its course to little Blakemere.

Ellesmere

Mary Webb may have been a rural romantic, but she knew her farming. The levying of a tax on imported grain – the Corn Law – in the aftermath of the Napoleonic Wars plays a significant part in the story, encouraging as it does Prue's hard-driving brother Gideon to put the whole of the family farm down to corn, and so almost inviting disaster. There are lovely descriptions of the processes of corn-growing and the differing feelings they inspire:

> *I called to mind ... Gideon and me walking up and down the fields with the bags of seed slung over shoulder, or with a deep round lid to hold enough seed for one crossing of the field there and back, and swinging out our arms with a great giving movement, as if we were feeding all the world, a thing I dearly loved to see. For reaping, though it is good to watch as be all the year's doings on a farm, is a grutching and a grabbing thing compared with sowing. You must lean out to it and sweep it into you, and hold it to your bosom, jealous, and grasp it and take it. There is ever a greediness in reaping with the sickle, in my sight. There is not in scything, which is a large destroying movement without either love or anger it, like the judgements of God. Nor is there in flailing, which is a thing full of anger, but without any will or wish to have or keep. But reaping is all greed, just as sowing is all giving.*

That passage may also serve as an example of the poetry which Mary Webb brings to her novels, most notably in *Precious Bane*. Poetry was, in fact, her first love, inspired by her schoolmaster father, George Meredith, who was a bit of a poet himself. Walter de la Mare selected three of her poems – *Green Rain*, *The Water Ousel* and *Market Day* – for his 1923 anthology *Come Hither*, which from him was quite an accolade. But it is *Viroconium*, inspired by the ruins of the Roman city which we now know as Wroxeter, which brings us nicely full circle, back to the country under the Wrekin, where she was born.

> *Virocon – Virocon –*
> *Still the ancient name rings on*
> *And brings, in the untrampled wheat,*
> *The tumult of a thousand feet.*

To Mary Webb, the ruins symbolised the transience of the works of man in contrast to the eternity of the natural world:

> *One that lives while empires die,*
> *A shrineless god whose songs abide*
> *Forever in the countryside.*

Viroconium (or Uriconium – take your pick) was the fourth largest settlement in Roman Britain, covering, at its peak, almost 200 acres alongside the Severn, a few miles east of Shrewsbury. What fires the imagination about the site is partly the very visible remains of walls and pavements – the so-called 'Old Work' most prominent amongst them – but mainly the fact that, unlike virtually every other Roman city in Britain, this site was not built over. It was abandoned, probably in the mid-sixth century, and gradually reverted to farmland. Stone from the ruins was quarried for use in local walls and buildings – not least in the church of St Andrew in the modern village of Wroxeter – but below the surface, the skeleton of Viroconium lay undisturbed. Serious archaeological investigation did not begin until the mid-nineteenth century, a prominent early visitor to the excavations being Charles Dickens, who recorded his impressions:

> *There is a bright spring morning overhead, the old wall standing by looks blank at us; here and there a stray antiquary clambers among the rubbish, careless of dirt stains; an attentive gentleman on the crest of a dirt heap explains Roman antiquities to some young ladies in pink and blue, who have made Wroxeter the business of a morning drive. An intelligent labourer, who seems to be a sort of foreman of the works, waits to disclose to the honorary secretary the contents of a box in which it is his business to deposit each day's findings of odds and ends ...*

It all sounds delightfully informal, a far cry from the gravelled paths, neatly trimmed lawns and carefully signposted visitor trail which you will find today. I found it quite hard to get myself into the frame of mind to be thinking about dead Romans with a smart visitor centre on one side of the road and an unconvincing reconstruction of a Roman villa on the other.

On the other hand, once you appreciate that the excavated section is only a tiny fraction of the entire site, and that most of the rest still lies buried under green fields as it has been for a millennium and a half, and when you look to the south-east and see the Wrekin looming on the skyline, fortress and symbol of the Celts whom the civilised Romans conquered, there is more than enough to fire the imagination, as another Shropshire poet, Wilfred Owen discovered:

Wrekin from Viroconium

It lieth low near merry England's heart
Like a long-buried sin; and Englishmen
Forget that in its death their sires had part.
And, like a sin, Time lays it bare again
To tell of races wronged,
And ancient glories suddenly overcast,
And treasures flung to fire and rabble wrath.
If thou hast ever longed
To lift the gloomy curtain of Time Past,
And spy the secret things that Hades hath,
Here through this riven ground take such a view.
The dust, that fell unnoted as a dew,
Wrapped the dead city's face like mummy-cloth:
All is as was: except for worm and moth.

That is from *Uriconium – an Ode*, one of his earliest poems, inspired by his regular visits to the 1912-14 excavations, when he was living with his parents in Shrewsbury. It expresses, rather better than Mary Webb managed, the poignancy of a lost civilisation, left alone to moulder for so long.

Wilfred Owen had been born at Oswestry in 1893. He was, of course, first and foremost, a poet of the First World War, massively influenced by Siegfried Sassoon, whom he worshipped. But it was in the countryside that he discovered his poetic vocation; not in Shropshire, but on Broxton Hill in Cheshire, from where there is a magnificent view, stretching from Liverpool to the north, around to Shrewsbury and the Wrekin in the south. As a young poet, he was a romantic. Keats and Coleridge were his heroes. All of his great work was written in the 18 months leading up to his death in action, a week before the Armistice in November 1918. But it is at least arguable that the power and bitterness which he brought to his war poetry may have owed something to the contrast between the pointless horrors of the trenches and the peace and beauty of the countryside he had known, growing up; as, for example, in *Spring Offensive*, where the soldiers sit or lie, high on a hill, on a glorious spring day, waiting for the order to attack:

*Wilfred Owen
(1893-1918)
Shropshire's greatest poet*

> *Hour after hour they ponder the warm field –
> And the far valley behind, where the buttercups
> Had blessed with gold their slow boots coming up,
> Where even the little brambles would not yield,
> But clutched and clung to them like sorrowing hands;
> They breathe like trees unstirred.*

AE Housman would have recognised the sentiment. Unlike Owen, he was not a 'Shropshire lad', but no-one has written more memorably about the county, Viroconium and the Wrekin included:

> *On Wenlock Edge the wood's in trouble;
>   His forest fleece the Wrekin heaves;
> The gale, it plies the saplings double,
>   And thick on Severn snow the leaves.*
>
> *'Twould blow like this through holt and hanger
>   When Uricon the city stood:
> 'Tis the old wind in the old anger,
>   But then it threshed another wood.*
>
> *Then, 'twas before my time, the Roman
>   At yonder heaving hill would stare:
> The blood that warms an English yeoman,
>   The thoughts that hurt him, they were there.*
>
> *There, like the wind through woods in riot,
>   Through him the gale of life blew high;
> The tree of man was never quiet:
>   Then 'twas the Roman, now 'tis I.*

The gale, it plies the saplings double,
*   It blows so hard, 'twill soon be gone:*
To-day the Roman and his trouble
*   Are ashes under Uricon.*

The Wrekin was certainly heaving on the snowy Saturday morning when I decided to make my pilgrimage to Shropshire's most famous hill. Half of Telford seemed to have had the same idea. They were there in their hundreds, clad mostly in garishly coloured lycra, walking, running, even cycling up the Wrekin's icy slopes. It goes without saying that the track to the summit is well used, and that you shouldn't expect much peace and solitude in which to reflect on what Housman was driving at. But the view from the top is astounding, stretching as it does from the Berwyn mountains of North Wales, to the Peak District to the north-east, south to the Cotswolds and the Malverns and south-west to the Long Mynd and the Stiperstones. It struck me that this was possibly the best vantage point from which to ponder Wenlock Edge. You can't see much from the escarpment itself, other than in winter when the trees have lost their leaves. But from the summit of the Wrekin you can appreciate Wenlock Edge in all its glory, rearing like a great green wave about to break over the Shropshire Plain.

Curiously, given how different they are, the Wrekin and Wroxeter share a common name: Uricon. It was what the Cornovii called their fortress on the hill; and it was what the conquering Romans called their city down by the river. As a classical scholar, Housman would have appreciated the connection, and he may even have visited both these strangely complementary places.

Rock formation on Wenlock Edge

Shropshire – Exploring Mary Webb country

Walks

The possibilities are almost limitless, given that the settings for Mary Webb's novels cover such a large part of the county. The Mary Webb Society carries a list of all the main locations, with information on each, on its website: **www.marywebbsociety.co.uk**

The Shropshire Tourism website – **www.shropshiretourism.co.uk** – is equally helpful, offering four 'Mary Webb Trails', together with information on how to use public transport, and in particular the local shuttle buses, to reach the various starting points.

The walk that I most enjoyed is the one described in the text, to the top of the Long Mynd, starting and finishing at Bridges and taking in Ratlinghope.

Lordshill and its chapel and the Devil's Chair are also not to be missed.

Viewpoints

Again, any number from which to choose. Some of the best are:

Polebank, on the Long Mynd.

The Stiperstones Ridge

Lyth Hill, just south of Shrewsbury, where Mary Webb lived at Spring Cottage and walked in Spring Wood.

Pulverbatch, and the remains of its medieval castle, the setting for Mary Webb's final novel, *Armour Wherein He Trusted*.

Clun, and in particular its ruined Norman castle.

Wenlock Edge, where you can park in the car park at Presthope, although the best view is probably from Hughley.

The Wrekin: the main car park is to the north-east of the hill and is well signposted.

Uriconium: head for Wroxeter and park next to the visitor centre. The Roman ruins are in the care of English Heritage and there is a charge for entry.

Pubs

The Horseshoe in Bridges, is excellent, serving real ale from the Three Tuns brewery at Bishop's Castle, and the sort of hearty, locally produced food you'll appreciate after a trek across the Long Mynd.

Stiperstones Inn in Stiperstones village is a cosy little roadside pub offering good beer and food. You can stay there, as well.

The Anchor Inn, which Mary Webb calls *The Mermaid*, is high in the hills on the road from Clun to Newtown. Despite its lonely and slightly forbidding location, the pub is a haven of warmth and good cheer, serving excellent beer and food. Only open in the evenings, from 7 pm.

The White Horse in Clun, where I stayed, is comfortable, friendly and has its own micro-brewery.

The Horseshoe at Bridges

Select Bibliography

Mary Webb www.marywebbsociety.co.uk
Golden Arrow (1916)
Gone to Earth (1917)
The House in Dormer Forest (1920)
Seven for a Secret (1922)
Precious Bane (1924)
Armour Wherein He Trusted (1929)
Gladys Mary Coles (ed): *Selected Poems of Mary Webb* (1981)
Gladys Mary Coles: *The Flower of Light – A Biography of Mary Webb* (1978)
Gladys Mary Coles: *Mary Webb – A New Critical Biography* (1990)

AE Housman www.housman-society.co.uk
A Shropshire Lad and Other Poems: The Collected Poems of AE Housman (Penguin, 2010)
Richard Perceval Graves: *AE Housman – The Scholar-Poet* (1979)
Norman Page: *AE Housman – A Critical Biography* (1996)

Wilfred Owen www.wilfredowen.org.uk
Dominic Hibberd: *Wilfred Owen: A New Biography* (2003)

Chapter Six

A Worcestershire Lad

AE Housman

That is the land of lost content,
I see it shining plain,
The happy highways where I went
And cannot come again.

AE Housman

If you had asked me how I imagined the life and work of AE Housman before I knew any more of him than the name and his most famous collection of poems, *A Shropshire Lad*, I would have conjured up a vision of a solid Shropshire countryman – a shepherd, maybe – wandering the hills and vales of his native county, composing romantic, pastoral poetry, like a late nineteenth-century cross between William Wordsworth and John Clare.

Nothing, it turns out, could be further from the truth. AE Housman (it was always AE, never Alfred, except on occasion to members of his close family) was born and brought up in Worcestershire, lived most of his adult life in either London or Cambridge and was an austere academic with homosexual tendencies. His poems, lyrical and romantic as they undoubtedly are, were inspired by a profound nostalgia for a lost, mostly imagined world, of innocent rusticity.

Alfred Edward Housman
(1859-1936)
Lyrical and austere

All of which makes him, as a poet of the English landscape, something of an enigma: a writer inspired by places which he may never have laid eyes upon. No fewer than six of the poems in *A Shropshire Lad* were written before he'd even set foot in the county, and he seems to have made only one fairly brief visit before composing the other 57.

Does that make his employment of places like Wenlock Edge, the Wrekin, Clun and Ludlow entirely symbolic? Did he, as some have suggested, just like the sound of the place-names? Was he, in effect, merely a rebuffed homosexual using an imagined countryside as an allegory for his lost happiness? Might he just as well have chosen the Cotswolds or the Malverns as his 'blue remembered hills', his 'land of lost content'?

Well, yes and no. Housman is certainly not a poet of the countryside in the conventional sense. He did indeed use largely imagined landscapes to illustrate deeper emotions that came from within, rather than being inspired by landscape to a deeper understanding of himself and the world around him. The nostalgia that permeates the poems in *A Shropshire Lad* was Housman's personal nostalgia, both for the innocence of his youth before the realisation of his homosexuality and the guilt which it produced, and, as the other side of that particular coin, for the warmth and love which he had felt in his relationship with Moses Jackson, and which he had come to realise could never be properly fulfilled.

If nostalgia is one thread which runs through Housman's poetry, then death is the other. He seems to have been as profoundly affected as you would expect by the death of his mother from breast cancer on, of all days, his 12th birthday. Later in life, the illness (fatal, as it would prove) of Moses Jackson in 1922 was the trigger which produced his second great burst of poetic activity – nearly 30 years on from *A Shropshire Lad* – and gave us his *Last Poems*.

Housman poems rarely have happy endings! Yet, for all his fixation with love (lost) and death (untimely), he most definitely was a poet of the countryside. That he chose to express his feelings through the medium of landscape was no coincidence. He was brought up a country boy. His father, Edward, was a solicitor in Bromsgrove who fancied himself as a country squire. His mother, Sarah Jane, was the daughter of the rector of Woodchester, high in the Cotswolds above the Stroud Valley. He was born at the Valley House, Fockbury (part of the Fockbury House Estate). The family lived there for several months before moving on first to Perry Hall and then to Fockbury House, some two miles away, just to the north-

Valley House, Fockbury, where Housman was born

west of Bromsgrove. For all Edward Housman's financial fecklessness, and the tragedy of Sarah Jane's early death, the seven Housman children, of whom Alfred was the eldest, enjoyed a comfortable middle-class upbringing in what was then the unspoiled north Worcestershire countryside.

It was a countryside that the young Housman loved. He was a great walker, whether at home in Worcestershire or on his regular visits to his godmother, Mrs Wise, at Woodchester in the Cotswolds, and he developed a keen interest in botany. One of his favourite excursions at Fockbury was to walk the few hundred yards along the lane to the hill at Worm's Ash, a modest eminence at just under 500 feet, but one that commanded a magnificent view across a pastoral countryside of hamlets and small woods, with the blue Shropshire Hills in the distance. This view became hugely important to him. He would spend hours there, just looking out across what he must have felt was the promised land. His siblings seem to have been somewhere between baffled and amused by their brother's meditations on Worm's Ash. They took to calling it 'Mount Pisgah', in reference to Moses climbing to the top of that mountain and being shown by God the land that had been promised to his people but which he, Moses, would never reach. I rather doubt if the Housman children fully appreciated the subtleties of the reference, but it certainly proved remarkably prescient, given that this probably was the closest that Housman would ever get to his personal promised land.

Much later in his life, he would look back on those hours as a troubled teenage boy, looking out from the hill, in one of the most moving of his *Last Poems*.

> *When summer's end is nighing*
> *And skies at evening cloud,*
> *I muse on change and fortune*
> *And all the feats I vowed*
> *When I was young and proud.*
>
> *The weathercock at sunset*
> *Would lose the slanted ray,*
> *And I would climb the beacon*
> *That looked to Wales away*
> *And saw the last of day.*
>
> *From hill and cloud and heaven*
> *The hues of evening died;*
> *Night welled through lane and hollow*
> *And hushed the countryside,*
> *But I had youth and pride.*
>
> *And I with earth and nightfall*
> *In converse high would stand,*
> *Late, till the west was ashen*
> *And darkness hard at hand,*
> *And the eye lost the land.*

Worm's Ash Hill

The year might age, and cloudy
  The lessening day might close,
But air of other summers
  Breathed from beyond the snows,
  And I had hope of those.

They came and were and are not
  And come no more anew;
And all the years and seasons
  That ever can ensue
  Must now be worse and few.

So here's an end of roaming
  On eves when autumn nighs:
The ear too fondly listens
  For summer's parting sighs,
  And then the heart replies.

It is hard to exaggerate how central the view from the hill at Worm's Ash was to the images and metaphors which Alfred Housman chose to express his feelings about love and death.

Worm's Ash is barely half a mile from the junction on the M5 where the M42 heads off east, although to reach it, you have to make your way through Bromsgrove and out on the Dodford road. I wish I could recommend a pilgrimage, but sadly the hill is topped now by a tall and ugly communications mast, and there is no public access to the summit. However, a lane does run around the hill about halfway up and, by stopping at gateways, we can see enough to be able to experience at least a flavour of the panorama which so influenced Housman, from the Shropshire Hills away in the north-west, to Bredon Hill in the south. This place, this view, is what, in Housman's mind, must surely have bound Bredon to Shropshire.

The other sense in which Housman was a poet inspired by the countryside concerns his manner of working. All through his life, it was whilst he was walking in the countryside – which he loved to do, particularly in the afternoon – that ideas for poems, words, lines, sometimes even complete stanzas, would come to him, for subsequent meticulous re-casting and polishing. As an undergraduate at St John's College, Oxford, he would walk for miles through the surrounding countryside, to watch hay being scythed above Godstow Bridge, for example, or around the fringes of Bagley Wood. Long walks were a feature of his regular visits to the Wises at Woodchester. A particular favourite, according to one of his biographers, Richard Perceval Graves, was to go up the steep main street of Woodchester to Selsley Common, from where he could look out across the spreading pastures of the Severn Vale to the mountains of Wales. In London, when his duties, first at the Patent Office and, from 1892, as Professor of Latin at University College, permitted, he would go for long walks out into the Surrey countryside, often accompanied – most influentially, as it turned out – by his friend, MH Eyre, who had a great fondness for the South Shropshire hills, loved talking about them and who must have helped, if not to plant, then certainly to nurture the idea of Shropshire as the imagined country to which the young poet would look back wistfully when the time came.

Housman himself ascribed his choice of location to 'the sentimental feeling (which I had) for Shropshire, because its hills were our western horizon' (when he was growing up). Taken to task by his younger brother Laurence (who would himself become a notable illustrator, novelist and playwright) over the factual inaccuracies in *Hughley Steeple* (not least the fact that Hughley church doesn't actually have a steeple!) he made this revealing reply:

> On my visit to Shropshire I ascertained by looking down from Wenlock Edge that Hughley church could not have had much of a steeple. But as I had already composed the poem and could not invent another name that sounded so nice, I could only deplore that the church at Hughley should follow the bad example of the church at Brou, which persists in standing on a plain after Matthew Arnold had said that it stands among mountains. I thought of putting in a note to say that Hughley was only a name, but then I thought that would merely disturb the reader. I did not apprehend that the faithful would be making pilgrimages to these holy places.

Well, pilgrimages Housman devotees – and they are many – most certainly do make, not least to Wenlock Edge. I have to say that, whilst Much Wenlock is a delightful

Across the Severn to Wales, from Selsley Common

Looking towards Stroud, from Selsley Common

little town, Wenlock Edge is a bit of a disappointment, for the simple reason that, whilst you're on it amidst all the trees, you can't really appreciate it. As I suggest in the Shropshire chapter, where the *On Wenlock Edge* poem appears, it is probably best appreciated from a little way away, so that you can see the trees along the line of the ridge tossing their heads on a windy day. The village of Hughley is as good a vantage point as any.

The other poem in *A Shropshire Lad* in which Wenlock makes an appearance is number XXXIX:

> *'Tis time, I think, by Wenlock town*
> *The golden broom should blow;*
> *The hawthorn sprinkled up and down*
> *Should charge the land with snow.*
>
> *Spring will not wait the loiterer's time*
> *Who keeps so long away;*
> *So others wear the broom and climb*
> *The hedgerows heaped with may.*
>
> *Oh tarnish late on Wenlock Edge,*
> *Gold that I never see;*
> *Lie long, high snowdrifts in the hedge*
> *That will not shower on me.*

It is a classic Housman poem, brimming with loss and nostalgia, as the exiled Salopian thinks back to spring on Wenlock Edge and to the joys now denied him. But in the poem's original form, it wasn't Wenlock to which the Shropshire lad looked back so wistfully, but a slightly less mellifluous settlement:

> *'Tis time I think by Stourbridge town*
> *The golden broom should blow.*

But he evidently decided that Wenlock had a better ring to it, so it is to that town, rather than the unfortunate Stourbridge, that the Housman faithful make their pilgrimages.

Of the 63 poems collected in *A Shropshire Lad*, 13 mention Shropshire place names. Ludlow is, if not necessarily Housman's favourite place, then certainly his favourite place name, featuring in five of them, including:

> *The lads in their hundreds to Ludlow come in for the fair ...*

> *When I come back to Ludlow,*
> *Amidst the moonlight pale*

> *When smoke stood up from Ludlow*
> *And mist blew off the Teme*
> *And blithe afield for ploughing*
> *Against the morning beam*
> *I strode beside my team.*

And, my own favourite Ludlow reference, *The Recruit*:

> *Leave your home behind, lad*
> *And reach your friends your hand*
> *And go, and luck go with you*
> *While Ludlow tower shall stand.*

It is not clear whether Housman had any particular war in mind as the recruit's destination. He tended to use wars in much the same way as place-names, as settings or props. But it is a less melancholy, more optimistic poem than many in *A Shropshire Lad* (unless Housman was being ironic), so that even if the recruit dies, at least he will be remembered:

> *Oh town and field will mind you*
> *Till Ludlow tower is down.*

The same might well be said of Housman himself. For it is in the churchyard at Ludlow that his ashes are buried.

Apart from Wenlock, the other Shropshire locations are: 'From Clee to heaven the beacon burns', 'High the vanes of Shrewsbury gleam, islanded in Severn stream', 'As through the wild green hills of Wyre', 'The vane on Hughley steeple', 'Shrewsbury Jail', the Wrekin and Uricon, which we will come to shortly, and, last but not least, Clun and the villages around it, as in the old jingle, with which Housman opens his poem:

> *Clunton and Clunbury,*
> *Clungunford and Clun,*
> *Are the quietest places*
> *Under the sun*

And so indeed they are. It is a long way to Clun from anywhere, and fewer people than ought to bother to make the journey. Which is a shame, because whilst it may be quiet, it is a friendly little town set in a striking countryside. As one drives north towards Clun through the blackcurrant fields, vineyards, orchards, hop yards and polytunnels of fertile, red-soiled Herefordshire, so the villages get smaller and more scattered, the farms more remote and the countryside emptier. By the time you reach Clunton you have penetrated one of the most remote and thinly populated stretches of countryside in all of England.

Clun itself was laid out by the Normans on the northern side of the steep-sided valley through which runs the river which gives the town its name (or possibly vice versa). There are two pubs, one of which, the White Horse, brews its own beer, a few shops, including a delightful gift shop called Caractacus and, Clun's pride and joy, its ruined Norman castle.

Housman's poem accepts that this is indeed

> *The country for easy livers,*
> *The quietest under the sun*

but goes on to point out that even 'Knighton lads' – Knighton being the much larger town, just down the road – knew trouble:

And if as a lad grows older
The troubles he bears are more,
He carries his griefs on a shoulder
That handselled them long before.

Where shall one halt to deliver
This luggage I'd lief set down?
Not Thames, not Teme is the river,
Nor London, nor Knighton the town:

'Tis a long way further than Knighton,
A quieter place than Clun,
Where doomsday may thunder and lighten
And little 'twill matter to one.

AE Housman hasn't had a particularly good press, down the years. He was obviously a fairly difficult man, who didn't suffer fools at all gladly, especially fools who liked to regard themselves as scholars or experts. He became, of course, a most eminent authority on the classics, first as Professor of Latin at University College, London and then, from 1911 until his death in 1936, Professor of Latin at Cambridge. He had, it is fair to say, a keen appreciation of his own intellect and scholarship and a matching disdain for sloppiness or a lack of intellectual rigour on the part of his peers. But even this sometimes aloof and austere man did have his more human side. He had a great fondness for good food and wine, Burgundy in particular, and once dined on hedgehogs and snails at the Carlton, after his brother Laurence had wagered his publisher, Grant Richards, that they couldn't be obtained and lost. The hedgehogs came from Scotland and were washed down with whisky. Housman reported that they tasted much like haggis!

Was Housman the original for his Shropshire Lad, 'Thomas Hearsay', as he was originally going to be named? His brother Laurence thought not, commending to all readers of his poems this truth: 'That whenever they are least like 'A Shropshire Lad' they are most deeply and truly like the man he really was who wrote them.' Housman himself put a slightly different complexion on the relationship. 'The Shropshire Lad is an imaginary figure, with something of my temper and view of life,' was his explanation. Perhaps the closest we can get to resolving those two views is to suggest that Thomas Hearsay was, in effect, Housman's alter ego, the imaginative country boy who inhabited the same skin as the formidable intellectual.

But whatever mixed emotions Housman the man may have inspired, there is no denying the wonderful lyricism of Housman the poet. It is no coincidence that so many of the poems in *A Shropshire Lad* have been set to music, most famously by Ralph Vaughan Williams in his song cycle *On Wenlock Edge*. Mostly written in ballad form they have a beguiling, loping rhythm, perfectly suited to their bittersweet subject matter of love and loss, the 'vaguely pleasurable melancholy' and 'deeply-rooted longing for the past' which Housman experienced when he visited the haunts of his childhood.

So it matters not that it was the idea of Shropshire that inspired AE Housman or that places like Wenlock Edge and Ludlow were important to him for the sound of their names rather than for the beauty of their actuality. His poems have become an integral part of what Shropshire is and how it is perceived. They enrich the experience of anyone who visits the county and walks through its countryside. Places like Wenlock Edge, or the Clee Hills, Wroxeter and the Wrekin, beautiful and fascinating as they are in themselves, mean so much more thanks to Housman, whether it is the simple beauty of his words and rhythms or the complex feelings of wistfulness and nostalgia which inspired them, never better expressed than in one of the shortest, but most moving and revealing poems in *A Shropshire Lad*:

> *Into my heart an air that kills*
> *From yon far country blows:*
> *What are those blue remembered hills,*
> *What spires, what farms are those?*
>
> *That is the land of lost content,*
> *I see it shining plain,*
> *The happy highways where I went*
> *And cannot come again.*

The blue remembered hills

In the footsteps of Housman

Walks

There are fine walks on **Selsley Common**, near Woodchester in Gloucestershire, where Housman stayed with his godmother, Mrs Wise, as a boy and got to know the surrounding countryside.

To reach the hill at **Worm's Ash**, from where Housman would look out to his blue remembered hills, go to Bromsgrove and take the A448 Kidderminster road. Half a mile after it crosses the motorway, turn right towards Dodford, but don't take the left turn into the village, instead staying on Fockbury Road until the lane reaches the hill, which it winds around. There are views from various gateways, but no public access to the hill itself. If you carry on down the lane (Cockshutt Lane) northwards towards Bournheath, you will reach Valley Road. Immediately opposite the road junction is the Clock House, complete with blue plaque, which is all that remains of the manor house in which the Housman family lived for a time, and about half a mile further on towards Bournheath, on the right, is Valley House, where AEH was born.

The Housman Trail, produced by the Housman Society, takes in all the main AEH locations in and around Bromsgrove and is well worth following.

For **Wenlock Edge** and other Shropshire locations, see chapter 5.

Viewpoints

Selsley Common, looking out across the Severn Vale to the Forest of Dean and the Welsh mountains beyond.

Worm's Ash, looking north-west towards Shropshire and south to Bredon Hill.

Pubs

The best pub in the Woodchester area is the *Royal Oak*, recently re-opened under new ownership, which offers good food and real ale.

The nearest pub to the hill at Worm's Ash is the *Dodford Inn*, situated outside the village in its own parkland, and very smart following a recent refurbishment. Good beer and aspirational food.

There are also two good pubs in Bournheath: the *Nailers Arms*, recalling what was once the main local industry, and the *New Inn*.

The statue of Housman in Bromsgrove and the Clock House,
the only remaining part of the manor house where he lived as a boy

Select Bibliography

AE Housman   www.housman-society.co.uk

A Shropshire Lad and Other Poems: the Collected Poems of AE Housman (Penguin, 2010)
Richard Perceval Graves: *AE Housman – The Scholar-Poet* (1979)
Norman Page: *AE Housman – A Critical Biography* (1996)

Chapter Seven

From the Malverns into Herefordshire

Bruce Chatwin, John Masefield, Elizabeth Barrett Browning, William Langland, WH Auden, William Wordsworth

Whenever I think of the bounty and beauty
of God, I think of parts of this county

John Masefield

The Border country of Herefordshire is dominated by the louring bulk of the Black Moutains. From Hay Bluff in the north to Hatterall Hill in the south, the easternmost ridge of the mountains looms over the valley of the River Monnow like a great dark rampart. There is no need for a dyke to be built to separate the two nations in this stretch of country. Yet curiously, despite the helpfully divisive topography, the two cultures have contrived to mix and mingle, so that the scattered farmsteads and Celtic field-patterns of parishes like Craswall and Llanveynoe feel as Welsh as genteel, bookish Hay-on-Wye feels English.

This is one of the most remote corners, not just of Herefordshire, but of all England. The parish of Craswall, in the shadow of the Black Hill, covers some 8,000 acres, but is home to just 150 people. Its Norman church stands alone, on a ridge above the river, small and plain, with just a stump of a spire, as testimony to the toughness of earning a living from the land up here, but also honest, strong and ancient – the sort of church in which Piers Plowman might have worshipped, and have felt at home. The fields are small and closely hedged, the farms may be weather-beaten and rather scruffy but they are, most of them at any rate, still working farms, and there are cattle and sheep in the fields, not solar panels and poly-tunnels. If you had decided to write a novel about twin brothers who cut themselves off from the world on their small farm and live their lives as if time has stood still, you could find no more suitable stretch of country in which to set it.

Which is precisely the conclusion that the journalist and writer Bruce Chatwin reached when Penelope Betjeman introduced him to the Howells brothers, Jonathan and George, at New House Farm, on the lower slopes of the Black Hill, in 1980. Chatwin was a bit of a golden boy, certainly in his own estimation. Handsome, charming, adventurous, unpredictable, and fatally attractive to both sexes, he had made his name as a travel writer with *In Patagonia*, published in 1977. But his next book,

Bruce Chatwin
(1940-1989)
Brilliance cut short

a novel based on the story of a slave trader who became *The Viceroy of Ouidah* and lived a life of rococo decadence, whilst well received by the critics, had failed to sell. So, being the ever-contrary Chatwin, he decided to write a novel which would be the polar opposite of an exotic tale set in faraway places – a story 'about people who never went out'.

It may have been Penelope Betjeman who sowed the initial seed. She had met Chatwin when he had been working for Sotheby's fine art department and, like so many others, had fallen under his spell. After reading *In Patagonia*, she had written to him from her remote cottage in the hills behind Hay-on-Wye to suggest that 'you really ought to come here because the stories are just as good as all those things in Patagonia you write about.' He needed no second bidding, for this was an area he already knew and loved. As a schoolboy at Marlborough, he had helped renovate an old farmhouse at Chapel-y-ffin near Llanthony, which the school had bought as a place in which the boys could learn to fend for themselves in a remote location.

"This area of the Welsh border I regard as one of the emotional centres of my life," he said in 1984. "It's what Proust calls the soil on which I still may build."

The story of *On the Black Hill* is simple enough. It is the story of a farming family: Amos and Mary Jones, and their twin sons, Lewis and Benjamin Jones, who are bound to each other as strongly as they are bound to the land. The saga stretches from the 1890s, when Amos and Mary meet and marry, almost up to the time that Chatwin was writing, taking in the two world wars and all manner of farming and personal vicissitudes along the way. The scene never moves away from the border country south of Hay-on-Wye. At the start of the novel, the newly married Amos and Mary take on the tenancy of 'The Vision', a run-down 120-acre farm on the Lurkenhope estate, so called for the vision of the Virgin Mary seen hovering over the rhubarb patch by a previous tenant in the early eighteenth century. The farmhouse is said to straddle the border between England and Wales – one of the main bedroom windows looking out over the green fields of England, the other looking back to the mountains of Wales. Chatwin had got the idea from the Reverend Francis Kilvert. On a visit to a farmhouse called The Pant, which does indeed straddle the border just south of Hay-on-Wye, the diarist had been told the story of how a previous occupant, heavily pregnant, had been told to stand in a particular corner of the house, so that her child could be born in England, which, happily, it was.

There is no real original for The Vision. The interior is undoubtedly based on New House Farm, just as the twins are based on Jonathan and George Howells, and Amos on their father. But New House Farm is squarely in England, tucked in under the escarpment, with no view of Wales. The nearest equivalent that I came across for the setting of The Vision was Black Hill Farm, which you pass as the lane winds up the southern tip of the Black Hill spur towards the razor-edged escarpment called the Cat's Back. It doesn't straddle the Welsh boundary – that runs along the top of the ridge to the west, on the other side of the Olchon Valley – but it is a working farm on a steep slope with views both east and west. A dirty-grey longhouse of uncertain age looks out through grimy green-framed windows to a cluttered farmyard in which

The original for The Vision

two derelict tractors are beached; a black cat scurries away. It certainly does have something about it of Chatwin's description of The Vision:

> *In the yard, a young ash-tree reared its trunk through the boards of a hay-waggon. The roofs of the buildings were yellow with stonecrop; and the dungheap was overgrown with grass.*

The other farm which features prominently in the story is The Rock, home of the Watkins family, between whom and the Joneses a terrible feud develops, sparked off, as so often when neighbouring farmers fall out, by a boundary dispute. And this most certainly does have an exact original, in Coed Major (known previously as 'The Barn'), a couple of miles north of Craswell church, on the eastern slope of Black Hill. Penelope Betjeman had taken Bruce Chatwin there as well, to meet the eccentric occupiers, Joe the Barn and Jean the Barn, arriving on horseback.

'The dogs howled as we dismounted,' wrote Chatwin subsequently, 'and a procession of geese and ducks flew off among the wreckage of red tractors and pullets.' One end of the barn had fallen down, the other end was open and everything inside was covered with goose and duck droppings. In the book, the description becomes:

> *Then they crossed a stone stile onto the moor, and followed a pony-trail northwards, with the screes of the mountain rising sharply on the left. Beyond a spinney of birches, they came to a barn and longhouse, standing amid heaps of broken wall. A jet of smoke streamed sideways from the chimney. There were a few contorted ash trees, a few pussy willows, and the rim of the muddy pond was covered with bits of goose fluff.*

And today, well, a bridleway called the Three Rivers Ride runs right past Coed Major. It crosses the narrow road from Hay-on-Wye to Craswall not far from the ruins of Craswall Abbey. We followed it on a cold March morning under a lowering sky, threatening rain. And after a mile or so across sheep pasture, adorned by an abandoned tractor, there it was, still almost exactly as Chatwin had described it – a rusting coach and caravan in the foreground, a half-finished wooden shed beyond, and a chilly-looking slate-roofed dwelling house, with a punctured horse-box keeling over outside. I have been to very few farms or small-holdings more bleakly set. The hillside which looms above the farm is magnificent, a great slab of mountain, shaped like a gigantic wedge of Cheddar cheese, runnels and rills cutting into its face like wrinkles in ancient skin.

The best place from which to appreciate the character of this country is not at the foot of the hill, but at the summit, and the best way of reaching it is up the Cat's Back. There is a car park, two-thirds of the way up the hill, above Black Hill Farm. From there, it is a short but steep climb to the vertiginous ridge along which a rocky and badly eroded path makes its way north towards the highest point on the ridge, the Black Hill itself. The slopes on either side fall almost vertically to the Olcthon Brook on the west and the River Monnow on the east. The hilltop was black with peat and winter heather in March, but the views on either hand are magnificent – of pastoral England rolling away like a great green sea into the misty distance on the one side; of the Black Mountains, living up to their name in all their Celtic grandeur, on the other.

There is no better vantage point from which to appreciate one of the several dichotomies which give the novel its central motif: decadent England and puritan Wales. As Jonathan Chatwin (no relation) observes in *Anywhere Out Of The World*, his excellent biography of his namesake, 'The action in *On the Black Hill* is divided between two opposing physical and moral worlds. On one side of the divide stands

On the Cat's Back

the civic world: represented by England, and all its associated institutions and associations: the Anglican church, the aristocracy and the middle class; and the urban centres of Rhulen, Hereford, Coventry and London. On the other stands the rural world: Wales, the nonconformist chapel, the agricultural class and the asceticism and seasonal virtues of country life.' The contrast is re-emphasised, not only by the print of *The Broad and Narrow Way* which hangs in The Vision – England being the primrose path that leads to destruction, Wales the stony track towards salvation – but also in the walks on which the twins, as boys, are taken by their grandfather. The 'English walk' leads to the green pastures and handsome trees of Lurkenhope Park; the Welsh walk up the steep slope of the ridge, past the honest poverty of the Rock, to the summit of the Black Hill and the Eagle Stone (which Chatwin transplanted from the Peak District, where he had lived for a time as a child).

There have been suggestions that Bruce Chatwin may have had a different Black Hill in mind when he wrote his novel, the Black Hill between Knighton and Clun, in south Shropshire. Indeed, this alternative setting was first suggested by Chatwin himself, when he was rebutting accusations that the book was a 'faction' based on real people in real places, i.e. the Howells brothers and their farm. He pointed out that it was at Cwm Hall, the home of his friends, the Wilkinsons, not far from this second Black Hill that he actually started writing the book. Even so, the setting of the Herefordshire Black Hill, with Hay-on-Wye (Rhulen in the book) to the north, Craswall (Lurkenhope) to the west and Cefn Hill nearby fits the narrative pretty well, quite apart from being perfect in its atmosphere.

On the Black Hill was mostly well received. The *New York Times* compared Chatwin with Hardy and DH Lawrence for the 'dramatic intensity' of his portrayal of British rural life, whilst Auberon Waugh declared that 'it is the first novel I have seen in two years which begins to merit the accolade of "masterpiece"'.' Not everyone was so taken with the novel. In the *London Evening Standard*, Paul Bailey criticised it as cliché-ridden, adding that, at its worst, the book had the quality of 'Mary Webb, on a very off day', which must have stung!

But that view was very much the exception. Although the book failed to make the Booker Prize shortlist, it did win the Whitbread Prize for Best First Novel and the James Tait Black Memorial Prize and was made into a feature film, written and directed by Andrew Grieve, starring Bob Peck as Amos Jones, which follows the story more or less faithfully, without, it must be said, a great deal of imagination.

Sadly, for he was a hugely talented writer, Bruce Chatwin never really fulfilled his potential. His next book, an account of life with the aboriginals in the Australian outback, entitled *The Songlines*, was another critically acclaimed success but, even as he was writing it, he was beginning to show symptoms of the AIDS-related illness from which he would die in 1989, at the age of just 48. I suspect that he will be remembered for *On the Black Hill* long after his travel books have been forgotten. Very few writers, certainly of the modern era, have captured the atmosphere of a stretch of country and its people quite so compellingly as Bruce Chatwin did with this remote corner of Herefordshire.

From some of the bleakest countryside in England, we will pass through some of the most fertile as we cross Herefordshire from Craswall in the north-west to Ledbury in the south-east. It would be fair to say that the Herefordshire countryside isn't quite what it was. Even the famed 'Golden Valley', so called by virtue of the River Dore running through it, now has more than its fair share of poly-tunnels, and other quasi-industrial installations. The NFU has long liked to refer to the countryside as 'the farmer's factory floor'. In large parts of modern-day Herefordshire, you can now see exactly what that looks like in practice.

Literary associations are rather thin on the ground in central Herefordshire. John Moore wrote a novel, *September Moon*, about love and lust among a group of hop pickers, based at Thinghill Court Farm near Withington, and Thomas Traherne, the metaphysical poet, was born at Hereford in 1637. But the Herefordshire area with much the strongest claim to literary fame is Ledbury and the Malvern Hills just beyond, thanks to four very different poets.

John Masefield
(1878-1967)
'Ties of beauty' to Herefordshire

The first of our quartet is John Masefield, who was born in Ledbury in 1878. He had the perfect childhood for a poet: idyllic in its setting, looking out from the family's homes in Ledbury across the rich Herefordshire countryside to the mountains in the distance; yet traumatic in its human relationships. It had all begun so promisingly. John Masefield would refer in later years (not least in his autobiography *Grace Before Ploughing*) to his early childhood at the imposing half-timbered family home called The Knapp as 'paradise'. His grandfather, George Masefield, had founded what seemed a very successful (and still surviving) legal practice in the town, in which his father, Edward, was a partner with his brother, William. His mother, Caroline, was musical, literate and would read poetry to the children. John, or Jack as the family called him, was the third of six, and at a remarkably early age, he not only came to appreciate the beauty of his surroundings, but – rather like Richard Jefferies – to lose himself in them:

> *All that I looked upon was beautiful, and known by me to be beautiful ... I was sure that a greater life was near us; in dreams I sometimes seemed to enter a part of it, and woke with rapture and longing. Then, on one wonderful day, when I was a little more than five years old, as I stood looking north, over a clump of honeysuckle in flower, I entered that greater life; and that life entered into me with a delight that I can never forget.*

Nor was the area around Ledbury the only stretch of countryside that he came to know in these early years. His mother's father, the Reverend Charles Hubert Parker, was rector of Great Comberton on the slopes of Bredon Hill. So there were regular trips there, as well as to Jack's godmother, Annie Hanford-Flood, who lived at ancient and fascinating Woollas Hall, built on a platform in the hillside under Banbury Tower. He and his brothers and sisters would explore the woods, the old quarries and the strange stone outcrops of this magical place. Young Jack even claimed to have discovered the site of an ancient chapel. The influence both of his godmother and of Bredon Hill would continue to shape John Masefield's life and poetry long into his adult life.

In his *Grace Before Ploughing – Fragments of Autobiography*, written late in his long life and looking back to his childhood, Masefield remembers Ledbury and Bredon Hill as 'linked Paradises'.

> *My early memories are of these two places and of spots very near to them. My early memories are therefore of fertile orchards full of fruit; of hills much marked with old tribal settlements; of rivers prone to flood, of many ancient buildings; and peopled by most kind folk who yet kept alive, deep in their hearts, a memory of the Civil War 'against Oliver'.*

He also formed an early attachment to the Malverns, Herefordshire Beacon in particular, after he'd been taken to the hill on a childhood excursion. The ramparts on the hillside, or 'trenches' as he called them, left a particularly deep impression. They 'gave me the feeling that they have never failed to give me, of vastness, of roughness and of something vast, rough and uncanny with a life of its own, like itself everlasting and strange; not inhuman, but not human. I have that sense of it still, and marvel at it. The rough wild hill is impressed with a rough wild life that is strangely greater than anything alive now.'

But this childhood paradise would all too soon be lost. In 1885, when he was six, his mother Caroline, who had first introduced Jack to poetry, died of pneumonia. The following year, both his paternal grandparents died and then the family was engulfed by financial crisis. More out of a sense of duty than any particular affection for the children, they were taken on by Uncle William and Aunt Kate, who lived at the Priory, another handsome Victorian pile, at the other end of town. Kate Masefield seemed to entertain a particular dislike of Jack, and especially for his love of books. A harsh and unsympathetic governess, Mrs Boers, added to the children's woes and then, to top it all off, their father Edward suffered a complete breakdown in 1889 and died the following year.

Could fate have any more slings and arrows with which to torment poor John Masefield? Well, yes, it could. In 1891, at the insistence of his aunt and at the age of just 13, he was sent to the naval training ship, HMS *Conway*, moored in the Mersey. Yet, after a rough, lonely and miserable start, this turned out to be the making of him. He passed out with a good record in 1894 – not good enough to get himself into the Royal Navy, but sufficient to win a berth on a four-masted White Star line barque called the Gilcruix, bound for Chile, with Cape Horn to be rounded on the way. This proved to be a terrifying experience, and when the ship finally reached Iquique, he fell seriously ill from a combination of sunstroke and a nervous breakdown and nearly died. Eventually, he was sent home across the Atlantic, deciding en route that he'd had enough of the sea-faring life, and would become a writer, not a sailor. Sadly for Jack, Aunt Kate saw things rather differently. Once he had recovered his strength at the Priory she sent him back to sea, this time on board the *Bidston Hill*, bound for New York.

But Jack's mind was made up. Once in New York, he jumped ship and, after drifting around doing odd jobs and working in bars, he found himself a job in a big New York carpet factory. Bear in mind that he was still only 17, had been orphaned, had twice looked death in the face, around Cape Horn and in Iquique, was alone in a big city in a foreign land, was suffering intermittent bouts of malaria and, like his father before him, was prone to depression. No wonder he became a poet!

He had, in fact, been writing poetry since the age of ten. But it was during his two years at the carpet factory, after discovering Keats, Chaucer and Milton, and reading them avidly in what little spare time he had, that he started writing in earnest. Despite vowing to become a journalist, he continued with his poetry when he returned to England in 1897, weak and ill. After yet more convalescence, his mother's family, the Parkers, found him a job in London as a bank clerk. After the usual disappointments, he began to get his poems published in periodicals. He may not have been long at sea – one voyage around Cape Horn and three times across the Atlantic – but the experience had left a profound impression on him. Almost all of his early published poems – the *Salt Water Ballads* – relate to the sea and the men who sailed on it. As you might expect, given Masefield's own experiences, they are not universally cheerful. But in amongst the rolling ballads of storm, shipwreck and death are just a handful of poems which speak of the time before John Masefield went to sea, and of the countryside in which he grew up.

There are four in a row: *Personal*, in which the poet wistfully looks back to 'the merry days in the old home before I went to sea', as he is passing a lighted inn at night; *On Malvern Hill*, which recalls the bloody battle when the Roman legions stormed the British Camp; *Tewkesbury Road*, with its undercurrent of wanderlust; and the delightfully arcadian *On Eastnor Knoll*.

Now, Eastnor Knoll is a hill a mile or so north-east of Ledbury, overlooking the mock-medieval Eastnor Castle, with its lake, campsite and Land Rover testing track (which was used as a film location for the television adaptation of Masefield's *The Box of Delights*). A footpath runs up the hill from the church, skirts the wooded summit and carries on down the hill, past 'Dead Woman's Thorn', and so into Ledbury. As the nearest high vantage point to his home, John Masefield must often have walked here as a boy, and the place had evidently left its mark:

> *Silent are the woods, and the dim green boughs are*
> *Hushed in the twilight: yonder, in the path through*
> *The apple orchard, is a tired plough-boy*
> *Calling the cows home.*
>
> *A bright white star blinks, the pale moon rounds, but*
> *Still the red, lurid wreckage of the sunset*
> *Smoulders in smoky fire, and burns on*
> *The misty hill-tops.*
>
> *Ghostly it grows, and darker, the burning*
> *Fades into smoke, and now the gusty oaks are*
> *A silent army of phantoms thronging*
> *A land of shadows.*

On Eastnor Knoll

Published in 1902, the *Salt Water Ballads*, complete with *Sea Fever*, were a modest success. The first 500 copies sold out within six months. Masefield's name was made. He had given up his job at the bank to become a full-time writer and moved in the same sort of London literary circles as Laurence Binyon and his friend and a major influence on his early work, WB Yeats. He got married, to Constance Crommelin, an English teacher nearly 12 years his senior (which is perhaps an indication of how much older than his years Masefield had become), and he discovered the Cotswolds, helping to produce Ben Jonson's play *The New Inn* at Chipping Campden.

More ballads followed in his next volume of poetry, *Ballads and Poems*, many of them, as before, drawing upon his experiences at sea, the most famous being, of course, *Cargoes*. But there are love poems, to Constance, as well, some nostalgic reflections on his childhood and his mother, and several poems which confirm the fact that, whilst Masefield was happy enough to be living in London with his new wife, he was still pining for the woods and fields of his native countryside. *London Town* expresses this perfectly, with that lovely loping Masefield rhythm – though it is a great pity that he tarnishes it by giving expression in the penultimate stanza to the prevalent anti-semitism of the period:

> *Oh London Town's a fine town, and London sights are rare,*
> *And London ale is right ale, and brisk's the London air,*
> *And busily goes the world there, but crafty grows the mind,*
> *And London Town of all towns I'm glad to leave behind.*

Then hey for croft and hop-yard, and hill, and field, and pond,
With Bredon Hill before me and Malvern Hill beyond,
The hawthorn white i' the hedgerow, and all the spring's attire
In the comely land of Teme and Lugg, and Clent, and Clee, and Wyre.

Oh London girls are brave girls, in silk and cloth o' gold,
And London shops are rare shops, where gallant things are sold,
And bonnily clinks the gold there, but drowsily blinks the eye,
And London Town of all towns I'm glad to hurry by.

Then, hey for covert and woodland, and ash and elm and oak,
Tewkesbury inns, and Malvern roofs, and Worcester chimney smoke,
The apple trees in the orchard, the cattle in the byre,
And all the land from Ludlow town to Bredon church's spire.

Oh London tunes are new tunes; and London books are wise,
And London plays are rare plays, and fine to country eyes,
But craftily fares the knave there, and wickedly fares the Jew,
And London Town of all towns I'm glad to hurry through.

So hey for the road, the west road, by mill and forge and fold,
Scent of the fern and song of the lark by brook, and field, and wold,
To the comely folk at the hearth-stone and the talk beside the fire,
In the hearty land, where I was bred, my land of heart's desire.

John Masefield was very far from being just a poet. He wrote plays, in both verse and prose, lyrics, non-fictional prose, a hugely popular series of children's books, and even, during World War One, Government-backed 'reinterpretations' of Gallipoli and the Somme which verged on propaganda. His next major work of poetry was very different from the ballads of his youth. By the time *The Everlasting Mercy* was published, in 1911, John and Constance had produced two children, Judy and Lewis, and had moved out of London into the countryside at Great Hampden in Hertfordshire. It was, and would remain, a fundamentally happy marriage, even if John had fallen briefly but heavily in love with another older woman, Elizabeth Robins. Probably fortunately for all concerned, she didn't share his passion and emigrated to Dresden in 1910, leaving Masefield both bereft and guilt-ridden, even though the relationship never seems to have been consummated. It was in this rather conflicted state of mind – outward content, inner turmoil – that *The Everlasting Mercy* was conceived, relating as it does how a wicked and unhappy man finds redemption through Christianity. The spark which lit Masefield's poetic flame on this occasion was accompanying a friend on a walk to the station one bright early morning in May.

A ploughman was working with his team of horses in a field alongside the road to the station, coming up the hill towards them, 'followed by the advancing breaking wave of red clay cast aside by the share'. It reminded Masefield of Piers Plowman or Chaucer's ploughman, especially as the ploughman himself – 'a staid, elderly, honest and most kindly man' – was the epitome of honest toil in a good cause. Later that same day, Masefield took again to the Hertfordshire woods and fields. At the upper edge of a wood, he came upon a stretch of common land 'most lovely in the tranquillity of the May evening'. For a moment, it was if he had rediscovered his childhood secret of becoming lost in nature. By his own account, as he burst through the fence, he said to himself, "I will write a poem about the blackguard who becomes converted", the first lines of the poem forming in his head even as he spoke.

It is a simple story, vividly told, set firmly in the Ledbury of his youth. It is by 'Dead Man's Thorn' on Eastnor Knoll, that Saul Kane picks a fight on false pretences with his fellow poacher and supposed friend, Billy Myers. The two of them fight it out at dead of night in a field at the top of the hill, with a drunken crowd, betting heavily on the outcome. Saul having knocked his man out in the 18th round, he is borne in triumph down to the town to celebrate the victory in 'The Lion', which is opened for the purpose at midnight. Much boozing and wenching ensues, to the point where Saul goes almost mad with drink, tears off his clothes, wakes the entire town from its beds by ringing the firebell and leads the pursuing authorities a merry dance before slipping back to the pub. More debauchery ensues on the following day until, back in the Lion at closing time, Saul is told the error of his ways by a Quaker 'mission lady', Miss Bourne. Almost instantly, he sees the light, vows never to touch another drop and when, like Masefield, he encounters a plough team on the following day, realises that

> *Christ had taught me what to be*
> *That I should plough, and as I ploughed*
> *My Saviour Christ would sing aloud,*
> *And as I drove the clods apart*
> *Christ would be plough in my heart,*
> *Through rest-harrow and bitter roots,*
> *Through all my bad life's rotten fruits.*

The fact that he then looks up to see the copse on the summit of May Hill looking for all the world like a ploughman and his team, merely serves to confirm what was now his life's choice.

It is a long poem, running to over 1,600 lines, and is rather over-moralistic for modern tastes. But it is well worth reading all the way through, not just for the vividness of the characters and the scenes, but also for the picture which it paints of Ledbury, as it would have been in Masefield's childhood. It is all there: the stony path coming down from Eastnor Knoll, Cabbage Walk, the Market Place, the almshouse pump where Saul encounters the purple-faced parson, Bye Street and Worcester Walk (which presumably ran off Worcester Road, where the Masefield Solicitors office is). Sadly, Dirty Lane either no longer exists or has been re-named, and I can't find a modern equivalent of the Lion pub (it's not the ancient Prince of Wales, as that gets a mention of its own, and I doubt if it is the pub, formerly the White Lion, which re-opened in 2016 as The Lion in Bye Street). But this is a poem with the strongest possible sense of place, and that place is Ledbury.

The Everlasting Mercy caused quite a sensation when it was published, not least for the uncompromising, almost Hogarthian grotesquerie of its descriptions of the seamier side of Herefordshire life in the nineteenth century. 'It was read, declaimed, interrupted, discussed with a sort of inflamed fever of controversy such as, in the case of poetry, I cannot in memory match,' wrote the critic Frank Swinnerton, who would subsequently hail Masefield as 'the first of the Georgians'. Not every critic was so impressed. Fellow writers JC Squire and Rupert Brooke mocked and parodied his 'jog-trot ballad' style. Nonetheless it transformed John Masefield from being a well-known poet into a famous one. He was even touted as Poet Laureate when Alfred Austin died and, although Robert Bridges got the nod, Masefield's turn would come.

Whether he was ever quite such a good poet again as he was during his Georgian period is perhaps open to question. Further long narrative poems followed, in *The Widow in the Bye Street*, *Dauber*, *The Daffodil Fields* and *Philip the King*. Some of the shorter poems that he wrote after the family moved to the Berkshire Downs during the First World War – *Lollingdon Downs*, for example, or *August 1914* – offer a striking evocation of a very different countryside to that in which Masefield had grown up. And *Reynard the Fox*, *Right Royal* and *King Cole* saw him returning to country themes after the move to Boars Hill in 1917.

He was an obvious choice for Poet Laureate when his Boars Hill neighbour Robert Bridges died in 1930. His first speech in his new role was made when he accepted the freedom of the City of Hereford in October that year. He spoke movingly of what his native county had meant to him as a poet: "I am linked to this county by subtle ties, deeper than I can explain," he said. "They are ties of beauty ... Whenever I think of the bounty and beauty of God, I think of parts of this county."

Ironically, his appointment was the start of a long decline in his reputation as a poet. He was a dutiful Poet Laureate, churning out verses for all the main royal occasions, as well as for other nationally significant events, like the launching of the *Queen Mary*. But whilst the technique remained, it would be fair to say that the muse had departed. In the 1930s, John and Constance lived at Pinbury House on the Bathurst estate in the Cotswolds, before moving to Clifton Hampden on the Thames in 1939. And there they stayed, Constance dying in 1959 at age of 93, and John surviving until he was carried off by gangrene in 1967. He will always be most famous for his poems of the sea, but the countryside of his native Herefordshire was arguably just as important an inspiration, throughout his long life.

Herefordshire's other most notable poetic association is with Elizabeth Barrett Browning. She was actually born in County Durham in 1806, the first of 12 children, into a wealthy family of Jamaican plantation owners. But she spent most of her childhood at Hope End, a couple of miles north of Ledbury, in the lee of the Malvern Hills. Her difficult, distinctly vainglorious father, Edward Barrett Moulton Barrett – who insisted that 'Barrett' appeared in the surname of every member of the family, and who in his own case, made that doubly sure – had bought the 500 rolling acres of the Hope End estate. On it, he proceeded to build one of the oddest houses in the county – a sort of Moorish palace, complete with minarets at either end, opulently furnished and lavishly decorated, set in exquisitely landscaped gardens. The young Elizabeth loved it, feeding as it did an already fertile and poetic imagination. Dubbed by her father 'The Poet Laureate of Hope End', she started writing poetry at the age of six, and had her first full length poem published (albeit privately, by her father) when she was just 14.

That was at about the same time when her life was blighted, permanently as it turned out, by a mysterious illness, which caused her acute pain in her head and spine. It may or may not have been brought on by a fall from her pony, but in any event the doctors could offer neither diagnosis nor cure. She took to taking laudanum to ease the pain, and would later develop a further condition, probably tuberculosis, which, for a period in her 20s and 30s, would render her effectively housebound. By this time, the entire family's fortunes had taken a turn for the worse. A combination of mismanagement and the abolition of slavery, which Elizabeth detested, had decimated their Jamaican earnings, forcing the sale of Hope End in 1833, and moves, first to Sidmouth and then to Wimpole Street in London, where Elizabeth, ill and heart-broken at the death of her favourite brother Edward, drowned whilst staying with her at Torquay, kept mainly to her room.

Elizabeth Barrett Browning
(1806-1861)
The Poet Laureate of Hope End

But that did at least give her the time and freedom from other distractions to start writing in earnest. Sonnets and ballads were her two favourite formats, and it is one of her early ballads, *The Lost Bower*, that draws most expressively upon her childhood at Hope End, and the countryside that she had clearly come to love:

II
Green the land is where my daily
Steps in jocund childhood played,
Dimpled close with hill and valley,
Dappled very close with shade:
Summer-snow of apple-blossoms running up from glade to glade.

III
There is one hill I see nearer
In my vision of the rest;
And a little wood seems clearer
As it climbeth from the west,
Sideway from the tree-locked valley, to the airy upland crest.

VII
On your left, the sheep are cropping
The slant grass and daisies pale,
And five apple-trees stand dropping
Separate shadows toward the vale,
Over which, in choral silence, the hills look you their 'All hail!'

VIII

Far out, kindled by each other,
Shining hills on hills arise,
Close as brother leans to brother
When they press beneath the eyes
Of some father praying blessings from the gifts of paradise.

IX

While beyond, above them mounted,
And above their woods also,
Malvern hills, for mountains counted
Not unduly, loom a-row –
Keepers of Piers Plowman's visions through the sunshine and the snow.

She finds the bower hidden in the trees, a marvel of entwining ivy, eglantine, wild hop and columbine, with red and white roses growing either side of the door, and enters, wonderingly

So young muser, I sat listening
To my fancy's wildest word.
On a sudden, through the glistening
Leaves around a little stirred,
Came a sound, a sense of music, which was rather felt than heard.

Softly, finely, it enwound me;
From the world it shut me in, –
Like a fountain, falling round me,
Which with silver waters thin
Clips a little water Naiad sitting smilingly within.

Was this, one wonders, Elizabeth's 'Masefield' or 'Jefferies' moment, when she found herself transported to a different, more spiritual, soul-world? If so, it didn't last:

Mystic presences of power
Had up-snatched me to the timeless, then returned me to the Hour.

In a child-abstraction lifted,
Straightway from the bower I past,
Foot and soul being dimly drifted
Through the greenwood, till, at last,
In the hill-top's open sunshine I all consciously was cast.

Face to face with the true mountains
I stood silently and still,
Drawing strength from fancy's daunting,
From the air about the hill,
And from Nature's open mercies, and most debonair goodwill.

The next morning, when she went to find her bower, there was no sign of it. It had vanished, and with it everything it signified: the secret world of innocence and childhood, before the pain of her illness and the complications of womanhood.

Although Hope End House was demolished in 1873, the gardens survive, as does most of the surrounding parkland. Until quite recently, the house that replaced it offered five-star bed-and-breakfast and, although that is no longer the case, the gardens are sometimes opened to the public under the National Gardens Scheme. There is no difficulty about access to the parkland. A well-signposted and maintained footpath runs up the valley from Hope End Farm past ancient oaks and sweet chestnuts to Oyster Hill – Elizabeth's 'airy, upland crest'. The views from here are, indeed, magnificent: to the north-west, 'shining hills on hills arise', stretching as far north as the Long Mynd in Shropshire; to the north-east, the Malverns – 'keepers of Piers Plowman's visions in the sunshine and the snow'. Considering that the poem was written a good ten years after the family had had to leave Hope End, the hilltop and its views must have left a deep impression on Elizabeth.

The woodlands where she found her lost bower are still there as well, climbing up the hill from the west, exactly as she describes, until they reach the open hill-top – 'there, in green arrest, the branches see their image in the ground' while

> On your left, the sheep are cropping
> The slant grass and daisies pale

The description fits the scene as well now as it must have done 180 years ago.

Compass Hill, looking north to Shropshire

The Lost Bower was included among the *Poems* which Elizabeth Barrett Moulton-Barrett, as she still was, published in 1844. It was warmly received, and cemented her reputation as the foremost woman poet of the time. No-one was more impressed by the poems than a still relatively unknown Robert Browning. A meeting between the two was arranged, and their love affair developed from there, conducted largely in secret, as Elizabeth's tyrannical father profoundly disapproved of the relationship. Eventually, in 1846, they married and fled immediately to Italy; first Pisa and then Florence. The love poems which Elizabeth had written during their courtship were published in 1850 as *Sonnets from the Portuguese*, the most famous being that all-time wedding favourite *How do I love thee, let me count the ways*. Her health improved for a time, and she remained as prolific as ever, whilst Robert's reputation slowly grew. She died in Florence, in her husband's arms, in 1861, aged 55.

Elizabeth Barrett Browning wasn't really a poet of the countryside. Her themes and her styles were many and varied. She loved to tell a story; she was, of course, passionately concerned about the role and treatment of women; she cared deeply for the poor and downtrodden; and then there was her love for Robert. She probably regarded these as higher poetic themes than landscapes. Yet, in her longest work of poetry, the nine book 'novel in verse' *Aurora Leigh*, there is just one section, at the end of Book One, where her appreciation and love of the countryside of her childhood comes shining through. After the death of her father, the 13-year-old Aurora is uprooted from her home in Italy and sent to live with her aunt near Malvern. At first, she despises her new surroundings, complaining that the countryside is no more than a garden, compared to the untamed wildness of Italy. But gradually she came to love 'that England':

> *I flattered all the beauteous country round,*
> *As poets use ... the skies, the clouds, the fields,*
> *The happy violets hiding from the roads*
> *The primroses run down to, carrying gold, –*
> *The tangled hedgerows, where the cows push out*
> *Impatient horns and tolerant churning mouths*
> *'Twixt dripping ash-boughs, – hedgerows all alive*
> *With birds and gnats and large white butterflies*
> *Which look as if the May-flower had sought life*
> *And palpitated forth upon the wind, –*
> *Hills, vales, woods, netted in a silver mist,*
> *Farms, granges, doubled up among the hills,*
> *And cattle grazing in the watered vales,*
> *And cottage-chimneys smoking from the woods,*
> *And cottage-gardens smelling everywhere,*
> *Confused with smell of orchards. 'See,' I said,*
> *'And see! is God not with us on the earth?*
> *And shall we put Him down by aught we do?*
> *Who says there's nothing for the poor and vile*
> *Save poverty and wickedness? behold!'*
> *And ankle-deep in English grass I leaped,*
> *And clapped my hands, and called all very fair.*

Maybe the countryside of Ledbury and the Malverns does not quite answer to that description these days, but it is still more than sufficiently glorious to suggest a touch of divine intervention.

There is something very unexpected, out of place almost, about the Malvern Hills. As Elizabeth Barrett Browning observes, they look more like mountains. Seen from the east, they do not so much rise from the broad floodplain of the River Severn, as erupt from it: a stegosaurus spine of grey-green, sharp-edged peaks, rising ever higher as the eye travels from Hangman's Hill in the south to Worcestershire Beacon in the north.

This is one of the most recognisable ranges of hills in England, and one of the most celebrated, although perhaps more so in music than in words. Edward Elgar was born at Lower Broadheath, between Worcester and the Malverns in 1857, and for most of his life loved nothing better than walking through the hills (unless, that is, it was cycling through them!). His musical influences may have been mainly Germanic – Schumann, Brahms, Wagner and Richard Strauss in particular – but the inspiration which produced works like the *Enigma Variations*, *Pomp and Circumstance* and *The Dream of Gerontius* was profoundly English, not to say Malvernian.

Elgar liked to compose in the open air, as he was walking the hills, writing it all down when he got home in the evening. "The music is what I have all day," he told a friend. "The trees are singing my music – or have I sung theirs?" According to his biographer WH Reed, Elgar's childhood in the Malverns and the wider Worcestershire countryside had an influence that 'permeated all his work and gave to his whole life that subtle but none the less true and sturdy English quality.' You can't walk the Malverns without the music of Sir Edward Elgar ringing in your ears.

The excellent Elgar trail will take you to all the key Elgar locations, which include our first literary port of call, at British Camp. It was walking here that inspired Elgar to write his cantata *Caractacus* in 1898. It was walking here some half a millennium earlier that inspired William Langland to write one of the great works of medieval literature, *Piers Plowman*.

Or that at least is what is assumed. We know little enough directly about Langland himself, beyond that he was the son of Stacy de Rokayle of Shipton-under-Wychwood in Oxfordshire and was either born or brought up somewhere near the Malverns in the 1330s. For the rest, we have to rely on the clues provided in *Piers Plowman*, which does draw heavily on the life and beliefs of its author, whoever he – or possibly they – may have been. What is beyond dispute is the Malvern connection, for it is there in the very first lines of the poem:

> *In a summer season when soft was the sun*
> *In rough cloth I robed me, as I a shepherd were,*
> *In habit like a hermit in his works unholy*
> *And through the wide world I went, wonders to hear.*

> *But on a May morning, on Malvern hills,*
> *A marvel befell me – sure from Faery it came –*
> *I had wandered me weary, so weary I rested me*
> *On a broad bank by a merry-sounding burn;*
> *And as I lay and leaned and looked into the waters*
> *I slumbered in a sleeping it rippled so merrily,*
> *And I dreamed – marvellously.*

Will, the narrator, dreams that he is looking east, towards a handsome tower on a hill, beneath it a dell, and in the dell a dark and deathly dungeon. And all in between, between the tower and the dungeon, he looked upon 'a fair field full of folk' – the folk, all manner of them, who would become the subjects of this and all of Will's subsequent dreams about the relationship between God and men, and much else besides.

Even today, almost 700 years later, it is not hard to understand why, standing on Herefordshire Beacon and looking eastward, Langland should have been struck by the variety and the industriousness of the prospect: all those villages, farms and cottages; the woodlands and the fields, arable and grassland, stretching to the horizon – a fair prospect indeed. And how many people must that landscape encompass – rich and poor, young and old, hard-working and idle, spiritual and secular, selfless and greedy. Still today, it feels as if you are looking out across a microcosm of England.

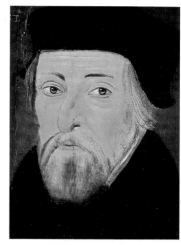

William Langland
(1332-1386)
Malvern dreamer

Of course, in Langland's day, there would have been many more trees, many fewer houses and no industrial sheds at all. But there would probably have been more people to be seen, given that in the fourteenth century most of the adult population worked on the land, whilst open-field farming would have meant they were visible, especially from a vantage point like the Malverns. However, whilst the scene that Langland looked out upon – quite possibly from the slopes above Little Malvern Priory, where he probably studied as a youth – may have given the appearance of being prosperous and industrious, the reality was anything but. The fourteenth century was a time of intermittent plague, famine and rural unrest, culminating in the ill-fated Peasants' Revolt in 1381. *Piers Plowman* was prayed in aid by the Revolt's Kentish leaders, although Langland had certainly never intended it to be a revolutionary tract, and seems to have been appalled at what was taking place. But you could argue that it was the inevitable result of the rottenness he had portrayed.

Ironically, given that initial setting high on the Malverns, what *Piers Plowman* did do, even before Chaucer was writing, was to provide a view of medieval society and religion from below, rather than from above. Almost all literature of the time was of and for the church or the aristocracy. But this is the work of a common man – an itinerant clerk – railing against the idle rich, the feckless poor, the grasping lawyers, a corrupt chuch and an inadequate monarchy. Its hero is the Plowman, who works his half-acre honestly, looks after his family dutifully and trusts in God. One cannot fairly claim that it was inspired by the Malverns – the inspiration was Langland's own beliefs, shaped and distilled by the experiences of his life – but it may well have been his time on the Malverns, looking out across the Worcestershire plain, which gave him the idea of writing an overview of a society in which the reality was so much at odds with the perception.

'A fair field full of folk'

The view to the west of the Malverns offers a striking contrast with that to the east. The landscape is more wooded, more hedged, more rolling as it stretches away across Herefordshire to the Black Mountains. The nearest village on this side of the ridge is Colwall, which rather straggles up the B4218 as it readies itself for the steep climb to Upper Wyche, in the Malverns' central cleft. Colwall's claim to literary fame rests on the considerable figure of WH Auden, who taught at The Downs prep school here in the early 1930s, when he was in his twenties. Auden certainly wasn't a poet of the countryside. He wrote of love, politics, the human condition and religion, this last being the central theme of his most obviously 'Malvern' poem. But, rather as with Langland, the top of the Malverns, looking out over England provided the perfect vantage point on which to reflect on broader, deeper themes.

> *Here on the cropped grass of the narrow ridge I stand*
> *A fathom of earth, alive in air,*
> *Aloof as an admiral on the old rocks,*
>   *England below me:*
> *Eastward across the Midland plains*
> *An express is leaving for a sailor's country;*
>   *Westward is Wales*
> *Where on clear evenings the retired and rich*
> *From the French windows of their sheltered mansions*
> *See the Sugarloaf standing, an upright sentinel*
>   *Over Abergavenny.*

William Wordsworth

William Wordsworth, his wife Mary and his ever-present sister Dorothy visited Herefordshire several times in the late 1820s/early 1830s. They stayed in the moted medieval manor house of Brinsop Court, a few miles north-west of Hereford. It had been the ancestral home of the Dinsey family, but was snapped up by the financier, David Ricardo (along with several other estates), after he had made a huge financial killing on the Battle of Waterloo.

The 900-acre estate was rented by Mary Wordsworth's brother, Thomas Hutchinson, who moved down from the Lake District to farm it. The Wordsworths first visited in December 1827, William enjoying the rich Herefordshire countryside and the proximity to his beloved Wye Valley; Dorothy remarking in her diary that it was 'no cheerless spot, and flowers in the hedges and blossoms in the numerous orchards will soon make it gay' and being adopted by the Hutchinsons' dog Prince. Further visits would follow over the next few years, but it was probably on this first visit that William made a day-trip to Ledbury and, after visiting St Katherine's Hospital there, wrote this sonnet:

St Catherine of Ledbury

When human touch (as monkish books attest)
Nor was applied nor could be, Ledbury bells
Broke forth in concert flung adown the dells,
And upward, high as Malvern's cloudy crest;
Sweet tones, and caught by a noble Lady blest
To rapture! Mabel listened at the side
Of her loved mistress: soon the music died,
And Catherine said, "Here I set up my rest."
Warned in a dream, the Wanderer long had sought
A home that by such miracle of sound
Must be revealed:– she heard it now, or felt
The deep, deep joy of a confiding thought;
And there, a saintly Anchoress, she dwelt
Till she exchanged for heaven that happy ground.

Church Street, Ledbury

The Catherine in question was Katherine Audley (1272-1322), a cousin of Edward II. The story goes that, after her husband had died, she heard the bells of Ledbury church ringing out to mark his passing, without the assistance of any bell-ringers. She took this as a sign that she and her attendant Mabel should settle there and found a hospital for the poor. In point of boring fact, the hospital had actually been founded some 80 years before, but a bequest in Katherine's will certainly helped it to expand.

The Malverns and Herefordshire

Walks

Hay-on-Wye is a good centre for exploring the country of **On the Black Hill**. The Offa's Dyke path takes you from the town, up the escarpment past Hay Bluff and onwards along the ridge. Branch left just after you cross the boundary into Herefordshire and follow the path along the top of the eastern ridge towards Black Hill, looking down on the village of Craswall, and so on to the steepest, narrowest section of the ridge, known as the Cat's Back. Return by the bridleway running along the bottom of the escarpment, past Newhouse Farm – the original for *The Vision* farm in the book – to rejoin Offa's Dyke path below Hay Bluff. Detours to the *Bull's Head* in Craswall and to Craswall's idiosyncratic little church are recommended. The bridleway also passes close to Coed Major, the smallholding on which *The Rock* is modelled.

For the less energetic, the best way to reach the top of the Black Hill is to make the fairly tortuous drive to the car park at the Cat's Back, then scramble up the steep slope to the narrow ridge at the top, and along that to the triangulation station at the summit.

Eastnor Knoll and Ledbury: A footpath runs up Eastnor Knoll from Eastnor church, past the field near *Dead Woman's Thorn* where Saul Kane fought Billy Myers, and on down through the woods into Ledbury. You will find all of the main *Everlasting Mercy* locations in the town (barring, sadly, the original *Lion*). The John Masefield Society has organised a 'John Masefield guided walk' as part of the Ledbury poetry festival, held in July.

The **Hope End** estate where Elizabeth Barrett Browning lived as a girl is three miles north of Ledbury, just beyond the village of Wellington Heath. A footpath, part of the Herefordshire trail, runs from the entrance gates, up through a handsome stretch of parkland with woods on either side, to Compass Hill, the main setting for *The Lost Bower*. There are fine views to north and west, and a bench on which to sit and enjoy them.

The **Malvern Hills** Area of Outstanding Beauty has produced a comprehensive Literary Trail Around the Malverns. Visit: www.malvernhillsaonb.org.uk

Walk on **Herefordshire Beacon and British Camp** and visit Little Malvern Priory to experience the country of William Langland and John Masefield.

Viewpoints

Black Hill • The Cat's Back • Compass Hill • Eastnor Knoll • Herefordshire Beacon • British Camp • Worcestershire Beacon

Pubs

On the Black Hill: At the time of writing, the *Bull's Head* at Craswall was sadly closed. However, the *Bridge Inn* at Michaelchurch Escley is within comfortable walking distance of the Cat's Back, and offers excellent food and real ale in a beautiful setting.

Ledbury: The oldest and most famous pub in the town is the *Prince of Wales* in Church Street. Excellent beer, food and atmosphere.

Malverns: The best bet is the *Wyche Inn*, which offers good beer and cider, decent food and far-reaching views. Further south, in the vale, the *Farmers Arms* at Birtsmorton is another fine Worcestershire pub.

The Farmers Arms at Birtsmorton

Select Bibliography

Bruce Chatwin   www.brucechatwin.co.uk
On the Black Hill (1982)
Under the Sun – The Letters of Bruce Chatwin (2010)
Nicholas Murray: *Bruce Chatwin* (1992)
Nicholas Shakespeare: *Bruce Chatwin* (1999)
Jonathan Chatwin: *Anywhere Out Of The World – The Work of Bruce Chatwin* (2012)

John Masefield   John Masefield Society, The Master's House, Ledbury
The Collected Poems of John Masefield
Grace Before Ploughing – Fragments of Autobiography (1966)
Constance Babington Smith: *John Masefield: A Life* (1978)
Muriel Spark: *John Masefield* (2010)

Elizabeth Barrett Browning   www.browningsociety.org
The Collected Poems of Elizabeth Barrett Browning
Margaret Forster: *Eliazabeth Barrett Browning – A Biography* (1988)

William Langland
Piers Plowman, translated by Arthur Burrell (Everyman, 1912)

W.H. Auden
Look, Stranger! (1936)

Chapter Eight

The Dymock Poets

Lascelles Abercrombie, Wilfrid Gibson, Robert Frost, Edward Thomas, Rupert Brooke, John Drinkwater

Dymock and daffodils and days of song
Before the war had scattered us apart.
In singing dreams of dancing gold,
In days of old before the world went wrong.
Wilfrid Gibson

The countryside around the village of Dymock, in the Leadon Vale on the Gloucestershire/Herefordshire border, presents at first acquaintance nothing particularly out of the ordinary. There are no romantic combes, or craggy mountains, far-flung views or deep mysterious forests. This is not the Dorset heaths, the North Yorkshire moors or even the Cotswolds, some 20 miles away to the east. It is a stretch of typically under-stated English countryside, gently undulating, embroidered with decrepit orchards, the occasional copse and the remnants of a forest in the shape of Dymock Wood. For much of the year, the landscape is brown rather than green. Other than along the banks of the Leadon, the old pasture has been ploughed up. The fields are mostly down to intensively grown arable crops. It is oilseed rape rather than wild daffodils which turns the landscape yellow every spring. Many of the old hedges have gone, and most of the old farmhouses are now just country residences with pony paddock attached. The white-faced, ruddy-coated Hereford cattle have almost disappeared, along with most of the sheep. To the south of the area, the dull roar of M50 provides an incessant aural backdrop.

It is hard to believe that this unexceptional stretch of country should have been either a home or an inspiration to no fewer than six poets, all at the same time, in a period when poetic sensibilities were heightened as rarely before or since by the prospect of war engulfing Europe. Two of the six, Rupert Brooke and Edward Thomas, would go to war and not return. When they lay awake at night, pondering what they were fighting for, the Leadon Vale would have been much in their thoughts. I wonder what they would think, were they to see it now?

Of course, the countryside was very different 100 years ago, especially in lowland England. Farms were small and had a mix of crops, livestock and, in north Gloucestershire, orchards of every description. Despite the rich, red soil, it was a picturesque rather than prosperous scene. Arable farming had been in decline for over thirty years when Lascelles Abercrombie became the first of the so-called Dymock poets to move to the area in 1911. Only the very best land was cropped for cereals. The rest was under pasture, for the Herefords, kept for their milk as well as for their beef, and maybe for a few mahogany-and-white Gloucester cattle, whose naturally homogenised milk gave double and single Gloucester cheese its unique creamy texture. The apple and pear harvest was the highlight of the farming year. Neighbours helped out neighbours in picking, sorting, milling and pressing the fruit. No farm would have been without its cider press, so that, come late autumn, the air would be heavy with the glorious smell of fermenting apples and pears.

In a letter to her sister, Robert Frost's wife Elinor described the area around Dymock as 'a lovely country':

> *When we first came* [in March]*, the meadows were covered with yellow daffodils and the cuckoo had just begun to sing … The pastures here are so rich that they are just as green as the mowing and wheat fields, and they are separated by dark green hedges and bordered by huge elms. Great flocks of sheep and herds of cows are everywhere.*

It must have been, in every sense, an intoxicating countryside, perhaps made even more so for being so typical of the pastoral western half of England, and never more so than in the golden summer of 1914 when, for a few short weeks of almost unbroken sunshine, all of the six poets either lived there or visited.

Dymock daffodils

And then there were the daffodils, possibly planted originally for the dye which they produced, or maybe just naturally occurring, growing wild in the fields, hedgerows, woods and orchards, for which the countryside around Dymock and the neighbouring village of Kempley was – and is still – famous. William Wordsworth may have been one of the first to appreciate the poetic possibilities of a carpet of daffodils, but he certainly wasn't the last. As a spirit-lifting, life-enhancing signal of spring and re-birth, the daffodil stands alone, with the added poignancy in 1914, which was the Dymock poets' annus mirabilis, of being a golden flower to signal the passing of a golden era.

141

Dymock and daffodils and days of song
Before the war had scattered us apart ...
In singing dreams of dancing gold,
In days of old before the world went wrong.
[from Wilfrid Gibson's 'To John Drinkwater']

The other part of the explanation for the Dymock phenomenon lies with the poets themselves: Lascelles Abercrombie, Wilfrid Gibson, John Drinkwater, Rupert Brooke, Robert Frost and Edward Thomas. Technically, they weren't all 'Georgians', to use the label that the poetry publisher, Eddie Marsh, devised to distinguish his contributors from their Victorian predecessors. Robert Frost was American and Edward Thomas didn't even start writing poetry until late 1914. His role with the Georgians was to bring them to critical attention as a reviewer for the *Daily Chronicle*. But they all aspired to use simple words to explore everyday circumstances and emotions, in a conscious revolt against the heroic themes and overblown language of the Victorians. They were still using conventional poetic structure, with rhyme and meter or blank verse, which made their poetry immediately accessible and, by modern standards, hugely popular. And, crucially, they all shared a love and appreciation of the natural world.

The first of the poets to arrive at Dymock, and the common thread which links all of them, was Lascelles Abercrombie. He had been born in Cheshire and started writing poetry when he was working in a quantity surveyor's office in Liverpool. But he had always felt himself to be a countryman at heart and, when the opportunity came to move with his new wife Catherine to Herefordshire, where his sister Ursula was already living, not far from Malvern, where he'd been sent away to school, he needed no second bidding. This was in 1910, by which time Abercrombie had published his first book of poetry, *Interludes and Poems*, and was working as a freelance journalist. After an initial year at Monks Walk Cottage, Much Marcle, they discovered 'The Gallows', a substantial cottage in the tiny hamlet of Ryton, a mile or so east of Dymock, and moved in in April 1911.

Lascelles Abercrombie
(1861-1938)
The Dymock poets' convenor

Abercrombie may best be described as the 'convenor' of the Dymock poets. Purely as a poet, he may well have been the least of them, but it was his enthusiasm and example which drew first Wilfrid Gibson and then Robert Frost to come and live near Dymock, and his unfailing friendliness and hospitality which made Drinkwater a regular visitor and even, on a couple of occasions, tempted Rupert Brooke to include a visit to Gloucestershire in his tangled and sometimes exotic schedule. It is no exaggeration to say that the Dymock poets would never have existed as an entity, had it not been for Abercrombie.

The Gallows – where it all started

His most famous poem is probably *Ryton Firs*, written in 1919, in which he first mourns the felling of the trees in Ryton Coppice, to which his cottage looks out, but then goes on to celebrate the re-birth of the hill on which they had grown, symbolised – of course – by his beloved daffodils:

> But here's the happiest light can lie on ground,
> Grass sloping under trees
> Alive with shine of yellow daffodils!
> If quicksilver were gold
> And troubled pools of it shaking in the sun
> It were not such a fancy of bickering gleam
> As Ryton daffodils when the air but stirs.
> And all the miles and miles of meadowland
> The spring makes golden ways,
> Lead here; for here the gold
> Grows brightest for our eyes,
> And for our hearts lovelier even than love,
> So here, each spring, our daffodil festival.

A combination of the 'Friends of the Dymock Poets' and Gloucestershire County Council has helpfully devised and way-marked four 'Poets' Paths', as they call them, which follow some of the routes which the poets would have taken on their walks together, and link the cottages in which four of them lived or holidayed. Poets' Path number 1 is the one which takes you nearest to where Abercrombie lived, walked and wrote. It is also one of the best bets for finding wild daffodils, from late March

143

onwards. The 'miles and miles of meadowland that spring makes golden' may have long since disappeared (vast swathes of land just to the east of Ryton Coppice were covered by plastic sheeting when I last visited), but there are plenty of daffodils to be found along the hedgebanks and in the woods. There is a fine display at Ketford Bank, just up the hill to the south of where Poets' Path 1 crosses the River Leadon. To the east from here, the path runs through some of the most attractive country in the entire area, as it follows an old bridleway through the meadows alongside the Leadon, to Cutmill – notable for being still a family farm amongst the prevailing agri-business, as well as its elephant's graveyard of ancient cars and derelict farm machinery, some of which looks as if it might have been there since Abercrombie's day! From here, the seeker-after-daffodils would be well advised not to follow the way-marked path along the track, but to branch off on the footpath heading north, through a valley with a muddy pond at its base, to the wood known as Cobhill Rough. It was probably in this wood that Edward Thomas and Robert Frost had an unpleasant encounter with the gamekeeper for the local estate on one of their walks together, and there are echoes of that in the notice posted by a stile warning that use of the woodland paths is only permissive, and of the primacy of shooting. However, the important thing is that there are plenty of daffodils to be seen here in late March, particularly on the western edge of the wood, along which the footpath helpfully continues, cascading down the bank and swirling round the trees, just as they must have done a hundred years ago:

> *Now I breathe you again, my woods of Ryton:*
> *Not only golden with your daffodil light*
> *Lying in pools on the loose dusky ground*
> *Beneath the larches, tumbling in broad rivers*
> *Down sloping grass among the cherry trees*
> *And birches.*   [Ryton Firs]

After a quick dive into the wood, the footpath rejoins Poets' Path 1 at the top of the hill, and so on along the northern edge of Ryton Copse to Ryton itself. Abercrombie's Gallows Cottage – long since demolished – used to stand in the grounds of Gallows House, a few hundred yards on the left along the narrow lane leading back to Ketford Mill.

There is also a much longer circular route, the Daffodil Way, with the villages of Kempley Green and Dymock at either end of its equator, which takes in part of Dymock Wood. No doubt parts of this route were also walked by the poets, but it doesn't take in any of their cottages, which are all to the north or north-east of Dymock. Sadly, as with the Poets' Paths, most of the surviving daffodils along the route are to be found in the hedges and woods, rather than in the fields.

If Abercrombie was the Dymock poets' convenor, then Wilfrid Gibson was his first lieutenant. The two had got to know each other as part of the Eddie Marsh 'Georgian' circle, when Gibson moved to London from his native Northumberland in 1912. He was already an established and very popular poet, known for his everyday subject matter and plain, sometimes colloquial, use of language, as epitomised in the title of his first volume of poetry *Daily Bread*, published in 1910. To Robert

Frost, he was 'the people's poet'. His personality seems to have been as warm and approachable as his poetry. Although a rather shy man, in contrast to the ebullient Abercrombie, he made friends easily, and became particularly close to Rupert Brooke, whose letters are full of references to what a nice man he was. It was Gibson, more so than Abercrombie, who was responsible for drawing Brooke into what became the Dymock fraternity.

Gibson's move to Dymock in early 1914 was prompted by a desire to move to the country, greater financial security, his recent marriage to Harold Monro's secretary, Geraldine, and to the urgings of his friend Abercrombie who, with his wife Catherine, was planning a West Country offshoot of Monro's *Georgian Poetry*, a poetry magazine to be called *New Numbers*, to promote his own poetry as well as that of his fellow Georgians, John Drinkwater

Wilfrid Gibson
(1878-1962)
Poet of the everyday

and Rupert Brooke. The cottage they found was The Old Nailshop, by a crossroads at Greenway, about two miles west of The Gallows. It was, and is, a half-timbered, red bricked, thatched cottage, typical of the area, which must once presumably have served the purpose which its name suggests. Wilfrid and Geraldine seem to have been blissfully happy there, revelling in the countryside, and the companionship, first of the Abercrombies and not long after, of Robert and Elinor Frost, whom Gibson persuaded to move to Dymock that March.

The Old Nailshop

145

The cottage now is much as the Gibsons would have found it. I approached it for the first time along the lane from Broomsgreen, on Poets' Path 2, thinking how much more pleasant this stretch of woods and pasture was than the wall-to-wall oilseed rape to the north of Dymock, and how well the cottage fitted into it, standing alone at the crossroads at Greenway. It is half thatched – presumably the original cottage – and half tiled – presumably the nailshop – with a pretty little garden. But, carrying straight on over the crossroads towards the Leadon, just as I was thinking how happy Wilfrid would have been to find it so little altered, modern agricultural reality hit me over the head like a sackful of wet sand, in the shape of two enormous farm sheds, standing at the top of a vast field of half-grown winter wheat. Poetic, this was not. As for the elms, well, therein lies the other most dramatic change in the landscape since the days of the poets. North Gloucestershire was classic elm territory; and the loss of them, to Dutch elm disease in the 1970s, was by far the biggest injury inflicted on this countryside in the last century, with no sign yet that the disease has lost its potency.

Wilfrid Gibson would have headed off this way to visit his friends Robert and Elinor Frost, after they had moved into another thatched cottage, Little Iddens, a couple of miles up the road at the hamlet of Leddington. In front of him, the dome of May Hill, crowned by its coppice of firs, which seems to dominate the scene wherever you are around Dymock; behind, what I always think of as the 'back' of the Malverns, just a few miles away to the north-east. There is a rare, well-tended standard orchard on the right as you head towards Leddington, just the sort of orchard which might have inspired Robert Frost's *Apple Picking*, and although that was written in his New England home, he loved spending time in the Little Iddens orchard.

Frost had arrived in London with his family in 1912, unknown as a poet either there or in his native land. Happily, he fell in with the Georgians at a reception held to mark the launch of Eddie Marsh's *Georgian Poetry* at Harold Monro's Poetry Bookshop. Abercrombie, Gibson, Rupert Brooke and John Drinkwater were fellow guests, as was Edward Thomas, in his capacity as one of the leading poetry reviewers, although he and Frost didn't actually meet. That didn't happen until almost two years later, when Ralph Hodgson brought them together in the smoking room at St George's restaurant in St Martin's Lane for what proved to be the start of a momentous literary friendship.

It didn't take Frost long to make his name as a poet in England. First *A Boy's Will* and then *North of Boston* were published, to critical acclaim, not least from Edward Thomas. According to Frost's own account, the poems were written either before he had left his farm in New England, or in 1913, so we can't really claim any Gloucestershire influence on them. However, his poetry did greatly impress

Robert Frost
(1874-1963)
'Rich and ripe' New England farmer

Wilfrid Gibson, prompting him to suggest to the Frosts that they leave their rented house in Beaconsfield, and move to live near him and Abercrombie at Dymock. This they duly did, arriving at Little Iddens in March 1914 to move into what is a long, narrow, black-and-white, half-timbered cottage, end-on to the lane.

At this stage, we need to introduce a woman who has some claim to be regarded as the seventh Dymock poet, Eleanor Farjeon. By now in her mid-twenties, she was an aspiring writer from a well-known literary family, who numbered several of the Georgians, including Walter de la Mare and DH Lawrence among her circle of friends. Edward Thomas was her hero. She followed him wherever she could, including to Leddington in that summer of 1914, and in her deeply personal account *The Last Four Years* described what life was like for the Frost family.

The cottage she describes as 'a labourer's cottage, standing on a rough patch of land planted chiefly with potatoes', although it did also have its own small orchard, where Robert loved to sit.

The rent was no more than a few shillings a week, which was just as well, for the Frosts had barely a penny to bless them. They lived a simple, slightly chaotic life, unworried by timetable or routine, spending as much time as possible outdoors. Elinor Frost sounds a bit like Laurie Lee's mother in her disdain for conventional home-making, without Annie Lee's cheerful robustness. Thanks to his long life (he died in 1963 at the age of 89) and literary eminence, one tends to think of Robert Frost as a slightly patrician, imposing figure. But in his Gloucestershire days he was just an ex-farmer, ex-teacher, struggling to support his wife and four children as he strove to fulfil his dream of earning a living as a poet.

Little Iddens

'I remember his figure as middle sized and compact,' recalls Eleanor Farjeon, 'his manner friendly and undemonstrative; he looked at you directly, his talk was shrewd and speculative, withholding nothing from nobody but himself. His New England speech came readily and leisurely, and of all the writers of worth whom I had met he spoke with the least sophistication.'

Helen Thomas, Edward's wife, was equally taken with the American, with his clear blue eyes shaded by bushy grey eyebrows: 'a thickset man, not as tall as Edward, with a shock of grey hair; his face tanned and weather-beaten and his features powerful.'

Although Robert Frost clearly enjoyed enormously his year at Little Iddens and would be shaped by it for the rest of his life, he doesn't seem actually to have produced much poetry whilst he was there. In 1919 he was at pains to inform a biographer that what he called 'Gibsonian or Abercrombian influence' might only have been at work in four of the poems in his next collection *Mountain Interval*: *Birches*, *The Hill Wife*, *Putting in the Seed* and *The Sound of Trees*, to which one must add the Edward Thomas influence on *The Road not Taken* and *Iris by Night*.

Those last two apart, it is *Putting in the Seed*, composed in the orchard at Little Iddens, which perhaps has the Dymock stamp most clearly upon it:

> *You come to fetch me from my work to-night*
> *When supper's on the table, and we'll see*
> *If I can leave off burying the white*
> *Soft petals fallen from the apple tree.*
> *(Soft petals, yes, but not so barren quite,*
> *Mingled with these, smooth bean and wrinkled pea;)*
> *And go along with you ere you lose sight*
> *Of what you came for and become like me,*
> *Slave to a springtime passion for the earth.*
> *How Love burns through the Putting in the Seed*
> *On through the watching for that early birth*
> *When, just as the soil tarnishes with weed,*
> *The sturdy seedling with arched body comes*
> *Shouldering its way and shedding the earth crumbs.*

We cannot really go any further in discussing Robert Frost's time at Dymock without bringing in Edward Thomas, because the two were so important, both to each other and to each other's work.

They were very different characters. Where Frost could seem solid, relaxed and easy-going (albeit with a quick temper and a depressive streak), Thomas was nervy, hyperactive and prone to bouts of severe depression. He'd been born in Wandsworth, London in 1878, to Welsh parents, and learned to love the countryside and everything in it on holidays spent with his father's mother at Swindon. According to one of his many biographers, John Moore, of 'Brensham' fame, 'Swindon was always the best place in the world.' Richard Jefferies was an early hero and influence. The young Thomas was particularly taken by *The*

Edward Thomas
(1878-1917)
From prose to poetry at Dymock

Amateur Poacher, which described precisely the sort of life he wanted to live. By his early teens, he had also discovered poetry. Byron, Shelley and Keats, those most romantic of poets, were his particular favourites. 'The combination of nature, poetry and the writings of Jefferies had, by the end of 1893, almost given birth to Thomas the writer,' concludes his most recent biographer, Jean Moorcroft Wilson.

There remained one further ingredient, and that was the influence of James Ashcroft Noble, critic, poet, editor and man of letters, who took Thomas under his wing in 1894, after being impressed by one of his early efforts. He encouraged his protégé's writing ambitions, guided him in developing his talent and published some of his work. But it would be James Noble's middle daughter Helen, who would change Edward Thomas' life.

The two soon fell in love. Helen's father's early death, from tuberculosis in the spring of 1896, brought them even closer together and three years later they married, in secret, Helen already pregnant, whilst Edward was still an undergraduate, reading history at Lincoln College, Oxford. It was a loving, but not an easy marriage. Helen was a fine mother to their three children, Merfyn, Bronwen and Myfanwy, and completely devoted to her tall, slender, distinguished-looking writer of a husband. But Edward could sometimes be overwhelmed by the pressures of work and, whenever he fell into one of his periodic bouts of depression, it was Helen who bore the brunt of his melancholy.

Edward was by now set on a career as a writer. But with a wife and young son to care for, he had to earn money, which was the one thing Helen couldn't bring him. So he became a jobbing writer, picking up work wherever he could, churning out the words to keep his editors happy. Thanks to the faith shown in him by HW Nevinson, literary editor of the *Daily Chronicle*, book reviewing became the mainstay of his income. Jean Moorcroft Wilson has estimated that, by 1914, Edward Thomas had written no fewer than 1,900 book reviews, totalling more than a million words. That is one review every three days for 14 years! And that was as well as all the topographical books he produced – most notably *The South Country* (1906) and *In Pursuit of Spring* (1914) – his biography of Richard Jefferies and a host of other essays, articles and books.

He and Helen lived at two addresses in London before moving to the country, first at Bearsted near Maidstone, then in the Weald of Kent and finally at Steep near Petersfield in Hampshire. But whenever his writing commitments allowed it, the restless Edward would be off on his travels, walking or cycling prodigious distances, usually to gather material for his travel books, but sometimes just to get away from the claustrophobia of life at home.

He was hugely talented, yet painfully shy and lacking in self-confidence; the most conscientious of wordsmiths, who always gave of his best and met his deadlines, yet who was disdainful of most of the 'hack-work' as he called it, that he felt obliged to do to keep his family housed, clothed and fed; on his good days, no-one could be better company; on his bad, he was misery personified. John Moore's portrait of him is, I am sure, how Thomas himself would have liked to be remembered:

> *a man who could walk thirty miles across country between dawn and dark and then with his friends, at home or in the pub, sing songs half the night; a man to whom a lost footpath, on the map or in the reality, was as joy and a challenge to rediscover it; who could find his way if need be by starlight across the loneliest and most secret parts of every Southern county; who deeply loved both sky and earth, and could name all the stars in their constellations and all the humble insignificant flowers of woodside and hedgerow, and who taught his children to call them by their old country names; who took Helen fishing and forgot all his cares in teaching her to catch slimy tench in a pond; who never failed to send a Christmas present to David Uzzell, the old poacher friend of his boyhood; who found as much pleasure in his sweet peas as in a poem; who enjoyed digging up potatoes, or taking cuttings of herbs, or grafting a fruit tree, or planting a stolen sapling in his garden; who could find a bird's nest quicker than a schoolboy could; who, like his friend Hudson, could pick up a snake, or hold a frail fluttering bird in his strong hands without hurting it; a man whom children loved, and dogs, and whom wild things did not fear.*

There, in a paragraph, you have the essence of Edward Thomas, on a good day!

His friendship with Robert Frost did not change the fundamental man but it did mark a crossroads in his life, and did eventually send him in a new direction. Frost was not the first to suggest that Edward should try his hand at poetry. Various others of his friends, including Walter de la Mare and Eleanor Farjeon, struck by the rhythms and cadence of his prose, had made similar suggestions, and Thomas had even written a few experimental lines in his field notebook a month or so before he first met Frost in October 1913. But it was Frost, on their long walks together through the countryside around Leddington, who gave him the confidence to start writing poems, just over a year later, and whose use of words – 'getting back to pure speech rhythms,' as Thomas described it – was such a powerful influence on how those poems sounded to the ear.

Edward Thomas visited Frost and his family on five occasions after they had moved to Little Iddens in March 1914, in April, June, August, October and November. He was there for only a week in April, but the impression made by both Frost and the countryside where he was living, was immediate and telling:

> *In April here I had heard, among apple trees in flower, not the first cuckoo, but the first abundance of day-long calling cuckoos; here the first nightingale's song, though too far off and intermittently, twitched away by gusty night winds; here I found the earliest mayblossom which, by May Day,*

while I still lingered, began to dapple the hedges thickly, and no rainfall, yet
the land was sweet. [This England]

Robert Frost wasted no time in identifying one of the sources of his friend's discontent – his subordination, as a critic, to his poetic inferiors – and urged on him the idea of writing the undoubtedly poetic passages in *In Pursuit of Spring* and other prose works 'in verse form in exactly the same cadence'. Within weeks Thomas was writing to Frost to tell him of his experiments with prose-poems and vowing to return.

Which he did, on 24 June, with Helen, but without the children. They were travelling down on the main line from Paddington, via Oxford, when the train made what to Edward Thomas seemed an unexpected stop at Adlestrop, a few miles east of Stow-on-the-Wold, not far from the Oxfordshire border. It was a glorious English summer's day and Thomas, no doubt, given his destination, on the look-out for experiences that might form the basis of poems, fixed it in his memory, recording later in his notebook:

Then we stopped at Adlestrop, through the willows could be heard a chain
of blackbirds' songs at 12.45 and one thrush and no man seen, only a hiss
of engine letting off steam.

Stopping outside Campden by banks of long grass willowherb and
meadowsweet, extraordinary silence between the two periods of travel –
looking out on grey dry stones between metals and the shining metals and
over it all the elms, willows and long grass – one man clears his throat – a
greater than rustic silence ...

From that it is clear that it was two unscheduled stops which inspired the poem, which wasn't actually written until the following January. It has become the definitive Edward Thomas poem. It is a beautifully crafted poem which manages, in a few short lines of plain English, to convey loss, nostalgia, peace, summer, nature, the essence of the English countryside and, finally, optimism. It deserves its fame.

Yes, I remember Adlestrop –
The name, because one afternoon
Of heat the express-train drew up there
Unwontedly. It was late June.

The steam hissed. Someone cleared his throat.
No one left and no one came
On the bare platform. What I saw
Was Adlestrop – only the name

And willows, willow-herb, and grass,
And meadowsweet, and haycocks dry,
No whit less still and lonely fair
Than the high cloudlets in the sky.

And for that minute a blackbird sang
Close by, and round him, mistier,
Farther and farther, all the birds
Of Oxfordshire and Gloucestershire.

Sadly for lovers of Edward Thomas, and no doubt as well for the North Cotswold tourism industry, nothing of the station now remains. In an act of cultural vandalism, it was flattened by British Rail soon after it fell victim to Dr Beeching's axe in 1966. All that remains to mark the spot are some ugly sheds and rusting scrap vehicles. One of the station signs was salvaged from the wreckage, and is now in the bus shelter in Adlestrop village, but whether that is enough to merit a pilgrimage, only the reader will know.

But we digress. Our destination, as was Mr and Mrs Thomas's, is Dymock. It was during that mid-summer visit that the Gibsons held that famous party at the Old Nailshop, the only occasion, as far as we know, that five of the six Dymock poets were together in Gloucestershire. The evening would be memorably recalled in Wilfrid Gibson's *The Golden Room*:

> *Do you remember that still summer evening*
> *When, in the cosy cream-washed living room*
> *Of the Old Nailshop, we all talked and laughed –*
> *Our neighbours from The Gallows, Catherine*
> *And Lascelles Abercrombie; Rupert Brooke;*
> *Elinor and Robert Frost, living a while*
> *At Little Iddens, who'd brought over with them*
> *Helen and Edward Thomas? In the lamplight*
> *We talked and laughed; but, for the most part, listened*
> *While Robert Frost kept on and on and on,*
> *In his slow New England fashion, for our delight,*
> *Holding us with his shrewd turns and racy quips*
> *And the rare twinkle of his grave blue eyes?*
>
> *We sat there in the lamplight, while the day*
> *Died from rose-latticed casements, and the plovers*
> *Called over the low meadows, till the owls*
> *Answered from the elms, we sat and talked –*
> *Now a quick flash from Abercrombie; now*
> *A murmured dry half-heard aside from Thomas;*
> *Now, a clear laughing word from Brooke; and then*
> *Again Frost's rich and ripe philosophy*
> *That had the body and tang of good draught-cider*
> *And poured as clear a stream.*
>   *'Twas in July*
> *Of nineteen-fourteen that we talked;*
> *Then August brought the war and scattered us.*

So how come Rupert Brooke was there, and how does he qualify as a Dymock poet? He was, as we have seen, one of the 'Georgian' circle and was an enthusiastic supporter of Abercrombie's idea to publish a poetry magazine from Gloucestershire. Gibson and Drinkwater were partners in the venture and the first edition of *New Numbers*, as the quarterly was called, was published in late 1913, with Brooke escaping the tangled knot of his love-life in the South Seas. His borderline sacrilegious poem *Heaven* appeared in the second issue, published in March 1914, and by early July, he was back in England and paid one of his only two visits to Dymock, staying with the Gibsons at the Old Nailshop.

It is, in all honesty, hard to detect much Gloucestershire influence in any of Rupert Brooke's poems. His 'Dymock' status really depends on his friendship with four of the poets (to the extent that two of them, Abercrombie and Gibson, were beneficiaries of his will) and the fact that his most famous poem, *The Soldier* was published in the fourth and final issue of *New Numbers*. It was written in January 1915, when Brooke – who had enlisted the previous summer – was with his regiment, preparing for the Dardanelles campaign, but it wouldn't be in the least surprising if he hadn't thought back to that happy evening, in Wilfrid Gibson's 'golden room', when he wrote of

Rupert Brooke
(1887-1915)
A gilded Dymock visitor

> *... laughter, learnt of friends; and gentleness*
> *In hearts at peace, under an English heaven.*

Rupert Brooke sailed for the Dardanelles in February. En route, he developed sepsis from an infected mosquito bite and died on board a hospital ship, moored off the coast of Skyros, on 23 April. He was buried on the island in an olive grove.

No-one mourned his passing more deeply than John Drinkwater, our final Dymock poet. His poem *Rupert Brooke* is one of the most touching of the many poetic tributes Brooke attracted, concluding, as it does:

> *So my mortality for yours complains,*
> *While our immortal fellowship remains.*

John Drinkwater
(1882-1937)
Cultural all-rounder

Like Brooke he was a non-resident, never anything more than a regular visitor, yet he was as enthusiastic as any of them about the countryside and the daffodils, and wrote several beautiful Dymock-inspired poems. Drinkwater had not enjoyed the privileged education of his fellow Dymock poets. He started life as an insurance clerk in Birmingham. But he soon became a cultural all-rounder: an actor, playwright and theatre producer with the Birmingham Rep, as well as a poet and essayist. It was in his theatrical capacity that he first encountered Gibson, when he staged a dramatic version of the latter's poem *Daily Bread* in 1911. Not long afterwards, he was pleased to read a favourable review of his own *Lyrical and Other Poems*, discovered that Abercrombie was the author and went to visit him at The Gallows, where the pair of them proceeded, as poets do, to drink too much cider, laced with rum.

It was the first of many visits. He, Abercrombie and Gibson got on like a house on fire, and were soon planning *New Numbers*. It was Drinkwater, as much as anyone, who got Brooke involved with the venture. John Haines, the Gloucester solicitor and patron of the arts, who knew the Dymock poets as well as anyone, remembered Drinkwater staying with the Abercrombies one spring-time at Ryton 'talking enthusiastically on Poetic Drama in that enchanted garden with a cherry orchard close by', with, for miles around, 'daffodils, daffodils everywhere'. It was an experience that helped produce *The Broken Gate*, which perhaps captures the magic of the Dymock phenomenon as well as anything any of the poets ever wrote:

> *I know a little broken gate*
> > *Beneath the apple-boughs and pines,*
> *The seasons lend it coloured state,*
> > *And round its hinge the ivy twines –*
> *The ivy and the bloomless rose,*
> > *And autumn berries flaming red;*
> *The pine its gracious scent bestows,*
> > *The apple-boughs their treasure shed.*
>
> *It opens on an orchard hung*
> > *With heavy-laden boughs that spill*
> *Their brown and yellow fruit among*
> > *The withered stems of daffodil:*
> *The river from its shallows freed*
> > *Here falls upon a stirless peace,*
> *The tides of time suspended lead*
> > *The tired spirit to release.*
>
> *A little land of mellowed ease*
> > *I find beyond my broken gate,*
> *I hear amid the laden trees*
> > *A magic song, and there elate*
> *I pass along from sound and sight*
> > *Of men who fret the world away, –*
> *I gather rich and rare delight*
> > *Where every day is holy day.*

Heavy blows though Rupert Brooke's death, the demise of *New Numbers* and the dissolution of the Dymock fraternity were to John Drinkwater, it would not be true to say that they marked the end of his poetic achievement. Having discovered Gloucestershire, through his friendship with Abercrombie and Gibson, he fell in love with the county, and especially with the Cotswolds, where he would go and stay with the artist William Rothenstein. The fruits of that association appear in other chapters.

Robert Frost had persuaded Edward and Helen Thomas to bring their three children with them for a month-long holiday at Oldfields House, just across the fields from Little Iddens. It must have been one of the happiest times of both of their lives. They went on long walks together, their children played happily together, they drank cider together and, most of all, they ate, drank, lived and breathed poetry together. All in a perfect English setting under a perfect English sun.

As Helen would later recall, Edward and Robert 'were always together and when not exploring the country, they sat in the shade of a tree smoking and talking endlessly of literature and poetry in particular.'

There was still tension between Edward and Helen, and she and Elinor had their differences as well. But the arrival of Eleanor Farjeon on August 20 brought a calming influence to bear, and the last week or so of the holiday proved to be the most joyful time of all. After a bit of a false start, Eleanor was safely installed with the perfectly named Mr and Mrs Farmer, in Glyn Iddens, a substantial farmhouse midway between the two poets. Her account of the dinner party which the Farmers laid on for her, the two poets and their wives, together with Gibson and Abercrombie, captures something of the atmosphere of that golden August.

Invitations had been issued, Mr Farmer had been squeezed into his best suit and the long farmhouse table was groaning with all the good things that had been laid out for supper: 'a ham, a great joint of beef, a raised pie and birds, among dishes of butter and pickles and salds, and sauce-boats of dressing, and slabs of home-made bread.' Full justice was done to this magnificent feast, and to the flagons of rough cider with which it was washed down. It was time for the cheese.

Oldfields House

She [Mrs Farmer] rose majestically, and from the sideboard produced an enormous Stilton in an advanced stage of ripeness. It was offered to the poets sitting beside her, and travelled down the board until it reached our end. I helped myself modestly, and presented it to Mr Farmer, now chuckling fruitily and showing his black teeth.

"I likes it," he said, "when they looks out o' their little winders and wags their tails, but I don't like it when they squeals between my teeth."

It is with the utmost sorrow that I have to report that the 'large orchards in which were grown the choicest of dessert plums, greengages and large golden and purple juicy plums' which, by Edward Thomas' own account, surrounded Oldfields that summer, are no more. A footpath still crosses the two-and-a-half fields which separate that house from Little Iddens, but these days, in August, you would be walking through the dessicated stubble of oilseed rape rather than plum trees laden with fruit. And in June, you would find difficulty making the journey at all, so tall, tangly, smelly and path-obstructing is this most unlovely of arable crops. Robert Frost and Edward Thomas would both be reduced to tears if they could see what their beloved orchards and meadows have come to. There is still an orchard, on the far side of the road from Little Iddens, but it is sadly neglected. When people talk of 'the death of the English landscape', you can see what they mean in this corner of England in high summer.

But we must not despair. There is one walk which a Thomas-and-Frost pilgrim can follow which does offer just a flavour of the countryside which the pair of them enjoyed in that Arcadian summer, and which inspired not one, but two, of the greatest 'Dymock poems'. It was on August 26, under a new moon, that the two poets set out on one of their longest walks together. From Leddington, they walked

A rare surviving traditional orchard

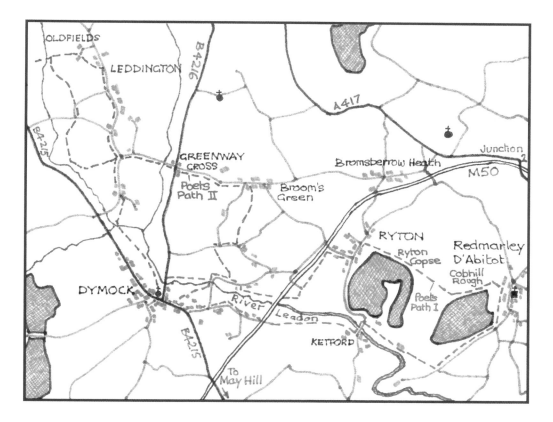

to Bromsberrow Heath, then via Hollybush to Castlemorton Common, and on past the reservoir to British Camp on the Malverns, coming back through Eastnor Park along the Ridgeway and so eventually, by now in darkness and damp from the late summer dew, back to Leddington.

Robert Frost would commemorate that walk in *Iris by Night*:

> *One misty evening, one another's guide,*
> *We two were groping down a Malvern side*
> *The last wet fields and dripping hedges home.*

But the experience would mean even more to Edward Thomas. Not only did it inspire his poem *The Sun Used to Shine*, it also played a big part in his decision not to follow Frost back to the US as they had been discussing, but to stay and fight for the England that he could see revealed to him that summer's night:

> *Then one evening the new moon made a difference. The sky was banded with rough masses in the north-west, but the moon, a stout orange crescent, hung free of cloud near the horizon. At one stroke, I thought, like many other people, what things that same moon sees eastward about the Meuse in France. Of those who could see it there, not blinded by smoke, pain or excitement, how many saw it and heeded? I was deluged, in a second stroke, by another thought, or something that overpowered thought. All I can tell is, it seemed*

157

to me that either I had never loved England, or I had loved it foolishly, aesthetically, like a slave, not having realised that it was not mine unless I were willing and prepared to die rather than leave it, as Belgian women and old men and children had left their country. [This England]

For the remainder of 1914, and through the first six months of 1915, Edward Thomas remained torn between returning with the Frosts to New England to write poetry, or enlisting and fighting for the England he knew and loved so well. To fight or to flee? In November 1914, he travelled down to Leddington to stay with the Frosts, by now living in the Abercrombies' cottage, which had been lent to them for the winter. On one of his and Robert's walks together, they wandered into the woods at Cobhill Rough, there to be confronted by Lord Beauchamp's game-keeper, a surly man called Bott. He ordered them off in no uncertain terms, referring to Frost as a 'damned cottager'. The two poets retreated, Frost furious, Thomas doing his best to be peace-maker. A further confrontation followed at Bott's cottage, when Frost threatened to 'beat up' the keeper, who again produced his shot-gun and aimed it at Thomas. At Bott's instigation, Frost was summonsed but, thanks probably to Jack Haines' intervention, the matter was eventually dropped. Some have suggested that the incident may have strengthened Thomas' resolve to demonstrate that he lacked nothing in physical courage by enlisting. More likely, it was just a storm in a teacup, which Thomas hardly mentioned afterwards, and then only jocularly.

It was only a matter of weeks after the gamekeeper incident that Edward Thomas began writing poetry, and it came in a rush. In December, he wrote some 20 poems, many of them based on writings in his notebook. *Adlestrop* was composed on January 8, when he was laid up with a badly damaged ankle, at around the same time that he started work on *This England*, an anthology of the poetry and prose which spoke to him most clearly of what England means to the English. The Frosts duly returned to New England in February, taking with them Merfyn Thomas but leaving a still-conflicted Edward behind.

There would be one more poetically significant visit to Gloucestershire. Towards the end of June, after four days' cycling in Wiltshire to celebrate the hurried completion of a commissioned biography of the Duke of Marlborough, Edward Thomas stayed with his friend and admirer Jack Haines at Hucclecote, on the edge of Gloucester. On June 25th, the pair of them cycled to May Hill, where he had walked with Frost during his stay at Leddington the previous summer. Happily, Jack Haines has left an account of the expedition and its aftermath:

A few days before he enlisted, we bicycled out to May Hill ... and all the way he mused, and I could note him musing as he asked me questions of the scarce flowers by the way, and whilst I botanised on the hill slopes, he sat on the hill ... composing the beautiful poem Words, *which he brought down completed for us at breakfast the next morning.*

It is indeed a beautiful poem:

Will you choose
Sometimes —

158

As the winds use
A crack in a wall
Or a drain,
Their joy or their pain
To whistle through –
Choose me,
You English words?

I know you:
You are light as dreams,
Tough as oak,
Precious as gold,
As poppies and corn,
Or an old cloak ...

May Hill is a dominating presence on the Gloucestershire/Herefordshire border: 'May Hill, that Gloucester dwellers 'gainst every sunset see,' wrote Ivor Gurney. It rises to 971 feet and became known as May Hill for the May Day celebrations that have pretty much always been held there. In common with almost every high hill in these parts, there was once an Iron Age fort on the summit, which is now crowned by that famous clump of trees. The trees have been there for many centuries, replenished in 1897 to mark Queen Victoria's Golden Jubilee and again in 1977 to mark the Silver Jubilee of Elizabeth II.

At one stage the trees looked from a distance – presumably because of a break in the profile caused by a lightning strike towards one end – like a ploughman and his team of oxen, an impression which John Masefield, who was brought up at Ledbury, on the Herefordshire side of the hill, employed to telling effect in his celebrated poem about redemption through Christian conversion *The Everlasting Mercy*:

Near Bullen Bank, on Gloucester road,
Thy everlasting mercy showed
The ploughman patient on the hill
Forever there, forever still,
Ploughing the hill with steady yoke
Of pine trees lightning-struck and broke.
I've marked the May Hill ploughman stay
There on his hill, day after day
Driving his team against the sky
While men and women live and die.
And now and then he seems to stoop
To clear the coulter with the scoop
Or touch an ox to haw or gee
While Severn stream goes out to sea.
The sea with all her ships and sails,
And that great smoky port in Wales,
And Gloucester tower bright i' the sun
All know that patient wandering one.

Edward Thomas and Jack Haines would probably have cycled along what is now the A40 towards Ross-on-Wye to reach May Hill, turning right just after Huntley to ride up the hill into May Village, where they would have left their bicycles and walked the last few hundred yards up the bridleway which is now part of the Gloucestershire Way. It is a fairly gentle climb up through the woods to the open heathland at the top, which was being grazed by a bunch of handsome, if not entirely indigenous, Belted Galloway cattle the last time I was there. The views to the north and east have, as is sadly so typical, been obscured by the hillside woodland of larch and fir. But there are stunning prospects to Herefordshire and the Black Mountains to the west, and of the Severn snaking its way to the sea between the Cotswolds and the Forest of Dean to the south.

Beautiful places like May Hill, and the beautiful vistas that they offer, are inspiring, not just in and of themselves, but of ideas and thoughts that run far deeper than the physical fabric of the landscape, however glorious that may be. One thinks of the relationship between man and the natural world, of the generations of people who have looked out over this same view for centuries past and how they lived their lives, or maybe just of how fortunate we are to be able to live amidst such natural beauty. In Edward Thomas's case, May Hill caused him to ponder on one of his favourite subjects, the words which we use to express our thoughts and feelings. He wrote lying on the grassy hilltop. If more recent visitors feel similarly moved – as well they might be – then benches have thoughtfully been provided around the perimeter of the clump, one of them – on which I sat to make these jottings – dedicated to the memory of Winfred Foley, of *Child of the Forest* fame, and her husband Sydney, who lived nearby and walked here often. It is a magical place.

Within two weeks of his flying visit to Gloucestershire, Edward Thomas had enlisted in the Artists Rifles. He was subsequently commissioned as a second lieutenant in the Royal Garrison Artillery, and after an extended and frustrating period of training and working-up, sailed for France on January 29, 1917. Ten weeks later he was dead; a shell fragment went right through his heart at the Battle of Arras. His wife Helen was sent almost mad with grief; Robert Frost was devastated. But the wider literary world shed not a single tear, for the simple reason that only a handful of his 144 poems had been published by the time of his death (and those under the pseudonym Edward Eastaway). He never saw even his first anthology of 18 poems, *An Annual of New Poetry*, in print. His second, *Poems*, which would be published in July, was in the press on the day of his death.

Of the other Dymock poets, Robert Frost became ever more distinguished and celebrated, dying in 1963 at the grand old age of 89. Lascelles Abercrombie became Professor of English at Leeds University in 1923 (preferred for the role to a certain JRR Tolkein!), continued to write poetry, none of it particularly inspired, and died in London in 1937. Wilfrid Gibson built a considerable reputation as a war poet, without ever actually seeing active service in France, drawing heavily on his time at the Old Nailshop, as he imagined himself on the front line, as in *Before Action*:

I sit beside the brazier's glow,
And, drowsing in the heat,
I dream of daffodils that blow,
And lambs that frisk and bleat —

Black lambs that frolic in the snow
Among the daffodils,
In a far orchard that I know
Beneath the Malvern Hills.

Next year the daffodils will blow
And lambs will frisk and bleat;
But I'll not feel the brazier's glow,
Nor any cold or heat.

After the war, he and his wife Geraldine moved first to Malvern and then to Pembrokeshire. He continued to write poetry, but his reputation gradually faded. By 1939, in a letter to Robert Frost, he was reflecting, with a wistful resignation, on the fact that 'I am one of those unlucky writers whose books have predeceased them.' Like Frost, he lived to a good age, dying in 1962 at the age of 84.

John Drinkwater's subsequent career followed an entirely different trajectory, although as a playwright, rather than a poet. His historical drama *Abraham Lincoln* was a hit on both sides of the Atlantic and was followed by similar success with *Oliver Cromwell* and *Mary Stuart*. He divorced his first wife after she had an affair with Benno Moiseiwitsch, a famous Ukrainian violinist. In revenge, Moiseiwitsch's then wife Daisy set her cap at Drinkwater and succeeded in capturig his heart. All of this amatory activity took place on board the White Star Line's SS *Adriatic*, as she was steaming from New York back to England. It must have been quite a voyage!

He died in 1937, of a heart attack reputedly brought on by the excitement of watching Oxford win the Boat Race for the first time in 14 years, and is buried in the churchyard at Piddington in Oxfordshire, where he spent childhood holidays and first came to know and love the English countryside.

Dymock and daffodils and days of song
Before the war had scattered us apart ...
[Wilfrid Gibson, 'To John Drinkwater']

At the time of the First World War, Dymock stood for much that Edward Thomas and countless others thought was worth giving their lives for. I can't help thinking how betrayed they would feel if they could see much of the countryside which they so loved as it is now. This hasn't been done deliberately, still less maliciously. It has been the inevitable result of economics, social change, mechanisation, the motor car, Dutch elm disease, developments in agronomy, subsidy regimes, population growth, you name it, and it's left its mark on rural north Gloucestershire, and not for the good. But on a spring morning, with the daffodils in bloom along the River Leadon, you can still feel just an echo of what made this place so special all those years ago and understand just a little of what inspired such a remarkable explosion of poetry.

Exploring the Dymock Poets' Leadon Valley

Walks

The Friends of the Dymock Poets has an excellent website – **www.dymockpoets.org** – which has a page on 'visiting the Dymock poets' countryside', including details of the Daffodil Way and the two 'Poets' Paths', all of which start and finish in Dymock. There is also an exhibition about the Dymock poets in Dymock Church at which you can buy leaflets on each of the poets, including selections from their works and a brief biography.

At the time of writing, both the 'Poets' Paths' were difficult to use on account of a variety of obstructions, some natural, others man-made, to the extent that the Friends of the Dymock Poets were campaigning to have them re-opened and properly maintained.

Two shorter routes, neither of which was seriously obstructed when I walked them, and which include most of the significant locations, are:

1. Pick up Poets' Path I at Ketford, and walk eastwards along the valley of the River Leadon, then up through the woods where Robert Frost and Edward Thomas had their encounter with the gamekeeper, following the path to Ryton, then back along the lane to Ketford, passing the site of the Abercrombies' Gallows House en route.

2. Pick up Poets' Path II at Greenway Cross, where Wilfrid Gibson lived in The Old Nailshop, follow it along the lanes to Robert Frost's Little Iddens at Leddington, across the field to Edward Thomas's Oldfields House and then southwards until it rejoins the road leading back to Greenway Cross.

Viewpoints

Given that the Leadon Vale is relatively flat, there aren't any obvious viewpoints near Dymock. The best perspectives of the landscape can be obtained by climbing either May Hill or the southern end of the Malverns.

Pubs

There is only one pub in the immediate vicinity of Dymock (although Ledbury is not far away) and that is the *Beauchamp Arms* on the edge of the village of Dymock. It is unusual, in being one of the very few community-owned pubs in England, and is a proper, welcoming village local, offering real ale and good traditional pub food.

The Poets' Paths – in varying states of maintenance

Select Bibliography

Linda Hart: *Once They Lived in Gloucestershire – A Dymock Poets Anthology* (1995)
Keith Clark: *The Muse Colony* (1992)

Lascelles Abercrombie
The Poems of Lascelles Abercrombie (1930)
Jeremy Cooper: *Abercrombie and the Origins of the Colony of Poets at Dymock* (1997)

Wilfrid Gibson
Collected Poems 1905-1925 (1926)

Robert Frost   www.robertfrostsociety.org *and* www.frostfriends.org
The Collected Poems of Robert Frost (1930)
Jay Parini: *Robert Frost – A Life* (2000)

Edward Thomas   www.edward-thomas-fellowship.org.uk
Edna Longley (ed): *The Annotated Collected Poems of Edward Thomas* (2008)
John Moore: *The Life and Letters of Edward Thomas* (1939)
Eleanor Farjeon: *Edward Thomas – The Last Four Years* (1958)
Jean Moorcroft Wilson: *Edward Thomas – From Adlestrop to Arras* (2015)

Rupert Brooke   www.rupertbrooke.com
Collected Poems, edited by Will Jonson (2014)
Nigel Jones: *Rupert Brooke – Life, Death and Myth* (1999)

John Drinkwater
Collected Poems Volume 1 (1923)

Chapter Nine
On Bredon Hill

AE Housman, John Moore, Fred Archer, Arthur Quiller-Couch

This was the unexplored jungle, the unclimbed
mountain, the unmapped hinterland!

John Moore

Bredon Hill is hard to miss. Anyone who has ever driven up or down the M5 between Worcester and Tewkesbury cannot fail to have been struck by the whale-backed hill which looms massively just to the east of where the Avon joins the Severn. It is not as spectacular as the Malverns, across the Severn Vale: its slopes rise gently, rather than abruptly, from the surrounding plain, but its sheer bulk takes and holds the eye. On the summit, overlooking the village of Bredon, stands Banbury Stone Tower – Parsons' Folly, as it's usually known – built during the eighteenth century by the local landowner and MP, John Parsons, so that he could enjoy in comfort the magnificent views across the vale and with the added benefit of taking the highest point on Bredon from 981 to exactly 1000 feet.

There are no villages or metalled roads on the hill itself (although there are plenty of footpaths and bridleways). It is pure, undiluted countryside. Including parts of nine parishes, and at roughly 8,000 acres in extent, it must be second only to Salisbury

Bredon Hill as seen from the River Severn

Plain as the largest area in lowland England uncrossed by any public road. It hasn't always been so unpopulated. On the broad plateau at the summit of the hill are the remains of three Iron Age forts, Kemerton, Elmley and Conderton, whilst Elmley Castle owes its name to what was originally a Norman castle, built by the powerful Beauchamp family on the hill's northern slope. In 779, the Kemerton Charter refers to 'the city of Bainintes Burh atop the hill Broedun', but by the time of Domesday, all that had gone, leaving the hill to the cattle, the sheep and the ghosts.

Given its size and location, it is not in the least bit surprising that Bredon Hill should have caught the imagination of painters, composers and, of course, writers. Even so, it has been exceptionally fortunate in its chroniclers and associations, led by AE Housman and his poem *Bredon Hill*:

> *In summertime on Bredon,*
> *The bells they sound so clear;*
> *Round both the shires they ring them*
> *In steeples far and near,*
> *A happy noise to hear.*

The poem isn't by any means a celebration of Bredon Hill as such. It is the 21st poem in *A Shropshire Lad*, Housman's lyrically melancholy, deeply nostalgic, extended elegy for lost innocence. The hopes of the lovers lying side by side on the summit of Bredon, looking out on the 'coloured counties', hearing the larks in the sky and looking forward to the day when the bells would be ringing out for their wedding, would crumble to dust.

> *But when the snows at Christmas*
> *On Bredon top were strown,*
> *My love rose up so early*
> *And stole out unbeknown*
> *And went to church alone.*
>
> *They tolled the one bell only,*
> *Groom there was none to see,*
> *The mourners followed after,*
> *And so to church went she,*
> *And would not wait for me.*
>
> *The bells they sound on Bredon,*
> *And still the steeples hum.*
> *'Come all to church, good people,' –*
> *Oh, noisy bells, be dumb;*
> *I hear you, I will come.*

Whether Housman ever actually walked on Bredon Hill and heard the bells himself isn't entirely clear. From the top of Worm's Ash Hill, to which he loved to walk from his boyhood home near Bromsgrove, the hill would have dominated the southern horizon. It would be surprising if he hadn't felt driven to explore it close up when the opportunity presented itself, especially as we know that he often visited his mother's family at Woodchester, further south on the Cotswold ridge above Stroud. The clue may be in the reference to 'steeples far and near'. Most of the parish churches in the immediate vicinity of the hill have towers, rather than spires. But the one closest to the summit, St Giles, just down at the bottom of the hill at Bredon, does indeed boast a splendid, slender steeple, complete with a peal of five bells. After an interval of some 80 years, when the belfry was deemed unsafe, these can most certainly now be heard ringing out so clearly from the top of the hill – although which the Gloucestershire steeple might have been isn't quite so obvious!

Anyway, as with Wenlock Edge, Housman's choice of Bredon Hill was symbolic rather than being based on any particular personal affection or experience. He wrote the poem before he had the idea of using Shropshire as his 'land of lost content', but Bredon stands every bit as powerfully for what would be lost and longed for about this part of England by anyone exiled from it and looking back.

And that is as true today as it was when Housman was writing in the 1890s. Perhaps it is the absence of roads, traffic and houses on the hill, but to climb its slopes is almost to make one's way back into an older, less crowded, less beleaguered English countryside. That isn't to say it's not farmed. The Overbury Estate, which owns large parts of the hill, is the very epitome of modern agricultural efficiency, albeit with an environmental conscience. For many years, the estate was owned by the Martin family, of Martin's Bank, and still uses the old Martin's Bank 'grasshopper' as its symbol. Its arable farming stretches far and wide across the summit plateau and along the eastern and southern slopes, the emptiness and silence of the big cornfields seeming almost to reinforce the sense of other-worldliness which Bredon Hill – on a quiet day! – has to offer.

Maybe it was because of this special quality that Bredon Hill came to inspire two of the most colourful and enjoyable writers about the English countryside of the twentieth century: John Moore and Fred Archer. Very different personalities, with very different motivations, who come at their subject both literally and metaphorically from very different directions, Moore from Bredon to the west, and Archer from Ashton-under-Hill to the east. Yet the pictures which they paint of Bredon Hill and the villages around it from the late nineteenth to the mid twentieth century, whilst sharply contrasting, are yet fundamentally consistent. It is in the style rather than the content in which they differ: Archer's approach reminding one of a sepia-tinted photograph, Moore's of a Bruegel painting.

John Moore is the senior and, unarguably the more important literary figure of the two. Like Fred Archer, he was a local man, born at Tewkesbury in 1907 into a comfortably prosperous middle-class family of auctioneers, doctors and lawyers. After failing to make the grade in the auctioneering business, he took to writing full-time in the 1930s, including spending some time reporting on the Spanish Civil War. When war broke out in 1939 he joined the Fleet Air Arm, before being effectively invalided out into the Ministry of Information, where his writing talents were put to good use as a propagandist alongside John Buchan. As journalist, chronicler, guide-book-writer, script-writer and, later in life, novelist, he was never less than prolific and his writing never anything but vivid and fluent. But Moore was very far from

John Moore
(1907-1967)
Campaigning countryman

Fred Archer
(1915-1999)
Chronicler of farming change

being just a jobbing wordsmith. He was one of the first of what we would now call 'conservationists'. He loved Tewkesbury and the villages around, people and places alike, with a passion. He was acutely conscious of the rapid changes taking place in both urban and rural life, and was instinctively hostile to them. He harked back to the England of Falstaff and of Hogarth and, if he recognised that he couldn't preserve it, he was determined at least to record it whilst traces of it still remained. It was that, as much as anything, which was the driving force behind the three books for which he will be most lastingly and affectionately remembered, the so-called *Brensham Trilogy*.

The three books – *Portrait of Elmbury*, *Brensham Village* and *The Blue Field* – were written in less than three years, between 1945 and 1948. The first deals mainly with his childhood in Tewkesbury, or 'Elmbury' as he calls it; the second two with life in Bredon and the other 'hill' villages, brought together as 'Brensham'. It is slightly irritating that he insists on using these made-up names, but he did have his reasons. The books are, as he himself always explained, based on a 'framework of truth', a 'ground-plan of a real town' and a 'synthesis of villages', without purporting to offer a strictly factual representation of Tewkesbury and the surrounding villages, still less of their more colourful inhabitants. (Mind you, I'll bet the locals had a wonderful time putting faces to names at the time the books were published!)

But the descriptions of town and country are most certainly from life, and beautifully painted they are too, as in this view of the Tewkesbury meadows, from the little hill known as the Toot:

> *Two broad streams joined at Elmbury among a confusion of small brooks.*
> *These snaking waterways almost isolated the town, even in summer; and*
> *when the floods rose in the winter they sometimes cut it off altogether, so*
> *that milk was delivered by rowing boat and people punted through the back*

streets. At such times, the meadows around Elmbury disappeared beneath a huge inland sea; and no doubt it was this annual flooding which made them so fertile and rich. There never was a greener countryside than those few square miles in which Elmbury was set and what gave it a particularly fat and sumptuous appearance was the size of those river meadows, which were large and liberal, pasturing fifty beasts apiece and yielding at haytime not one meagre rick but a whole rickyard.

Portrait of Elmbury is certainly the most personal, and probably the best of the three books, but its compass its limited mainly to Tewkesbury itself: to its pubs, its almost medieval slum, which Moore calls Double Alley, its magnificent abbey and, above all, to its cast of characters, like Black Sal, the Colonel, Mr Parfitt the crooked craftsman, Mr Rendcombe the editor, and the three reprobates whom he names after Falstaff's cronies, Pistol, Bardolph and Nym, to name just a few of so many. It is a joyous book, brimming with life and colour. But rather like John Moore himself, who moved from Tewkesbury to Bredon in 1949, we must turn our path from town to country and head for the hill.

Bredon is roughly four miles north of Tewkesbury, perched on a bluff above the River Avon, its church spire as prominently graceful to travellers along the M5 as it was to John Masefield when he used it to define the south-eastern boundary of his

Bredon Church

'land of heart's desire' in the poem *London Town*. Bredon remains, as Moore describes it, a 'long and straggling' village, running 'in a semi-circle more or less coincident with one of the lower contours' (of Bredon Hill), albeit with more than its fair share of half-timbered cottages – although to describe it as a village doesn't really do it justice, either in reality or in the context of Moore's Brensham. It is rather the mother-village of a collection of hamlets – Westmancote (Upper and Lower), Bredon's Hardwick, Bredon's Norton, as well as Bredon itself and the neighbouring parish of Kemerton. Of the three village pubs which Moore describes, the 'Adam and Eve', near the station, is a pub no more. 'The Trumpet', however, in reality the Royal Oak, is still much as John Moore described it, with its 'sizable back room where the Cricket Club and Farmers Union meetings and the annual dinners of organisations such as the British Legion were held.' It is a large, rather plain pub, now featuring an 'Eastern Thai' restaurant, three fruit machines, a cash point and a pool table. No sign of the dart board which was such an important feature of all three pubs in Moore's day. Unlucky the Royal Oak may once have been, but it is at least still open, and well supported locally, from what I could see. The bigger disappointment was the Fox and Hounds, in the village centre, which is the original for Moore's 'Horse and Harrow', or 'Horse Narrow' as he liked to refer to it. The 'eves jutting out over the small bedroom windows looking like beetling eyebrows' are still there, but within all of the amiable eccentricity which Moore describes has been swept away, in the name of gastro-isation. Shame.

The way to the hill which Moore describes, in *Brensham Village*, runs up through Westmancote:

> When you started to climb the hill you left the half-timbering behind; the village still straggled along beside the steep path, but the cottages were built of limestone quarried a few hundred yards away, and the hedges gradually gave way to stone walls. Then you came to the end of the path and to the last cottage, which was inhabited by an old man with a wooden leg and a long beard. He kept in his garden a billy-goat which also had a long beard. We called him Goaty Pegleg, and thought of him as the hill's janitor, for he was almost always to be found leaning on the gate at the road's end. If he were feeling good-humoured he opened the gate for us; and we went through into a rough chalky field full of furze-bushes, ragwort, thistles and rabbits. A stony cart track led upwards through the quarries, the banks covered in scrub and bramble, the hanging woods of oak, sycamore and ash, and the larch plantation on the hilltop, with the round preposterous tower of Brensham Folly just showing above the feathery tops of the conifers.
>
> This was the unexplored jungle, the unclimbed mountain, the unmapped hinterland!

Two cottages vie for the honour of being the original of Goaty Pegleg's, the last on the left up the hill, and the last on the right. I think I prefer the latter, as it would be the obvious place to put a gate. There are no gates – or goats – today, just a small parking area. Then it's away up the bridleway of Cotswold stone and golden sand. It's a fairly gentle climb, with quarries on the left and trees on the right and, if you pause and turn around, a wonderful view unfolds of the Severn vale running down to Tewkesbury and Gloucester with May Hill away in the distance. Halfway up, the path runs across open downland, before plunging into a finger of woodland running along the escarpment, with the River Avon visible (at least in winter) through the trees, meandering lazily across its flood plain to the Severn. A final wooden gate and there on the skyline in front of you is Parsons' Folly and the summit.

In John Moore's day, a mad hermit lived in Banbury Stone Tower, to give the folly its proper name, who would sometimes dress up in an ancient black suit and boater to conduct visitors up the 52 steps leading up through the folly to the roof, for a fee of threepence. He's long gone. These days, the tower has been put to work as a convenient platform for mobile phone masts, which sprout from its walls and roof like spines on a porcupine. I suppose it avoids a small copse of aerials being erected on the plateau, although the hum emitted by the air-conditioning system needed to keep the electronics at the right temperature does rather blight the reverie.

Still, the views are stunning. According to John Moore, there is an inscription in Latin on the roof parapet: 'From this elevated place, when the sky is untroubled by cloud nor mists lurk in the low places thou canst see, O Traveller, twelve rich counties, four great cathedrals , and sixteen abbeys.' All I can say to that is that it would need to be an exceptionally clear day. But given that, then I take the counties to be Worcestershire, Gloucestershire, Hereford, Shropshire, Staffordshire, Warwickshire, Somerset far away to the south and, across the border into Wales, Monmouthshire, Brecon, Radnor, Montgomery and, just possibly, either Glamorgan or Flintshire;

May Hill and the flooded Severn from Bredon

170

the cathedrals are presumably Gloucester, Worcester, Hereford and Litchfield; and as for the abbeys, I can't get much further than Tewkesbury, Pershore and Evesham. But at any event, it is a magnificent panorama, from the Wrekin in the north to the Mendips in the south, the Black Mountains to the west and the Cotswolds to the east.

In *The Blue Field*, Moore claims a Shakespearean connection for Bredon Hill, and not just because Stratford-upon-Avon can just about be made out.

> *Shakespeare seems very close when you walk on Brensham Hill. He had friends in this neighbourhood, but a day's good tramp from his home, and just across the river lived one who witnessed his will. You will find yourself wondering, when you see a very old tree, whether he sat in the shade of it; or when you come to a pub, whether he drank there.*

He cites the use of the word 'kecksies' in *Henry V* as another telling indication of the link, as in 'Nothing teems but hateful docks, rough thistles, kecksies, burrs ...' In the area around Bredon Hilll it means the crackly dry stems of the hemlock and hedge-parsley, and is found nowhere else.

'So, you see,' he concludes, 'he spoke our speech and thought our thoughts. These, our woods and fields, our lanes and rivers, served him as a backcloth for Arden or Athens, Burgundy or Illyria.' Wishful thinking maybe, but the connection is far from implausible.

Just a few yards from the folly is the Banbury Stone, a limestone outcrop commonly referred to as the Elephant Stone, for reasons which are immediately apparent. It is one of three on the hill, the others, in the woods further back down the hill, known as the King and Queen. The ramparts look as ramparts should, and the situation is a commanding one, at least when approached from the west and north. To the east and south, however, the hill slopes fairly gently away, which perhaps explains why another Iron Age fortification was thrown up above the village of Conderton. At any rate, Kemerton Camp, as it is known, proved to be anything but impregnable, when its Dubunni inhabitants were bloodily evicted not long before the Roman conquest, probably by the fierce and warlike Siluri from across the border in South Wales.

The views from here are at their finest in spring and early summer, in blossom time, even if the scene today is not quite the magnificent tapestry of floral abundance which Moore describes in *Brensham Village*:

> *The whole of the vale and the lower slopes of the hill were buried beneath a vast snowdrift of petals. As a rule, the effect as you look down on the flowering vale, is that of a lace curtain stretched loosely over it; for the plum blossoms are very small and even though they may be multitudinous the leafless sepia twigs will show amongst them. However, in this season of unparalleled prodigality I had the impression, not of a lace curtain, but of foam and lather, of curds overflowing a dish of cream. It was the loveliest June day you could possibly imagine, a day of blue and green and gold, and of light breezes, gilly-flower scented, and lullaby sounds of bees, wood pigeons and faraway cuckoos. The sky was immaculate, hedge-sparrow egg blue; the mowing grass rippled in all the water-meadows along the river, and like green foam were the leafy orchards on the lower slopes of the hill.*

The success of the Brensham trilogy brought John Moore financial security for a time. He and his wife Lucille, whom he'd married in 1944 after a whirlwind courtship, bought a house in Kemerton and he started broadcasting as well as writing, on programmes with names like *Sunday Out* and *Country Lover*, in harness with other renowned 'countrymen' like Freddie Grisewood and Phil Drabble. He also started writing a weekly column on countryside matters for the *Birmingham Post*, which he used to lambast 'chemical farming', hedge removal and all the perceived evils of modern farming. He was one of the very first campaigning conservationists and doubtless made himself very unpopular indeed with the NFU (which is never a bad thing!).

Besides his writing and his broadcasting, his other great interest was the Cheltenham Literary Festival, with which he was involved from its start in 1949 to his eventual retirement in 1963. The idea for the festival had been the Cheltenham Town Clerk's. John Moore was invited to chair the organising committee because of his successful experience with the Tewkesbury Music Festival in the 1930s, and his wide range of literary contacts. He proved to be a brilliant publicist for the festival, brimming over with ideas, initiatives and competitions. But despite the big crowds and public attention it commanded, the festival was dogged with financial problems, and it was as bumpy a ride for Moore as for any of the festival's leading lights. But it would be fair to say that without his energy, imagination and determination it is very doubtful if the Cheltenham Literary Festival would have become, as it eventually did, the biggest literary festival in Europe.

Further literary success would follow for John Moore as well, thanks to novels such as *September Moon*, set in the Herefordshire hopfields, and his historical saga *Waters Under the Earth*. Perhaps his most surprising success was with *You English Words* (the title taken from the Edward Thomas poem *Words*), a book on English usage, which sold over 25,000 copies. When he wasn't writing, Moore was fighting battles with officialdom, be that the taxman, the planners or the magistrates. His biographer, David Cole, wrote that he would be remembered by his many friends as a 'thoroughly decent chap', without adding, as perhaps he might have done, that to his many enemies, he was a real thorn in their flesh, who loved nothing better than a good feud. One such, and perhaps the biggest of them all, was over the demolition of much of Tewkesbury's medieval heart, at the hands of the self-proclaimed 'progressives' on the local council. Moore fought tooth and nail to preserve what he could, and with some success. Without his intervention, the fine old Abbey Lane cottages would certainly have gone, and the fact that one of them now houses the John Moore Museum could not be more appropriate.

He died suddenly, of cancer of the oesophagus, in 1967, at the age of 59; a fine, spirited writer and, as the title of his biography has it, 'a true countryman'.

Fred Archer, on the other side of Bredon Hill, at Ashton-under-Hill, was a very different sort of writer from John Moore, yet who was equally successful at capturing not just the beauty of Bredon Hill but the flavour of life there. The two knew each other slightly and, when Fred's first book was published, John Moore wrote to congratulate him on the quality of the writing. Fred was first and foremost a farmer, whose family had farmed the slopes of Bredon Hill for centuries. He took to writing thanks to a happy accident. In 1968 he was asked by the local Townswomen's Guild to give a talk and, inexperienced as he was, decided to play it safe by writing out a story, set in the local countryside, which he read out to the assembled ladies. He went down a storm and never looked back. Within a year or so, sitting at the kitchen table in Stanley Farm, almost opposite the Star Inn, he had written out a whole series of stories of farming in the 1920s. He sent it off to the publishers Hodder and Stoughton, they liked what they read and it was published as *The Distant Scene* in 1967.

Fred was already 52, but he quickly made up for lost time as story-teller and rural chronicler. For the rest of his long life, he produced virtually a book a year, every one of them an account of the characters of Bredon Hill and how they lived, yet each one finding something new and original to say. He particularly understood how the little things in country life could loom large in close-knit communities, acquiring a significance out of all proportion to their real importance. Like the time when Cyril Pumfrey, churchwarden at St Barbara's parish church in Ashton, decided to lock the lych gate, through which ran the footpath to the hamlet of Paris, leaving its inhabitants to use the narrow kissing-gate alongside. The parish council got involved, then the district council, but still Cyril wouldn't yield in his insistence that the gates had to remain locked, other than for church services, for fear that 'Milko's cows' would break into the churchyard. It is a slight tale but, as with all Fred Archer's stories, beautifully told, and it includes a lovely description of the footpath to Paris:

St Barbara's, Ashton-under-Hill

For centuries labouring men, women and children had walked the grassy
track each day. The action of leather soles, hob-nailed boots, kept the turf
in condition; it could have been the green of a golf course ... Two gushing
springs from the hill were crossed by the footpath just short of Paris. At the
lower end, it meandered through the tombstones of the churchyard, two
feet away from my grandfather's grave, then under the copper beech and
the yew tree that stands underneath it like a labourer sheltering from a
thunderstorm, then on past the spring snowdrops, purple crocuses which,
with lady smocks later, possess the land between the stream of spring water
and the row of drooping ash trees.

The footpath isn't quite so well used these days, but is otherwise much as Fred Archer
describes it. The same cannot honestly be said of Ashton-under-Hill. The village has
been comprehensively gentrified: two of the three pubs have closed, leaving only the
Star, where they seem more interested in running a restaurant than being a village
pub; and most of the old farmhouses have been renovated as smart country homes
for commuters and the comfortably retired. But it makes a good base from which to
explore Bredon Hill.

I followed the Wychavon Way, as it is now known, through the lych gate and
up the hill, passing some ancient rowan trees halfway up, and enjoying the views
eastward across the valley towards Broadway. As is sadly so often the case, the hill's
collar of trees has been allowed to grow up around its north-eastern ramparts, blocking
out the views to the north, but once you reach the pasture land around Parson's
Folly, the trees disappear and the views open out. Sadly, the path does not make a
complete circumnavigation of the summit plateau, so one is faced with a choice of
either going back the way one has come, or taking the bridleway that leads down the
hill to Overbury, and then using a mixture of lanes and footpaths to make one's way
back to St Barbara's. I chose the latter, and a very enjoyable walk it made for. There
is beautiful parkland around Overbury Court, golden-stoned Overbury itself is as
pretty as a picture and the walk 'under the hill' back to Ashton offers both good views
to the south and a nice mix of country.

If, as I did, you turn left at the eastern end of Overbury village, and then follow the
footpath that leads off the lane just a few yards up the hill, you will, after crossing half
a dozen fields, reach Grafton, with its three farms, upper, middle and lower. The poet
John Drinkwater visited Grafton in the years before the First World War, possibly on
his way to or from Dymock, and was inspired to write this rather lovely poem:

God laughed when he made Grafton
That's under Bredon Hill,
A jewel in a jewelled plain.
The seasons work their will
On golden thatch and crumbling stone,
And every soft-lipped breeze
Makes music for the Grafton men
In comfortable trees.

God's beauty over Grafton
Stole into roof and wall,
And hallowed every paved path
And every lowly stall,
And to a woven wonder
Conspired with one accord
The labour of the servant,
The labour of the Lord.

And momently to Grafton
Comes in from vale and wold
The sound of sheep unshepherded,
The sound of sheep in fold,
And, blown along the bases
Of lands that set their wide
Frank brows to God, comes chanting
The breath of Bristol tide.

But we must get back to Ashton and to Fred Archer, taking precisely the path from Paris to the church yard which he describes in *A Lad of Evesham Vale*. He wrote so much about the countryside round here that it is difficult to know where to start or finish when it comes to quoting him, but I offer you the following passage, illustrating as it does that Fred Archer's stories do not ignore what might be called the fleshier side of country life. It could hardly be otherwise, given the fondness for the fairer sex of one of the real heroes of his books, the ne'er do well Sacco:

> *By the little stone bridge over Carrants Brook a one-acre meadow was almost wedged between the two hams (water meadows). Here the unlopped willow trees leaned top-heavy over the water. The winter's flood had stanked or dammed the brook, forming little islands of brushwood, mud and stones. Sacco and Martha left the motor bike by the field gate … Going hand in hand towards the brook the couple disturbed the moorhens sitting on their eggs, nesting on the islands made by the flood. The moorhens' cry made Martha hold Sacco's hand that much tighter. Sacco instinctively laid his khaki coat under the trees and soon they were in each other's arms under the stars, his coat their bed, undisturbed apart from the labouring goods train on the nearby railroad.*

Fred Archer, whose ability as a story-teller was matched only by his quite remarkable memory, died in 1999, aged 84. As John Moore said of him in that letter of congratulation: The style is just right; it is absolutely genuine and some of the stories are extremely funny.

John Masefield's early experiences of Bredon Hill are recounted in the Herefordshire chapter, but we do have one final literary pilgrimage to make before we leave the hill, and it is to a place not far from where Masefield stayed with either his mother's family or his godmother, and that is Eckington Bridge.

The six-arched red brick bridge was built in 1720 to replace an older structure and carries the road from Bredon to Pershore over the River Avon. Quite how Sir (as he became) Arthur Quiller-Couch came to visit Eckington Bridge, I am not sure. His biographer, another formidable Cornishman, AL Rowse, makes no mention of any Worcestershire connections for his subject. But no matter. The bridge is a handsome structure in its own right, and the views from the niches in the parapet of Bredon Hill to the east, and the rich country of the Severn Vale unrolling towards the Malverns in the west, do make one feel as if this is possibly the very centre of, as Quiller-Couch's poem puts it, the heart of pastoral England:

Arthur Quiller-Couch
(1863-1944)
A Cornishman in Worcestershire

> *O pastoral heart of England! like a psalm*
> *Of green days telling with a quiet beat –*
> *O wave into the sunset flowing calm!*
> *O tirèd lark descending on the wheat!*
> *Lies it all peace beyond the western fold*
> *Where now the lingering shepherd sees his star*
> *Rise upon Malvern? Paints an Age of Gold*
> *Yon cloud with prophecies of linkèd ease –*
> *Lulling this Land, with hills drawn up like knees,*
> *To drowse beside her implements of war?*
>
> *Man shall outlast his battles. They have swept*
> *Avon from Naseby Field to Severn Ham;*
> *And Evesham's dedicated stones have stepp'd*
> *Down to the dust with Montfort's oriflamme.*
> *Nor the red tear nor the reflected tower*
> *Abides; but yet these elegant grooves remain,*
> *Worn in the sandstone parapet hour by hour*
> *By labouring bargemen where they shifted ropes;*
> *E'en so shall men turn back from violent hopes*
> *To Adam's cheer, and toil with spade again.*
>
> *Ay, and his mother Nature, to whose lap*
> *Like a repentant child at length he hies,*
> *Nor in the whirlwind or the thunder-clap*
> *Proclaims her more tremendous mysteries:*
> *But when in winter's grave, bereft of light,*
> *With still, small voice divinelier whispering*
> *– Lifting the green head of the aconite,*
> *Feeding with sap of hope the hazel-shoot –*
> *She feels God's finger active at the root,*
> *Turns in her sleep, and murmurs of the Spring.*

[Upon Eckington Bridge, River Avon]

176

Eckington Bridge

I don't know exactly when he wrote it, but it was probably quite early in his life as virtually all of his poetry, including this poem, was published in *Poems and Ballads* in 1896, when he was 33. Q, as he was always known, became Cambridge University's first Professor of English Literature, having previously edited the first edition of the *Oxford Book of English Verse*. You can read all about him and his writings, which were considerable, in *With Magic in My Eyes – West Country Literary Landscapes*.

There is a car park and a picnic area right next to the bridge, and a circular walk which is signposted, but you have to watch the traffic lights closely, and move pretty sharply, to reach the safe haven of one of the niches on the bridge parapet, and see the 'elegant grooves' worn into the sandstone by the bargemen's ropes over the centuries.

Exploring Bredon Hill's literary connections

Walks

There are footpaths to the top of Bredon Hill from all of the villages which surround it: Great Comberton, Elmley Castle, Ashton-under-Hill, Overbury, Kemerton and, of course, Bredon itself. From Bredon, the best way up is probably through Westmancote, as described. The Wychavon Way, from Great Comberton to the summit, is short but steep.

For a longer walk, you can start off at Ashton-under-Hill church, which is almost opposite half-timbered Stanley Farm where Fred Archer lived, following the Wychavon Way to the summit plateau and around the northern rim until you reach Banbury Tower, returning via Overbury Park.

There is a car park and picnic area in Elmley Castle, and the route to the summit passes close by the remains of the castle in its Iron Age fort. Details of a circular walk from Elmley Castle are given on the website of the *Queen Elizabeth Inn*: **www.elmleycastle.com**

Viewpoints

Almost anywhere on the summit plateau, although the views to the south, east and west are better than to the north.

Pubs

All of the Bredon Hill villages still have their pubs: the *Queen Elizabeth* at Elmley Castle, which is now a smart gastro-pub, the *Crown* at Kemerton, the *Yew Tree* at Conderton, the *Star* at Ashton-under-Hill and the two remaining pubs in Bredon, the *Royal Oak* and the *Fox and Hounds*.

However, if you want a trip back in time to the world of John Moore, the place to go is the *Monkey House* at Defford on the A4104 road from Upton-on-Severn to Pershore. It is one of only a handful of cider houses left in England and can have changed little, if at all, since Moore's day. It sells only cider or perry, and there is no food, but a visit is an experience not to be forgotten. Opening hours are limited to Friday and Sunday lunchtimes and Wednesday and Saturday evenings.

Museum

The John Moore Museum, which was set up in memory of the author in 1980, focuses mainly on natural history. It is in Church Street, Tewkesbury, close to the Abbey.

Website: **www.johnmooremuseum.org**
Contact: **curator@johnmooremuseum.org**

The Yew Tree at Conderton

Select Bibliography

John Moore   John Moore Society contact: johnshakles@btinternet.com
Portrait of Elmbury (1945)
Brensham Village (1946)
The Blue Field (1948)
The three books are available in one volume as *The Brensham Trilogy* (1985)
David Cole: *John Moore – True Countryman* (2007)

Fred Archer   www.fredarcher.co.uk
Fred wrote more than two dozen books about Bredon Hill and its surrounding villages.
The two quoted in the text are *The Distant Scene* (1967), his first book, and *A Lad of Evesham Vale* (1972).

Chapter Ten

Cotswold Poets

Frank Mansell, Laurie Lee, John Drinkwater

The dead leaves drift down the headland,
The grey clouds sweep over the hill,
The dog and his master are ploughing
The stubble that's standing in drill.

Frank Mansell

In many ways Laurie Lee and Frank Mansell were two of a kind: poets, countrymen, boozers, romantics with a well-developed fondness for the opposite sex and, perhaps most of all, both sons of the Cotswolds. Yet there was this crucial difference between them. Mansell was a poet of the Cotswold hill country; Lee of its steep-sided vales.

Laurie Lee
(1914-1997)
His writing saved the valley he loved

Frank Mansell
(1919-1979)
Cotswold balladeer

Of the pair of them, it goes without saying that Laurie Lee was vastly the more famous and successful. *Cider with Rosie* saw to that. But if you take his autobiographical books out of the equation, and assess them purely as poets, there isn't, I would suggest, much to choose between them. Their styles are as contrasting as the landscapes which inspired them: Mansell's ballads can be as bleak and spare as the thin-soiled fields which his forebears had farmed for centuries; Lee's choice of words and images as lush and sometimes over-blown as the valley in which he grew up. Rhythm is central to Mansell – the rhythms of work on the land. Seasons are what fascinated Laurie Lee, as he looked out across his valley. Frank Mansell looked out at the world from his cottage high on the hills. Laurie Lee looked into the world from his snug Cotswold valley.

This is Mansell:

The young wheat is green on the headland
The west wind blows clean on my brow,
The road that goes down to the valley
Leads back to the farm and the plough.

And this is Laurie Lee:

O the wild trees of my home,
Forests of blue dividing the pink moon,
The iron blue of those ancient branches
With their berries of vermilion stars

The pair of them were not exact contemporaries. Frank Mansell was five years the younger and died almost 20 years earlier. But after Laurie Lee had moved back to Slad in 1959, they became firm friends, soulmates almost. They drank deep together at the Woolpack, no doubt comparing notes on the local talent. It was Laurie Lee, as much as anyone, who persuaded Mansell to get his poems published, and who would tell anyone in the literary world prepared to listen about the uncut diamond of a poet he had unearthed on his very doorstep. He wrote a beautiful, generous foreword to the *Cotswold Ballads*, when they were published in 1969:

This poet's voice reverberates with the resonance of the Cotswold Highlands,
with all the smooth-wrapped hardness of moss-dressed stone. But the special
value, to me, of this present volume is that it collects and preserves, for those
who care about such things, a kind of poetry that may not be seen again. For
Frank Mansell has the ear and gift of a natural ballad-singer, and what is
remarkable about these poems is that they are neither ancient nor modern;
but have the timeless quality of a flowering hedgerow.

And, at a more practical level, he helped his friend sell almost 2,000 copies of the *Ballads* by hawking them round the pubs of Gloucestershire!

Frank Mansell was born into a Cotswold farming family in 1919. Not just any Cotswold farming family, but a family that could trace its roots back to the Norman Conquest. But, in common with all too many family farming businesses in the 1920s and '30s, the Mansells had fallen on hard times, as government support was removed and cheap imports flooded in. Frank's parents were forced to sell the farm when he was 12, a decision that would leave its mark on him for the rest of his life. He might not have made a very good farmer, but farming was what he felt in his bones he ought to have been doing:

'With me the line ended, turned back on itself, tore at its own vitals,' he would write in the introduction to *Cotswold Ballads*. 'The burden of the long centuries of land love and land labour was more than I could bear, and I had to write the pain of it out of my system. Only thus could I resolve the hereditary conflict and justify, in some fashion, my own existence.'

So whilst his poetry is a genuine celebration of life on the high Cotswolds, it is also shot through with melancholy; a mixture of regret and guilt at his own failure – as he saw it – to carry on the family tradition on the land, and everything that went with it. It is the theme of the very first poem in the collection, entitled *Heritage*:

He came of poor but ancient country stock
Of lineage fallen from a better day,
Who lived of late too near the Cotswold rock
To scrape more than bare living from the clay ...

Now he, the last and least in changing time,
Inept, inert, still heavy from the clay,
Labours with words and gathers them in rhyme
To tell the things they felt but could not say.

There was nothing much superficially melancholy about Frank Mansell the man. He may not have had many close friends, but he was widely known and liked. His job, as a telephone engineer, kept him out and about in the countryside he loved, he roared around the lanes on his motorcycle, he chased the girls, he sank his pints in the Carpenters Arms at Miserden, the Butchers Arms at Sheepscombe and the Woolpack and, every summer for the best part of 30 years, he played cricket.

He was a fast bowler; by reputation, a very fast bowler, who would terrify the life out of visiting batsmen as he came charging up Sheepscombe CC's famous slope to unleash his thunderbolts. John Light, a former chairman and president of the Gloucestershire county club, who knew Frank Mansell well and played with or against him many times, reckons it was more his accuracy than his sheer pace that brought him such a rich harvest of wickets. But however that may be, the figures speak for themselves: Frank Mansell played for Sheepscombe for 28 seasons (1946-73), taking 1,725 wickets at an average of just 8.25, with a strike rate of a wicket every 18 balls. Twice he took more than 100 wickets in a season and against Barnsley in 1961 he took all ten in an innings. Quite a cricketer!

And quite a poet! I think I like the farming poems best – *On Eldern Hill, Farm Sale, Farm Dog, Autumn Ploughing, I'd Sooner Go Hedging* and *Stone Wall* – combining as they do a deep pride in work on the land, with a deep sadness at the way farming life had changed, all in the context of a landsman's practical grasp of the tasks of the farming day and the rhythms of the farming year.

The dead leaves drift down the headland,
The grey clouds sweep over the hill,
The dog and his master are ploughing
The stubble that's standing in drill.

But there is love and loss as well, as in the lovely:

The roads go down to Gloucester town
And Severn seeks the sea;
But what road leads where I'd be gone
What river flows to thee?

There are two places to visit to feel the spirit of Frank Mansell. The first is the crossroads at Bunnage, high on the hill to the east of Sheepscombe. There stands the

The Salt Box

Salt Box, the lonely cottage where Frank Mansell lived for his entire adult life, mostly by himself, although he was briefly, and unhappily, married to a cousin. It was, by all accounts, a rather scruffy, unkempt little place when Mansell lived there. In one of his best-known poems, *The Cottager's Reply*, he imagines a potential buyer arriving from the city:

> *You say you'll pay ten thousands pound*
> *For this old house and piece of ground,*
> *You like these hills and have it planned*
> *To settle here on Cotswold land ...*

whom he sends away with a flea in their ear:

> *Enough for me this cott of stone,*
> *A mite of land to call my own,*
> *A friend to drink with, wench to smile*
> *And Cotswold country by the mile.*
>
> *So take your glass and drain it down*
> *You would-be peasant from the town,*
> *Go on your journey, let me bide*
> *Content in my own countryside.*

The people who live in Salt Box cottage now – they bought it after Mansell's sadly early death in 1979 – may not be strictly local but, from what I could see, they've done the old place proud. Just along the lane is where the tumbledown farm buildings used to be, now – like virtually every other set of old farm buildings for miles around – converted into a smart country residence.

The land which Frank Mansell's parents farmed stretches away to the south of the crossroads on both sides of the road. It is indeed the 'lean hill soil' which is not so much bemoaned as almost celebrated in *On Eldern Hill*. When I visited in February, a thin-looking crop of winter wheat was bravely pushing its way through the thin reddy-brown soil and its sprinkling of golden shards. It is a good spot to pause and think, as Mansell did, of all the sweat and toil invested in this land, year after year, and for what?

> *Here where I stand, my forebears swung the scythe*
> *And farmed the land where now the brambles grow*
> *Here had their home and here were young and blythe*
> *And full of hope – a century ago …*
>
> *With plough and harrow, reaping-hook and flail,*
> *They won their bread, and bore what had to be,*
> *Until at last in Sheepscombe's quiet vale*
> *They laid them down, as though in Arcady.*

And no-one should visit Sheepscombe without making a pilgrimage to its cricket ground, preferably in high summer, with a match in progress. It is not quite a plateau, and it is not quite at the top of the hill. The slope which runs down from the pavilion means that, to a bowler from the bottom end, only the batsman's head is visible, and fielding at that end of the ground must be a nightmare. But, oh, what views! – across the valley to the hill-top trees at Frank Mansell's Bunnage, and down the valley to Painswick and its steeple, with Stroud, Stinchcombe and the Severn beyond.

Laurie Lee loved Sheepscombe cricket ground – so much so that he used £600 of the proceeds of *Cider with Rosie* to buy it when, in 1971, it was put up for sale by its farmer owner, and the club itself couldn't afford it. "It is one of the real classic village

The cricket field at Sheepscombe

184

cricket grounds with one of the best views in Gloucestershire and I wanted to be sure it would not be built on," he explained. It is now officially known as the 'Laurie Lee Ground', even though his widow Kathy was forced by straitened circumstances to sell it after his death, with the England Cricket Board Trust gallantly chipping in to help the villagers find the £25,000 asking price.

In fact Sheepscombe, not Slad, was Laurie Lee's 'ancestral village', as he called it. That was on account of his mother Annie's family, the Lights. Annie's father, John Light, kept what was then Sheepscombe's 'other pub', the Plough, halfway up the hill on the eastern side of the valley, now and for many years a private home. It was to the Plough that Annie was recalled from service at Berkeley Castle to look after her father and four brothers after her mother died – an experience that foreshadowed what her marriage would be like

But it is with the Slad Valley, over the hill, that the name of Laurie Lee will for ever be linked. The valley did not inspire *Cider with Rosie*; that sprang from within. But it did provide the perfect context for an elegy to a countryside childhood:

> *narrow, steep and almost entirely cut off; it was also a funnel for winds, a channel for the floods and a jungly, bird-crammed, insect-hopping sun-trap whenever there happened to be any sun.*

The crucial words there are 'almost entirely cut off'. Laurie Lee was looking back to a way of life which, even by the time he was writing, in the late 1950s, was almost entirely cut off from the modern world, just as the valley itself was almost entirely cut off from the towns, villages and countryside around it.

Landscapes are much more than merely the sum of their physical parts. I have referred before to Simon Schama's argument, in *Landscape and Memory*, that landscapes are as much a product of minds as they are of materials, and nowhere is that more true than in the Slad Valley. You cannot even drive through it, let alone walk through its woods and fields, without scenes from *Cider with Rosie* being conjured up in your mind: the magnificently disorganised Annie Lee in the garden of her cottage with a great armful of flowers; Laurie and his friends playing in the road outside the village school; poor Miss Flynn, her dead naked body stretched on the pond, like Ophelia; or maybe Jones' terrifying goat, dragging his broken chain down the village street at midnight. The entire valley is haunted – in a good way – by scenes from the book.

And besides, one wonders what might have happened to the valley had its immortalisation not made it all but impossible for would-be developers to gain a foothold. What you see now is, with one important exception, which we will come to in due course, very much what Laurie Lee would have seen, growing up in the 1920s and '30s. One or two houses have been built in the interim, and the Woolpack now does a good line in quasi-rustic food. But it is still a real pub, just as Slad is still very much a real village, not some sort of *Cider with Rosie* theme park.

The place to start for a walk to explore the Slad Valley, and to feel something of what it meant to Laurie Lee, is Bull's Cross. It had supposedly been the scene of a terrible coaching accident by which it was haunted, as well as possibly being the site of a gibbet, and must have had a distinctly ominous feel to it, when he was growing up:

That ragged wilderness of wind-bent turves – I still wouldn't walk there at midnight. It was a curious tundra, a sort of island of nothing set high above the crowded valleys ... To the villages around, it was a patch of bare skyline, a baldness among the woods, a wind-scarred platform which caught everybody's eye.

Not any longer, it isn't. The open heathland has been allowed to become colonised by bushes, scrub and trees. By far the biggest change in the landscape of the Slad Valley since Laurie Lee's childhood – and you can see it immediately if you look at old photographs – is the way in which trees and hedges have been allowed to grow unchecked so that, in summer especially, almost the entire landscape has become over-grown and the views of the valley blocked out. This dawned on me first when I was pushing my bicycle up the hill from the Woolpack to a campsite at the top. Every so often, I would pass a bench at the side of the road, put there no doubt so that weary travellers or visitors could rest awhile and admire the view across the valley to the east. Nowadays, the only thing the seats look out upon is a great wall of trees, and judging by their decrepitude, no-one bothers to use them any longer.

Not much of a view

No doubt the vegetation has been allowed to grow up for the best of motives, and no doubt there would be an outcry if the Gloucestershire Wildlife Trust or the other landowners took out their chainsaws and gave the valley the thorough haircut that it needs. But it is a shame that so many of the vistas that Laurie Lee enjoyed are being denied the modern-day visitor, simply as a result of a sort of benign neglect. The landscape wouldn't be any the less rich in wildlife if some of the trees were cut down, the hedges laid and the drystone walls re-built. The wild-flowers growing in the old limestone pasture especially would probably enjoy a bit more sunshine and a bit less shade. All it needs is a bit more management – the sort of management which created Laurie Lee's landscape in the first place. For the moment, this is a landscape which is being smothered by kindness.

But it is still a glorious place for a walk, and there is no better walk through the Slad Valley than the 'Laurie Lee Wildlife Trail', laid out by the Gloucestershire Wildlife Trust, taking in its four nature reserves in the valley and punctuated by 'poetry posts' carrying both information about the animals and plants to look out for and extracts from Laurie Lee's poems. It starts, as I say, near the car-park at Bull's Cross, plunging down into Longridge Wood, with Deadcombe (now Detcombe) Bottom still further down on your right. This where the Bull's Cross hangman was supposed to have had his cottage, and hanged himself in remorse at having executed his own son. The remains of his cottage, where Laurie and his brothers played when they were young and found an ominous hook still jutting from a wall, may still be down there, but there is no path, and this is a dark, entangled, rather forbidding place.

Laurie Lee Wildlife Trail

In Laurie Lee's childhood, this was 'a dank yellow wood'. Now, in its upper reaches at least, it is full of great beeches and tall pines. I wondered if any of them had been planted by Lee's Uncle Charlie (Light), his mother's eldest brother, a renowned forester, who did more than anyone to restore the woods of Horsley, Sheepscombe, Rendcomb and Colne, in the wake of all the felling which, perforce, went on during the First World War.

His are those mansions of summer shade, lifting skylines of leaves and birds, those blocks of new green now climbing our hills to restore their remembered perspectives.

There is a steep climb up from the Slad Brook, but worth it when you emerge at the top to be greeted by a magnificent view of the valley stretching away to the south-west. To choose a poem entitled *Landscape* for this location must have seemed obvious, although one wonders if the chooser actually went on to read it, given that the landscape Laurie Lee was writing about was actually that of a woman's body and the poem is much more about sex than the countryside! Still, it is one of his best. From here, the path runs down through a beautiful example of an old Cotswold hay-meadow, bursting with wild flowers in summer, to Snowshill Woods and the remains of the Old Shop, supposed – probably fancifully – to have once been the local brothel. Then out into the sunshine on the sloping pastures of the Snows Farm Nature Reserve, down to the Dillay Brook and up the other side to Catswood. From here there is a stunning view across the valley to Snows Farm: big trees, old pasture, sheep, drystone walls and the big old farmhouse on the hill, the very essence of a Cotswold vale. *Three Winds* is the poem chosen for the gate into Catswood, and it is well chosen as one of the best examples of a Laurie Lee 'seasonal poem', painting as it does a lovely picture of how the countryside changes in response to wind and weather.

After Catswood, the way runs along a short stretch of metalled road through the hamlet of Elcombe. Near here is the cottage that was home to three more poets: Michael Horowitz, his wife Frances Horowitz and their son, Adam Horowitz, who wrote a delightful account of his own childhood in an offshoot of the Slad Valley and his memories of Laurie Lee, *A Thousand Laurie Lees*, to mark the centenary of Laurie's birth. Beyond Elcombe, we break off the lane into 'Laurie Lee Wood', which he bought for the local community to enjoy and which is now in the ownership of the Gloucestershire Wildlife Trust, and so up a steepish hill to the high point of the walk, both literally and metaphorically, on Swift's Hill. The views from the top of this cone of limestone, both down the valley towards Stroud and across it to Slad, are memorable. You feel as if the whole of Laurie Lee country has been laid out before you. I stopped for a picnic of pasty and cider to give me time to drink it all in, as I'm sure thousands more will have done over the years.

This was the hill to which Lee would look out across the valley from Rose Cottage, where he lived after moving back to Slad in 1961. As he explained much later, in a radio interview, it was a view that meant a lot to him:

I can sit and look at that hill and those fields; that wood which changes constantly with the light and the weather and which has remained unchanged since Elizabethan times.

It [Swift's Hill] glows like a heap of ashes of roses on an autumn evening because the sun sets down at the end of the valley, over the Severn, and there is this afterglow which catches the outcrops of limestone and it just sits there, glowing, holding the light to the last drop.

Slad from Swift's Hill

But one mustn't give the impression that Laurie Lee wrote his poems sitting in his cottage, or out in the fields, admiring the view like some sort of landscape painter, or latter-day Coleridge. Most of his poetry was written quite early in his writing career, in the 1930s and '40s, when he was living in London. The Slad Valley may have been an important inspiration to him, but, like Housman's 'blue remembered hills', it was the images and impressions of its landscape in his memory that inspired him, more than the actuality. He found it very difficult to work there. "I couldn't write about Slad in Slad any more than I could write about Spain in Spain," he said later. "I wrote *Cider with Rosie* in an attic in London." In typically dogmatic fashion, he reached the conclusion that creative writers could only work in cities: "Gloucestershire has never produced an artist of any great stature because it is too satisfying a place to live," he pronounced.

After making a cautious descent of the precipitous slope of Swift's Hill, we follow the lane for a short distance before turning right onto the footpath leading to Furner's Farm and the remains of its orchard. As you cross the stream below the farm, it becomes more obvious than ever that the Slad Valley is not a single valley, but a confluence of valleys, the streams divided by fold after fold of limestone grassland and handsome woodland. The only thing missing when I was last there was cattle. The small mixed farms, like farmer Wells' in *Cider with Rosie*, have all but vanished from the Cotswolds, the farm houses sold off as character country residences each with a few acres for ponies, the rest of the land parcelled up and either bought by a dwindling number of much larger, commercial farmers to add to their empires, or – as has happily been the case in the Slad Valley – turned into nature reserves. But a

189

living, working countryside, as this most certainly was for most of Laurie Lee's life? Well no, not really. At least the sheep are still there, and better empty pastures than battery chicken farms and wall-to-wall oilseed rape.

Apples is, with a certain inevitability, the poem chosen for this stretch of the walk, and a lovely poem it is too:

> *The russet, crab and cottage red*
> *Burn to the sun's hot brass,*
> *Then drop like sweat from every branch*
> *And bubble in the grass.*

It is a doubly appropriate selection for, on the left as you walk down the path from Furner's Farm towards the pond at the bottom where poor Miss Flynn drowned herself, is the field where Laurie Lee took what he describes as his 'first bite at the apple' – that fateful encounter with Rosie Burdock under the hay wagon. Not that there ever was a single Rosie Burdock, you understand. As Laurie Lee made clear on many, many occasions, she was a composite of the girls he knew at school, although that doesn't make the description of their cidrous afternoon of discovery any the less enchanting.

Rose Bank Cottage

And so, up the lane from the pond, past the entrance to Steanbridge House where lived the squire, to the main road. Here one is faced with a choice. Go up the hill, past the Lee family's cottage, Rose Bank, down a steep embankment on the right, and so on up until you reach a footpath branching off the main road to the left, to Frith Wood and, eventually, back to Bull's Cross. Or you can delay that final climb for an hour or so, and make your way down the hill to the Woolpack. It is a smashing pub. Structurally, it has changed. The pool room in the cellar is now the kitchen and what was the kitchen is a bar. But the small rooms, low ceilings, uneven floors and fascinating clutter that Laurie Lee and Frank Mansell would have known when they drank here in the 1960s are all still very much with us. And there has been one change for the better from the passing of the years. The food on offer is vastly more interesting, and probably fresher, than it would have been in the days when it was regarded simply as blotting paper to mop up the booze, while the beer offering has been transformed. Back in Laurie and Frank's day, the only real ale on offer would have been the distinctly gutless West Country PA, brewed at Cheltenham under the less than benign Whitbread umbrella. On my last visit, three contrasting beers were available on handpump, each from a different local brewery, and there's some excellent cider as well. The snug bar at the northern end of the pub has been converted into what is almost a Laurie Lee shrine, complete with one of his guitars, photographs and copies of his books. There is no better place to sit and ponder over a glass of cider Laurie Lee's contribution, not just to literature but to social history. With a poet's gift for words, a musician's feel for lyricism and an artist's visual memory, he has painted for us, in *Cider with Rosie*, a vivid and evocative picture of life in a Cotswold valley before the arrival of the motor car, which will enchant and inform for all time.

Laurie Lee tribute bar

Cider with Rosie was published in November 1959, to mostly rapturous reviews, and by January was top of the best-seller list. It changed the lives of Laurie and his long-suffering wife Kathy. From being an almost unknown minor poet one minute, he had become an international celebrity the next. Royalties from the book enabled them to buy a house in Slad – Rose Cottage, within what he called 'stumbling distance' of the Woolpack. That was in 1961 and, two years later, the icing on the cake arrived – a daughter, Jessy, after years of frustration and pain at Kathy's seeming inability to conceive. From then on for the best part of 35 years, Laurie would divide his time between his cronies in London, and his family in Slad. The second and third parts of what became an autobiographical trilogy followed, *As I Walked Out One Midsummer Morning* in 1969 and *A Moment of War* in 1991.

In 1975, the family moved to the larger house next door, Littlecourt, in which Laurie had a big plate-glass window installed, so that he could look down the valley and across to Swift's Hill. Vulgar it may have been but it was, he said, 'one of my great refreshments' for the rest of his life.

Despite his celebrity status and relative prosperity, his moods ebbed and flowed more abruptly than ever, not helped by a prodigious intake of alcohol, much of it imbibed at the Chelsea Arts Club and the rest at the Woolpack. He was mildly epileptic, his eyesight deteriorated as he got older and he had always been prone to fits of depression. Booze apart, he had three great consolations as he grew older: Kathy and Jessy, his friends, and the Slad Valley. He would sit by his big picture window and watch the landscape, thinking back to what it had meant to him: 'a grand kind of extravaganza with no beginning and no end.' To the valley and its people, Laurie Lee owed much. But the valley owed Laurie just as much, for it is thanks to the way he wrote about it, that it is now, surely, safe for all time.

He died in May 1997, a few weeks short of his 83rd birthday, and was buried exactly where he wanted, in the lower churchyard, between the Woolpack and the church. As he had said in one of the countless interviews he had given in the wake of his greatest triumph:

> *I've never found a place which has such intimate significance for me. The trees, the very slope of the valleys are so intensely special to me. I want to be buried between the pub and the church so I can balance the secular and the spiritual, and my long sleep will be punctuated by rowdy Saturday nights in the Woolpack, and Sunday morning worship in the church. It would give me a sense of continuity.*

And Laurie's fellow poet and long-time drinking partner, Frank Mansell? He'd died, much earlier, in 1979 at the age of 61, much mourned by all who had known him and still fondly remembered, as both poet and cricketer.

They were quite a pair.

John Drinkwater

John Drinkwater, the critic, poet and playwright, is probably best known as one of the six Dymock poets and we have written about his work there in the Dymock chapter. But Drinkwater also loved the Cotswold country – "the most beautiful in England," he declared. "There is no more tender or subtle landscape on earth."

Drinkwater discovered the Cotswolds while staying with his friend the painter William (later Sir William) Rothenstein, at Iles Farm, Far Oakridge, midway between Stroud and Cirencester, in 1917. He loved the place, its people as well as its landscape, and was persuaded to write a collection of essays about the craftsmen he got to know there, which was published as *Cotswold Characters* in 1921. He wrote a number of poems about the Cotswolds, of which probably the best is *Cotswold Love*, even if it is more about the charms of the Cotswold womenfolk than those of the local countryside:

> *Blue skies are over Cotswold*
>   *And April snows go by,*
> *The lasses turn their ribbons*
>   *For April's in the sky,*
> *And April is the season*
>   *When Sabbath girls are dressed,*
> *From Rodboro' to Campden,*
>   *In all their silken best.*
>
> *An ankle is a marvel*
>   *When first the buds are brown,*
> *And not a lass but knows it*
>   *From Stow to Gloucester town.*
> *And not a girl goes walking*
>   *Along the Cotswold lanes*
> *But knows men's eyes in April*
>   *Are quicker than their brains.*
>
> *It's little that it matters,*
>   *So long as you're alive,*
> *If you're eighteen in April,*
>   *Or rising sixty-five,*
> *When April comes to Amberley*
>   *With skies of April blue,*
> *And Cotswold girls are briding*
>   *With slyly tilted shoe.*

What a lovely, happy, little poem that is!

Laurie Lee and Frank Mansell

Walks

The Laurie Lee Wildlife Way, set up by the Gloucestershire Wildlife Trust, takes in all of the main Laurie Lee locations in the Slad Valley. It starts at a lay-by opposite Bull's Cross and is around seven miles long, including one very steep climb. There are way-markers featuring excerpts from Lee's poetry at intervals along the route.

Frank Mansell's Salt Box cottage is at the top of the valley, alongside the cross roads where the Sheepscombe to Miserden road crosses the B4070.

Viewpoints

Slad and its valley are probably best appreciated from Swift's Hill.

Sheepscombe cricket ground, with its Laurie Lee Pavilion, has strong associations with both poets and offers spectacular views of the surrounding countryside.

Pubs

The Woolpack, where both Laurie Lee and Frank Mansell spent so many happy hours, is not to be missed. It is still a proper pub, with one bar dedicated to Laurie Lee's memory, albeit offering excellent food.

The Butchers Arms at Sheepscombe is another fine pub, with real ale and good food – the perfect place to repair to after an afternoon watching cricket up the hill.

Frank Mansell's favourite watering hole was the *Carpenters Arms* at Miserden, a few miles east of Slad. The Carps, as it is known, has a fine local reputation for both food and real ale and was a key location in the most recent TV adaptation of *Cider with Rosie*.

The Woolpack from the churchyard

Select Bibliography

Laurie Lee
Cider with Rosie (1959)
Selected Poems (1983)
Valerie Grove: *Laurie Lee – The Well-Loved Stranger* (1999)
Adam Horowitz: *A Thousand Laurie Lees – The Centenary Celebration*
of a Man and a Valley (2014)

Frank Mansell
Cotswold Ballads (1974)

John Drinkwater
Cotswold Characters (1921)
Cotswold Love in *Collected Poems Volume 2* (1923)

Chapter Eleven

Hill, Vale and Forest

Ivor Gurney, Will Harvey, William Shakespeare, Winifred Foley, Dennis Potter

Big glory mellowing on the mellowing hills
And in the little valleys, thatch and dreams
Will Harvey

Ivor Gurney and Will Harvey were near contemporaries, friends and poets of Gloucestershire. The comparison with Laurie Lee and Frank Mansell is obvious, although Gurney and Harvey are more closely matched in terms of literary reputation. Unlike Lee and Mansell, who rarely looked much beyond the Cotswolds for their poetic inspiration, Gurney and Harvey were fundamentally Vale men; the one born in Gloucester, the other not far from the Severn at Hartpury.

Ivor Gurney
(1890-1937)
Touched by genius and tragedy

Will Harvey
(1888-1957)
Laureate of Gloucestershire

That isn't to say that they loved the line of hills which formed their eastern horizon as they looked up from Severnside any the less; both wrote passionately about places like Crickley Hill and Cooper's Hill. But they were, Harvey especially, poets for the whole of the county, not just part of it, and it is at least arguable that they were both at their best as poets down by the river, rather than high on the hills.

They first met, by chance, on a tram, in 1908, when Gurney was 18 and Harvey two years older. Gurney was a talented musician, a pupil of Dr Herbert Brewer, organist at Gloucester Cathedral; Harvey was working in a local solicitor's office, but had already started writing poetry. They took to each other immediately, with

Gurney's fellow music scholar Herbert Howells joining in to form what became a sort of cultural countryside triumvirate. The Harvey family home at Redlands in the village of Minsterworth, south-west of Gloucester, became their favourite gathering place. From there, they would set off on foot or bicycles to explore the Severnside meadows, tour the villages and sail on the Severn in the little sailing boat (called the Dorothy, after his sister) that Gurney had bought from James Harris, the lock-keeper at Framilode, an experience Harvey would recall in *Ballade of River Sailing*:

> *The Dorothy was very small: a boat*
> *Scarce any bigger than the sort one rows*
> *With oars! We got her for a five-pound note*
> *At second-hand. Yet when the river flows*
> *Strong to the sea, and the wind lightly blows,*
> *Then see her dancing on the tide, and you'll*
> *Swear she's the prettiest little craft that goes*
> *Up-stream from Framilode to Bollopool.*
>
> *Bare-footed, push her from the bank afloat,*
> *(The soft warm mud comes squelching through your toes!)*
> *Scramble aboard: then find an antidote*
> *For every care a jaded spirit knows:*
> *While round the boat the broken water crows*
> *With laughter, casting pretty ridicule*
> *On human life and all its little woes,*
> *Up-stream from Framilode to Bollopool.*
>
> *How shall I tell you what the sunset wrote*
> *Upon the outspread waters – gold and rose;*
> *Or how the white sail of our little boat*
> *Looks on a summer sky? The hills enclose*
> *With blue solemnity: each white scar shows*
> *Clear on the quarried Cotteswolds high and cool.*
> *And high and cool a fevered spirit grows*
> *Up-stream from Framilode to Bollopool.*

Of the many villages in the Severn Vale, Framilode would become probably Gurney's favourite, thanks not least to the time he spent there in 1913, reviving his spirits after two rather chequered years as a pupil of the formidable Sir Arthur Stanford, at the Royal College of Music, and suffering from the first intimations of what became his serious mental illness. Thanks in large part to Will Harvey's influence, he had started to write poetry by now, but it wasn't until after the War, when he came to look back on his Gloucestershire childhood, that he was able to put into words what Framilode and the Severn meadows meant to him. Around two thirds of his *80 Poems or So*, written between around 1918 and 1922, concern his time there, *First Framilode* being perhaps the most poignant:

When I saw Framilode first she was a blowy
Severn tided place under azure sky.
Able to take care of Herself, less girl than boy.
But since that time passed, many times the extreme
Of mystery of beauty and last possibility
Of colour, sea breathed romance far past any may dream.
With 'Treasure Island', 'Leaves of Grass' and Shakespeare all there,
Adventure stirring the blood like threat of thunder,
With the never forgotten soft beauty of the Frome,
One evening when elver-lights made the river a stall-road to see.

That particular night left an equally strong impression on Will Harvey. The 'elver-lights' were the lanterns which the elver fishermen would hang by their stations to attract the 'millions and millions of slithy elvers' which used to make their way down river every spring on their way to the Sargasso sea:

Up the gleaming river miles and miles along
Lanterns burn yellow: old joke and song
Echo as fishermen dip down a slight
    Wide frail net,
     Gauzy white net,
     Strong long net
In the water bright.

Framilode today is a prosperous little village. The lock-keeper's cottage is now a smart country residence, hidden behind high garden walls. The remains of a slipway opposite St Peter's Church suggest where Ivor and Will might have launched the Dorothy, to sail her upstream to the hamlet of Bollopool. From Framilode, you can walk either way along the river path, to enjoy the blowy Severn tides. Or you can strike inland, up the lane past the magnificently gabled fifteenth-century farmhouse of Wick Court, which is now one of the three farms which make up Michael and Clare Morpurgo's wonderful 'Farms for City Children' initiative, and up to Barrow Hill. The footpath to the summit branches off the lane opposite Oldbury Farm, where the schoolchildren learn all about modern dairy farming from the Merrett family. The climb to the top is neither particularly long, nor particularly steep, and the view from the top is splendid. Here, looking out from under the branches of the magnificent oak tree which graces the summit, you can see exactly what is meant by the 'Arlingham Horseshoe', as the Severn heads west towards Wales, and then comes back on itself as if having second thoughts. The countryside within the horseshoe is English pastoral. I was just reflecting on how sad it was that there weren't more cows to be seen – beautiful mahogany-coated Gloucester cattle especially – when, lo and behold, there in the field just beyond the top of the hill was a small but handsome herd of British Friesians, grazing peacefully in the afternoon sunshine. Beyond the silver ribbon of the river to the west, the wooded hills of the Forest of Dean; to the south, the spire of Frethern church, the Severn heading east and Stinchcombe Hill in the distance; to the north-west, May Hill, watching over the vale, and beyond, the miniature mountains of Malvern. No wonder Ivor Gurney

The Severn and May Hill from Barrow Hill

loved this view so much. 'Oh what a place!' he wrote to his confidante and guardian angel Marion Scott in June 1913. 'Blue river and golden sand and blue-black hills.'

From here, you can follow the route suggested by Eleanor Rawling in her book *Ivor Gurney's Gloucestershire*, back down the hill, across the lane, and on through big fields of rye-grass and wheat, until you eventually reach the outskirts of Arlingham. The pub here, the Red Lion, was bought by the local community in 2013 to save it from threatened closure, and is now a thriving, hospitable concern, serving excellent food and local beers. Four circular walks start and finish from Arlingham as well: the Hare Walk, the Skylark, the Salmon and the Gloucester Cattle. Between them, they explore virtually every nook and cranny of this remarkable, atmospheric peninsula.

And nowhere is it more atmospheric than on the walk back from Arlingham to Framilode, along part of the Severn Way. The river here is broad, and on a fine day, blue and smooth, flanked by beaches of yellow sand. I didn't see any salmon in the river, and the only Gloucester cattle to be found in these parts now are at Wick Court, but a hare dashed away in front of me as I was crossing the fields to reach the river, and larks were singing beautifully overhead. The river here has a stately tranquillity, and there is nowhere better than the river path to appreciate the three defining elements of the Gloucestershire landscape: the Cotswold edge to the east, the Forest of Dean to the west and the river – the very heart of the vale – at your feet. Ivor Gurney and Will Harvey are by no means the only poets to have been inspired by this glorious synthesis of water and land. Alice Oswald describes it as an 'uncountry of an estuary', in her poem *A Sleepwalk on the Severn*, written for the 2009 Festival of the

The Severn near Framilode

Severn; while to Philip Gross, it is the 'Betweenland' in the series of ten poems which make up his *The Water Table*. How spectacular it must be when the bore comes dashing up the river like a miniature tsunami, to shatter the tranquillity just for a moment, and then leave it as if nothing had passed.

Will Harvey, the 'thick-set, dark-haired, dreamy little man' of his own description, is the poet of this country, just as much as Ivor Gurney. The two young men went their separate ways in the First World War. After initially being turned down because of his poor eyesight, Gurney eventually manage to enlist with the Gloucestershire Regiment, arriving in France in the spring of 1916, and experiencing the full horrors of life in the trenches before being gassed at the Battle of Ypres in September 1917 and invalided home, never fully to recover. Harvey was in the same regiment, but had enlisted within four days of the outbreak of war and was soon in the front line. He was awarded the Distinguished Conduct Medal in 1915 for routing a group of German soldiers he had come across whilst on patrol, and relished the camaraderie he encountered in the trenches, as indeed did Gurney. He seems to have been fearless as a soldier, reckless even, for after being commissioned as an officer, he led a reconnaissance patrol into a German front-line trench, there to be captured and sent to a succession of prisoner-of-war camps.

Both men wrote prolifically and often nostalgically during their wartime experiences. Gurney regarded himself as primarily a composer, poetry was the second string to his bow. But the exigencies of life in the trenches meant that he had, perforce, to focus on words rather than music, and the result was the first flowering of his poetic talents. With Marion Scott's considerable assistance, his first slim volume of poetry *Severn and Somme* was published in 1917, to good reviews. PJ Kavanagh chose *Song*, with its simply expressed sense of longing and nostalgia, for his selection of Ivor Gurney poems. [*Ivor Gurney: Selected Poems*, Oxford Poets series, Carcanet Press]

Only the wanderer
Knows England's graces
Or can anew see clear
Familiar faces

And who loves joy as he
That dwells in shadows?
Do not forget me quite,
O Severn meadows

With Harvey, it was the shock of his capture which seems to have triggered his poetic muse. His first three volumes of poetry – *A Gloucestershire Lad at Home and Abroad*, *Gloucestershire Friends* and *Ducks* – were all written either in the trenches or in captivity, and earned him a considerable reputation as a war poet in the early 1920s. He too looked back to happy times in his beloved Gloucestershire, and to its hills seen from the vale where he was born and grew up, as in *In Flanders*:

I'm homesick for my hills again –
   My hills again!
To see above the Severn Plain
Unscabbarded against the sky
The blue high blade of Cotswold lie;
The giant clouds go royally
By jagged Malvern with a train
Of shadows. Where the land is low
Like a huge imprisoning O
I hear a heart that's sound and high
I hear the heart within me cry:
I'm homesick for my hills again –
   My hills again!
Cotswold or Malvern, sun or rain!
   My hills again!

Harvey's characteristic lyricism makes it sound like a song, and a song it soon became, thanks to Ivor Gurney, who set the poem to music. It is perhaps the perfect evocation of their friendship, their time at war and their love for Gloucestershire.

When Ivor Gurney thought back to the Severn meadows from his front-line dugout, he didn't just have Framilode and Arlingham in mind. The riverside country to the north of Gloucestershire, which he had first explored with his father, on visits to his grandmother, who lived at Maisemore, was just as important to him. Ashleworth, with its manor house, church, tithe barn, jetty and pub by the river was a particular favourite.

The Severn is a very different river on this side of Gloucester – deeper, darker, more compressed. At times of bad flooding, as in the summer of 2007 and the winter of 2014, it must be truly frightening. But in normal times, the Boat at Ashleworth is a blissful spot. The pub has only recently passed out of the hands of the Jelf family, who had it in Gurney's day (and for several hundred years before that!), but is otherwise very much as young Ivor and his father would have found it. The bar parlour and the little rooms leading off it have not been tampered with, and you can still moor your boat at the quay. To sit at one of the tables ranged along the flood-bank on a summer's evening, pint of good cider in hand, watching the river glide past, is one of the great Gloucestershire experiences. Edward Thomas would have been in his element here.

I doubt if Ivor Gurney would have sat at a table outside the pub; he might have been parked on a bench somewhere and told to keep quiet whilst his father enjoyed a glass or two, before or after their walk through the surrounding countryside. This part of Gloucestershire is exceptionally well served by footpaths and bridleways. There must have been some very dedicated walkers and riders around these parts when the definitive map was being drawn up in 1947! Not that all the paths are easily accessible or well signed. Many a kissing-gate is nettle-bound in high summer; some farmers are less than punctilious in reinstating cross-field paths after a crop has been planted and some of the stiles are daunting. But my strong impression is that a doubtless over-worked Gloucestershire County Council Rights of Way department does its best, and it is true that most of the obstructions are natural, rather than man-made.

The plethora of footpaths does mean that the possibilities for exploring this stretch of countryside are almost endless, although the one place that anyone seeking to follow in Gurney's footsteps simply must visit is Barrow Hill. Yes, another Barrow Hill, and offering views just as spectacular as the one in the Arlingham horseshoe. Setting off from the pub, you can reach it by taking the bridleway that leaves the lane just beyond the church and manor house, by the Dutch barns at Ashleworth Court Farm. The fact that Barrow Hill, topped with its coronet of horse chestnuts and limes (which looks rather as if a gigantic, long-legged centipede is making its way across the

Barrow Hill

summit of the hill) is in full view for most of the way makes navigation relatively easy. The route I followed took me to the hamlet of Whitehill, past handsome Ashleworth Manor, through some horseyculture, then turning sharp left to follow the rather tunnel-like bridleway which emerges on the lower slopes of Barrow Hill. There isn't actually a right of way to the summit, but Eleanor Rawling tells us that the landowner doesn't take any great exception to walkers making a small detour up what is a steep, grassy slope to the copse on the top.

Very much as with the other Barrow Hill, the magnificence of the view from the summit is out of all proportion to the relatively modest elevation of the hill: half of Gloucestershire is laid out before you – to the south-east, almost the full extent of the Cotswold ridge stretches along the horizon to Stinchcombe; to the south-west, the wooded hills of the Forest of Dean, culminating in ever-present, ever-commanding May Hill; and in between the Severn and its beautiful vale, with Gloucester Cathedral just visible, fittingly, at the very heart of the panorama. It is a view which inspired Ivor Gurney to write *Above Ashleworth*, in which he imagines some unimaginative philistine failing to appreciate what is spread out before him, whilst he, who truly loves and appreciates all it means, is stuck in France:

> *O does some blind fool now stand on my hill*
> *To see how Ashleworth nestles by the river*
> *Where eyes and heart and soul may drink their fill.*
>
> *The Cotswolds stand out eastwards as if never*
> *A curve of them the hand of Time might change;*
> *Beauty sleeps most confidently for ever.*
>
> *The blind fool stands, his dull eyes free to range*
> *Endlessly almost, and finds no word to say;*
> *Not that the sense of wonder is too strange*
>
> *Too great for speech. Naught touches him; the day*
> *Blows its glad trumpets, breathes rich-odoured breath;*
> *Glory after glory passes away.*
> *(And I'm in France!) He looks and sees beneath*
> *The clouds in steady Severn silver and grey*
> *But dead he is and comfortable in death.*

After the war, Will Harvey settled back into his career as a solicitor, living and working in Lydney. He was a better poet than he was a businessman, and more of a philanthropist than a lawyer. He would take up the causes of all-comers, sometimes regardless of their ability to pay, to the extent that he became known as 'the poor man's solicitor'. But whilst this earned him well-deserved popularity in the Forest of Dean – then, as now, the poorest part of Gloucestershire – it wasn't much of a business plan. Not surprisingly, the practice failed and in 1930 he was forced to sell it.

He continued to write poetry (despite at one stage in the mid-1920s trying to abandon his literary vocation) and his bond with Gurney was as strong as ever. But it was a very different Ivor Gurney who returned eventually to Gloucestershire, after his treatment in a succession of military hospitals, first for the after-effects of the gassing, and then for what was officially classified as 'shell-shock'. He seems in fact to have been suffering from a progressive form of depression, whose effects were compounded by his rejection by the only real love of his life, Anne Drummond, a nurse, and the death of his father from cancer. He also missed the structure and comradeship of military life. He became a lost soul.

Back in Gloucestershire after his discharge in October 1918, he found it difficult to settle to anything. He would walk for miles, by day or night, and suffered from an eating disorder which involved eating nothing for days, and then gorging himself on cream cakes. His friends, Marion Scott and the Gloucester solicitor John Haines, who had acted as a sort of informal patron for the Dymock poets, did their best to find him work and lift his spirits, but it was only in the Gloucestershire countryside, and in particular on Crickley Hill, that Gurney found any real solace.

In the spring of 1919, he took a job as a farm labourer at Dryhill Farm, just under Crickley Hill, about three miles north-east of Gloucester. It was a well-chosen location. The hill dominates the eastern skyline when seen from his boyhood home in Gloucester, and he must have walked out from the city and up the steep slope many times whilst he was growing up. In fact, judging by the number of times it is mentioned by name in his poems, Crickley was his favourite place of all – the place where he would go, either in reality or in his mind, in search of creative inspiration or to restore his mental equilibrium. For his depression – his 'bipolarity' as it would probably be described these days – was getting steadily worse. Although happy enough working at Dryhill Farm, he couldn't settle to anything for any length of time, living a tramp-like existence. His restlessness took him to London, where he was still theoretically enrolled at the Royal College of Music, to his friends, the Chapmans, at High Wycombe, then back to Gloucester, where he took to living in his Aunt Marie's house at Longford on the outskirts of the city. Physical exertion provided some relief from his mental torture. He would walk for hours, night and day, trying to find inner peace. In February 1920, he even walked all the way from High Wycombe back to Dryhill Farm, describing the experience in a poem called, with a touch of irony, *The Little Way*. Up at Dryhill, he attempted to take over a derelict cottage at Cold Slad, just under the Crickley escarpment, but if he ever lived there properly at all, it was only for a few weeks.

But for all his restlessness and unhappiness, this was a productive period. As both composer and poet, the years between 1919 and 1922 were the most prolific of his life. Songs poured from him, and in 1921 he composed what was arguably his magnum opus, his *Gloucestershire Rhapsody*, an orchestral piece which was first performed as recently as 2010 at the Three Choirs Festival. These years also produced some of his finest poetry, much of it looking back to his time in France, and recalling the deep nostalgia that he felt for Gloucestershire. His first stopping-off place when the Glosters arrived in France had been Riez Ballieu. It reminded him of the Severn Vale:

> *Riez Ballieu in blue tea-time*
> *Called back the Severn lanes, and roads*
> *Where the small ash leaves lie, and floods*

Of hawthorne leaves turned with the night's rime,
No Severn though, or great valley clouds.

Other poems from that era draw upon the his work at Dryhill Farm – *Felling a Tree*, for example, which perfectly and poignantly describes how physical effort produced mental relief – or his walks through the countryside, as in *Cotswold Ways*:

One comes across the strangest things in walks:
Fragments of Abbey tithe-barns fixed in modern
And Dutch-sort houses where the water baulks
Weired up, and brick kilns broken among fern,
Old troughs, great stone cisterns bishops might have blessed
Ceremonially, and worthy mounting-stones;
Black timber in red brick, queerly placed
Where Hill stone was looked for – and a manor's bones
Spied in the frame of some wisteria'd house
And mill-falls and sedge pools and Saxon faces;
Stream-sources happened upon in unlikely places,
And Roman-looking hills of small degree
And the surprise of dignity of poplars
At a road end, or the white Cotswold scars
Or sheets spread white against the hazel tree.
Strange the large difference of up-Cotswold ways;
Birdlip climbs bold and treeless to a bend,
Portway to dim wood-lengths without end,
And Crickley goes to cliffs are the crown of days.

It is not hard to understand why Crickley Hill came to mean so much to Ivor Gurney. It may now be a country park, where you pay and display for parking, and the landscapes and townscapes over which it looks may be very different from Gurney's day, but it is still a magnificent vantage point from which to look out upon the Cotswold edge, the Cotswold outliers, Robinswood Hill and Chosen Hill, May Hill to the west, with the Herefordshire hills beyond, and the great sweep of the Severn Vale stretching northwards through the gateway formed by the Malverns and Bredon Hill.

Gurney loved the Cotswolds, but I think loved them more for the views they afforded of Gloucester and the vale than for themselves. If you wanted somewhere to go where you could try to put your troubled state of mind into some sort of perspective – to reduce it from being an all-consuming nightmare to just a speck of worry in the greater scheme of things – then Crickley Hill would be the place. The escarpment drops abruptly from the brink of the quarry to the white-veined ridge below, but on either hand are the close-cropped grassy slopes where, on a fine day, you can stretch out, drink in the views and think great thoughts, just as Ivor Gurney did. There can be few finer spots for a picnic in all of Gloucestershire. On the summit is the amphitheatre which enclosed a substantial Iron Age settlement. The turf underfoot is soft and springy, be-jewelled in spring-time with cowslips.

Crickley looking west

However, Ivor Gurney loved Crickley as much for its solitude as for the views that it offered:

> *Up there on the Roman Hill all was quiet.*
> *Only harebells nodded.*
> *And the pieces of limestone scattered in the spaces white,*
> *Wondered not what I did.* [Quietude]

You won't find much solitude, still less quietude, for that matter, up on Crickley these days. It is a popular spot, especially at week-ends, and the drone of the M5 is ever-present. But it is still one of the very best places to go to think about Ivor Gurney and read his poems. One of the best ways of exploring it is to follow the walk suggested by Eleanor Rawling in *Ivor Gurney's Gloucestershire*: through the Iron Age fort, dropping down the hill to what may have been Ivor Gurney's cottage in Cold Slad, then back up Greenfield Lane, to where a bridleway branches off left along the line of the hillside, through the fields where Gurney worked in his time at Dryhill Farm, and then back along the Cotswold Way above the old quarry. Just before re-joining the Cotswold Way you will pass the site of the Roman villa, with which Gurney seems to have been so obsessed. He can hardly mention Crickley without some reference to the Romans. He called it 'the Roman Hill' and felt that he could feel the ghosts of Roman soldiers when he walked there, particularly at night.

However, not even Crickley Hill could keep his progressive schizophrenia at bay for long. In August 1922, convinced he was being targeted by radio waves – "broken by electrical torment," as he described it – he abandoned what proved to be his last job, at the local tax office, moved out from Aunt Marie at Longford, and arrived uninvited at his brother Ronald's house in Gloucester. The pair had never got on and Ivor's increasingly erratic behavior was just too much for Ronald and his new wife. When Ivor produced a gun and threatened to shoot himself, the police were called. By October, Ivor had been certified insane and committed to the Barnwood House asylum in Gloucester. When he attempted to escape a month or so later, the authorities decided that he would have to be moved out of Gloucestershire. Thanks again to the intervention of Marion Scott, he was sent to the City of London Mental Hospital at Dartford in Kent, which did at least mean that he could be visited regularly by herself and his other London-based friends.

And there he stayed, for the remaining 15 years of his life, still composing music, and still writing poems, including many – especially in the *Rewards of Wonder* collection – in which he recalls the sights and sounds of the Gloucestershire countryside. But for all Marion Scott's devoted efforts, Gurney seems to have been profoundly miserable and increasingly disturbed. In 1932 she took Helen Thomas to visit him, knowing that her late husband Edward was one of Ivor Gurney's heroes. Helen Thomas has left a moving account of the experience in *World Without End* (now re-published with *As It Was* as *Under Storm's Wing*). She found him depressed and room-bound, 'a tall gaunt disheveled man clad in pyjamas and a dressing gown', reluctant even to walk in the gardens of the hospital, because it wasn't proper countryside. He only came to life when, on a subsequent visit, she hit upon the idea of taking him Edward's one-inch Ordnance Survey maps of Gloucestershire:

> This proved to have been a sort of inspiration, for Ivor Gurney at once spread them out on his bed and I spent the whole time I was there tracing with our fingers the lanes and byways and villages of which he knew every step and over which Edward had also walked. He spent that hour in revisiting his home, in spotting a village or a track, a hill or a wood and seeing it all in his mind's eye, with flowers and trees, stiles and hedges, a mental vision sharper and more actual for his heightened intensity ... It was most deeply moving ... I became for a while not a visitor from the outside world of war and wireless, but the element which brought Edward back to life for him and the country where they two could wander together.

Ivor Gurney died at Dartford, of pulmonary TB, on Boxing Day 1937, at the age of just 47. He cuts a tragic figure in many ways: a budding genius of music and words cut down in his prime by war and mental illness, the last painful years of his short life spent exiled from his beloved Gloucestershire imprisoned in a lunatic asylum. Yet there is another, very different, side to him. In his boyhood years, and periodically thereafter, he could be the life and soul of any party: ebullient, adventurous, happy in the company of his friends and deeply conscious of the beauty of the natural world around him, with all the inner joy which that can bring. His poetry is uneven in quality: 'a mixture of genius and muddle,' to quote Michael Hurd's assessment. He is thought to have written almost 900 poems but, of those, only around 300 could be regarded as both complete and worthy of publication. Even his best work is often rough and unfinished – 'gnarled,' to use Edmund Blunden's description – as polish was sacrificed for immediacy and vividness. But anyone who loves Gloucestershire will forgive him all of that for the pictures that he paints and the atmosphere he evokes, of its countryside a century ago.

Meanwhile, what of Will Harvey? Thanks largely to the popularity of *Ducks*, he had enjoyed a brief period of relative fame, if not of fortune, in the immediate aftermath of the end of the war and his release from prison in Germany. He and Ivor Gurney remained close friends, giving recitals together, although the bond inevitably weakened when the poet-composer was sent away to Kent. In 1921, he married an Irish nurse, Anne Kane, and announced his retirement from the literary world with what was intended to be a final volume of poetry, entitled *Farewell*. In fact, although his main preoccupation from here on was using his legal training and considerable force of personality to stand up for the less fortunate, be they his ex-comrades or the local people of the Forest of Dean, he continued to write, without ever quite touching the heights of his war-time poetry. He and his family lived a Bohemian, hand-to-mouth, sort of existence at Yorkley, in the Forest of Dean, his main source of income in later years being talks on the BBC, which reinforced his reputation as the 'Laureate of Gloucestershire' and 'Voice of the Forest'.

To an extent, Will Harvey was to poetry what Thomas Hughes was to Christianity. As the dramatist Theodore Hannam Clark put it in his introduction to the 1947 volume of Harvey's poems, entitled simply *Gloucestershire*, 'he never became a pansy poet'! A promising weight-lifter in his youth, a daring and fearless soldier in the Great War and a fanatically keen cricketer all his life and a great fighter for his fellow men, there was nothing pale or retiring about Will Harvey. He died in 1957, aged 68, and is remembered by a plaque in Gloucester Cathedral inscribed 'Soldier and Poet of Gloucestershire'. Of his many Gloucestershire poems, perhaps my favourite is *A Rondel of Gloucestershire*:

> Big glory mellowing on the mellowing hills,
> And in the little valleys, thatch and dreams,
> Wrought by the manifold and vagrant wills
> Of sun and ripening rain and wind; so gleams
> My country, that great magic cup which spills
> Into my mind a thousand thousand streams
> Of glory mellowing on the mellowing hills
> And in the little valleys, thatch and dreams.
>
> O you dear heights of blue no ploughman tills,
> O valleys where the curling mist upstreams
> White over fields of trembling daffodils.
> And you old dusty little water-mills,
> Through all my life, for joy of you, sweet thrills
> Shook me, and in my death at last there beams
> Big glory mellowing on the mellowing hills
> And in the little valleys, thatch and dreams.

Shakespeare in Gloucestershire

Considering how much Shakespeare wrote, and how well known he was even in his own lifetime, remarkably little is known about his life, and about two periods in particular. The first is the three years from 1579 to 1582, between leaving school and Stratford and returning to court and marry Anne Hathaway; the second is the so-called 'lost years', from 1586, when he again left Stratford probably to join one of the troupes of travelling players, and his re-emergence in London in 1592.

It is in the first of those two periods that he may have spent time in Gloucestershire. Shakespeare was 15 at the time. He seems to have been a precocious youth, fond of girls and beer and maybe a spot of minor criminality on the side. Legend has it that, at about this time, he was forced to flee his home town, in order to avoid a prosecution by Sir Thomas Lucy for poaching deer in the grounds of Charlecote Park. And, having fled, he would have needed to earn some money. John Aubrey reports hearing an account that, 'in his younger years', which is presumably a reference to this time, Shakespeare was 'a Schoolmaster in the Countrey'.

But where might he have flown, and taught? Lancashire has a good claim, by virtue of a favourable mention in the will of one William Hoghton, of Hoghton Hall near Lea in Lancashire, of 'William Shakeshaft now dwelling with me'. The Hoghtons were Catholic, as was William's father, but even if one accepts that 'Shakeshaft' was a mis-transcription, the connection seems tenuous.

Far more plausible is the suggestion that the refuge to which he escaped to flee the wrath of Sir Thomas was Dursley, in Gloucestershire. Not only were there Shakespeares living in the town at that time – quite possibly relations – but, especially given how few geographical locations are mentioned anywhere in his writings, this particular part of Gloucestershire does enjoy a quite striking prominence. The textual case for the Gloucestershire/Dursley connection rests on three passages in Shakespeare's plays and, in my view, one sonnet.

The first of the references is that to 'hateful docks, rough thistles, kecksies, burs' in *Henry V*. As John Moore has pointed out, 'kecksies' is a dialect word meaning 'hollow plant stem' found only in north Gloucestershire and south Worcestershire.

The second is from *Henry IV pt 2*, Act V Scene I, set in Gloucestershire, when Davy says to Justice Shallow: 'I beseech you, sir, to countenance William Visor of Woncote against Clement Perkes a' th hill.' Both families were known to Shakespeare, for they were both wool merchants who did business with his father, the Perkes possibly more fairly than the Visors. So where is Woncot, and which hill is Shakespeare referring to?

Woncott is the long-established pronunciation of Woodmancote, of which there are three in Gloucestershire: one at Bishop's Cleeve, near Cheltenham, another near Cirencester and a third on the edge of Dursley. The two strongest contenders are the Bishop's Cleeve Woncot, which is only a few miles from Sudeley Castle where William Brydges had his own troupe of actors and regularly put on plays, in which Shakespeare may well have taken part; and Woodmancote on the edge of Dursley, overlooked by Stinchcombe Hill.

Both are perfectly plausible. What I think tips the balance in the Dursley direction is the second part of the line: 'against Clement Perkins o' the hill'. We know from documentary evidence that there was a family of Perkins living not far from Stinchcombe Hill at this time; and Visor, or Vizard, is a well-known local name. What could be more natural when referring to two rival wool-dealers to choose two living not far from each other and in an area with which, as we have seen, there may well have been family connections? If Shakespeare was indeed forced to flee Stratford as a teenager in 1579, Dursley would have been an obvious bolt-hole.

That theory receives further reinforcement from the exchange in *Richard II*, Act II Scene 3, set in 'the wilds of Gloucestershire', when Bolingbroke asks Northumberland how far it is to Berkeley Castle, to which the Earl replies that he doesn't know because

> *I am a stranger here in Gloucestershire:*
> *These high wild hills and rough uneven ways*
> *Draws out our miles and makes us wearisome …*

Then Harry Hotspur, Northumberland's son, turns up, who knows the country better and points the way:

> *There stands the castle, by yon tuft of trees,*
> *Manned with three hundred men, as I have heard.*

Which is more or less exactly how you would see Berkeley Castle to this day from Stinchcombe Hill and which strongly suggests that Shakespeare was familiar with that view.

Then finally there is *Sonnet 33*, which certainly wasn't written between 1579 and 1582, but which could very well have been based on a memory from that time:

> *Full many a glorious morning have I seen*
> *Flatter the mountain-tops with sovereign eye,*
> *Kissing with golden face the meadows green,*
> *Gilding pale streams with heavenly alchemy;*
> *Anon permit the basest clouds to ride*
> *With ugly rack on his celestial face,*
> *And from the forlorn world his visage hide,*
> *Stealing unseen to west with this disgrace:*
> *Even so my sun one early morn did shine*
> *With all triumphant splendor on my brow;*
> *But out! alack! he was but one hour mine,*
> *The region cloud hath mask'd him from me now.*
> *Yet him for this my love no whit disdaineth;*
> *Suns of the world may stain when heaven's sun staineth.*

The poem is a reference to some form of slight received from the young male friend – possibly the Earl of Southampton – to whom the early sonnets are addressed. But the imagery, of the morning sun lighting up the meadows and mountain tops to the west, only for the clouds to roll in and spoil the view, is exactly what you might employ if you had spent long hours walking on Stinchcombe Hill, looking west across the Severn Valley to Wales.

The connections between William Shakespeare and Dursley and Stinchcombe Hill may not be proven, but for me at least, they are convincing enough to give any visit to that magnificent promontory, overlooking the glorious Severn Vale, that extra touch of magic.

We cannot leave Gloucestershire without a visit to the Forest of Dean, that strange, heart-shaped hinterland of wooded hill-country, bracketed by the Rivers Severn and Wye, that seems to belong neither to England nor to Wales. The Forest is a land unto itself. It has its own laws, its own customs, its own dialect and its own landscape. Its distinct industrial character, of coal and iron, has now almost disappeared, but the influence of that legacy lingers on, in the shape of the Forest's unmistakably mining villages, its few remaining 'free-miners' still digging for coal and, sadly, in a post-industrial economy which has made the area one of the most deprived in the South-West.

That the Forest still seems like a land apart is down to its history, as much as its geography. Since the Norman Conquest, it has been a Royal Forest, owned by the Crown and reserved for the Crown's own uses, principally hunting, timber and minerals. For that reason, it lacks not only the typical land use mixture of the English countryside, but also its social structure, of villages and market towns, and, to a large extent, the class structure that went with it. The villages that did grow up were effectively created by squatters, who built their houses despite having no legal right to the land on which they stood. It has left us with a landscape of utilitarian (to put it kindly) settlements, in a beautiful wooded, mostly wild countryside. There is nowhere else like it in England.

The Forest has had brushes with literary celebrity. JK Rowling lived at Tutshill not far from Chepstow when she was growing up and JRR Tolkien visited briefly in 1929 to help out Sir Mortimore Wheeler with the excavation of a Roman Temple on the Lydney Park Estate, in an area riddled with the remains of ancient mine workings and associated with both goblins and a cursed ring – an experience of which *The Hobbit* and *The Lord of the Rings* may or may not bear the imprint. But the two writers most closely associated with the area, Winifred Foley and Dennis Potter, are Foresters to the core.

They were born within a few miles of each other, Foley in the village of Brierley, Potter at Berry Hill. Both came from mining families who struggled to make ends meet. And with both of them, their childhoods in the Forest – Foley's in the 1920s, Potter's in the 1940s – had a huge influence on what they came to write.

Winifred Foley was the Forest of Dean's answer to Laurie Lee and Flora Thompson. She was encouraged to write down her reminiscences of childhood by her niece, Elizabeth Ann, and eventually submitted some rather scruffy notebooks to John Burnett, Professor of Social History at Brunel University, who was working with the BBC's *Woman's Hour* programme to record the experiences of working-class listeners. He encouraged her, and the notebooks found

Winifred Foley
(1914-2009)
Uncut diamond

their way to Pamela Howe, a producer with the BBC in Bristol. She could spot an uncut diamond when she saw one, and set out to polish it. After much editing and re-writing, Winifred Foley's reminiscences were serialised on *Woman's Hour* in 1973 and subsequently published, also by the BBC, as *A Child in the Forest*. The book was an overnight success, selling well over half a million copies and being eventually re-published, shortly after its author's death in 2004, as *Full Hearts and Empty Bellies*.

Personally, I prefer the original title, but you cannot argue that the second incarnation doesn't fairly summarise the book's subject matter. Winifred Foley's childhood was one of genuine grinding poverty, in Great Aunt Lizzie's two-up, two-down cottage in the straggling little village of Brierley, a few miles north-east of Coleford. Food was always short, new clothes virtually unheard of, there was no running water or sanitation, her parents living in a state of semi-exhaustion from working down the mine in her father's case, struggling to keep her family clothed and fed in her mother's. But, as comes across so clearly in Winifred Foley's vivid account, whilst the Mason family and others like them may have been poor, that didn't necessarily mean they were unhappy. For a start, there was the beauty of their surroundings:

> With our heads uncomplicated by lessons in botany or geology we took it for granted that hundreds of massive oak trees bordered our village, that the woods were full of ferns, that our fathers worked in coal mines. What was it to us that such a luxuriance of ferns was peculiar to oak forests? They were just there to play and hide in.

Then there was the sense of community, the pride, the independence, the sheer cussedness of the Forest people. Winifred Foley recalls a visitor the Forest snootily expressing pity for an elderly crippled man in Brierley.

> Looking slowly round, the old man said, "Doosn't thee fret for I, me booy; I ban't tired o round ere yet." The Forest was that sort of place. As my father once said, "Nobody wants to come 'ere if they can 'elp it; but once they do settle down, you'd atter shoot 'em to get 'em to muv."

As you would expect, the Forest is ever present in Winifred Foley's writings. She paints wonderful pictures of the landscape: of the humiliating experience when she, her mother and her sister were caught scrumping apples by the angry farmer; or, at the other end of the happiness scale, the joyous summer Sunday afternoon when she and her brother walk the two miles across country to their grand-parents' cottage at Lydbrook to take them a cabbage, to be proudly shown the view over the River Wye:

> "Hello, me butties, is Grancher showin' you 'is dailies then? What a lovely day you've 'ad to come over! Just see the river from 'ere. There! What do ye think o' that? Ben't it a beautiful sight? All they fields and trees, and ups and downs, for miles and miles."

Oak trees and ferns still surround Brierley, the walk over the hill to Lydbrook remains a joy, and a beautiful sight the Wye Valley most certainly still makes.

The Wye Valley: "Ben't it a beautiful sight?"

Dennis Potter was born in 1936, 22 years after Winifred Foley, at Berry Hill on the outskirts of Coleford. His too was a mining family, not perhaps quite as hard-up as Winifred's, but poor enough by any standards, and squarely in the non-conformist, radical, fiercely independent Forest tradition. His childhood coloured his books, his journalism and, especially, his television plays, not in the sense that he wrote about it to any great extent, but because of the way his family background and childhood experiences – and maybe one experience in particular – shaped his outlook on life. The one experience in particular was being interfered with as a ten-year-old by his Uncle Ernie, when he was staying with his mother's relatives in London. When Potter came to be interviewed by Mark Lawson in 1993, he explained its influence:

> *It's obviously there in my consciousness, and is there in the work, if people want to see it. A lot of the characters are the abused, the helpless ones.*

What with that, the family's financial troubles, and his own situation as a bit of a clever-clogs, and a redhead to boot, who needed to use every ounce of his intelligence to avoid becoming a victim of bullying, Dennis Potter's childhood was by no means idyllic. And when it came to writing his television plays, that showed.

Dennis Potter
(1935-1994)
Son of the Forest

The Potter family finally left Berry Hill to move to London in 1949, although Denis would return to live at Ross-on-Wye on the fringe of the Forest, after his marriage to Margaret Morgan in 1959. By that time, he had won a State Scholarship to New College, Oxford, where he earned himself a considerable reputation as a left-wing firebrand and edited the university magazine *Isis*, done his national service, had a crack at writing a semi-autobiographical novel and had his first book published. This was *The Glittering Coffin*, a polemic on social change in England, heavily coloured by Potter's left-wing politics. It was a subject he returned to, much closer to home, in 1962 with his account of *The Changing Forest*. It is a fascinating read – an important sociological document in its own right, based on deep personal knowledge and perceptive observation, which leaves us with a vivid picture of how the Forest was, a generation on from the period that Winifred Foley has immortalised.

He writes about the decline and fall of the coal mines, the rise of coffee bar culture and pop music, the changes to pubs and clubs, televisions invading the sanctity of the old front room, young people, and most of all the diminishing of the old sense of working-class solidarity, which was stronger in the Forest than anywhere else, if only because the working class made up a higher proportion of the total population in the Forest than anywhere else in southern England. It was effectively a one-class community.

One thing which he didn't see as changing was the landscape:

> *Surprise still revolves through the year – the myriad greens, the walks down an old stony road to the rapids, the bracken turning and crumbling into a dusty and universal golden brown, and, even in winter, the stark black trunks and icy stubble has its own bitter loveliness.*

Two things happened at around the same time that Potter was writing *The Changing Forest* which would shape the rest of his career: he joined the BBC and he started showing the first symptoms of the psoriatic arthropathy which would blight the rest of his life. He stood, unsuccessfully, for Labour in the safe Tory seat of Hertfordshire East in the 1964 General Election, but after that devoted himself to writing plays for television – plays which have come almost to define that era in terms of serious television drama.

Many of his plays and serials draw on his own life and experiences. The Forest of Dean is woven into much of his work. Eileen, the Madonna turned whore in *Pennies from Heaven*, is 'the ingénue from the Forest of Dean'; *The Singing Detective*, Philip

Marlowe, is a clever miner's son from the Forest of Dean who moves to London; *The Beast with Two Backs* is based on an incident when rioting Forest miners, incited by false rumour, killed four performing bears and badly injured their French handlers, in 1889.

And then there is *Blue Remembered Hills*, in which adult actors (who included Colin Welland, Helen Mirren and Robin Ellis) play the parts of children. The title was chosen by Potter ironically, for, as he explains in a preface to the published text of the play (in *Waiting for the Boat*) he wrote it as an attack on what he called 'a misplaced nostalgia for those "blue remembered hills" of Housman's aching little verse.' Adult actors were used because, he explained, he did not want the raw emotions of the play 'to be distanced by the presence of young limbs, fresh eyes, or falsetto voices.' It is a bleak, almost brutal play with a shocking denouement, set ostensibly in 'the west country' in 1943, although the commons, woods and hollows in which the action takes place would place it firmly in the Forest of Dean, even without the fact that the protagonists speak in the unmistakable Forest dialect.

The play concludes with a narrator speaking those famous lines:

> *Into my heart an air that kills*
> *From yon far country blows.*
> *What are those blue remembered hills,*
> *What spires, what farms are those?*
> *That is the land of lost content,*
> *I see it shining plain.*
> *The happy highways where I went*
> *And cannot come again.*

I rather fancy that AE Housman, prone to melancholy as he was, would have approved.

Dennis Potter wrote dozens of television plays and film screenplays between the early 1970s and his sadly early death in 1994. It was entirely typical of the man that he named the cancer which killed him 'Rupert' as a mark of his detestation of the mass media.

Winifred Foley outlived him by 15 years, dying in 2009 at the age of 94. She continued to write, romantic novels as well as further volumes of memoirs, without ever quite touching the heights of *A Child in the Forest*.

The Forest can be proud of having produced two such writers as Winifred Foley and Dennis Potter, and they in turn have done the Forest proud. Between them, they have left an imperishable account of how the Forest of Dean changed during the twentieth century without, I'm glad to say, losing its own very distinct identity.

Exploring the country of Ivor Gurney and Will Harvey

Walks

Framilode and the Arlingham Horseshoe: The best starting point is probably Arlingham, from which four circular walks radiate, each starting at the *Red Lion*. A map of them can be picked up from the pub or downloaded from **www.redlionarlingham.co.uk**. I mixed the walks, going north-east from Arlingham to the Severn, then along the Severn up to Framilode, where Ivor Gurney lived with James Harris, the lock-keeper. From Framilode I walked up Overton Lane past the entrance to Wick Court to Oldbury Farm, where a footpath on the left takes you to the summit of Barrow Hill. There is a magnificent oak tree at the top, and lovely views of the Horseshoe, the Severn and May Hill beyond. The path back to Arlingham is almost straight, running through big fields of grass and corn.

Crickley Hill Country Park: There are spectacular views and plenty of possible walking routes, including one which takes you past Dryhill Farm, where Ivor Gurney worked for a time after the First World War, and what was probably the cottage in which he lived. From the south end of the Roman fort, the route goes down the hill to Cold Slad, then back up the hill to the base of the escarpment, branching off left above Dryhill Farm to Greenway Lane. Turn right there and almost immediately on your right, the Cotswold Way will take you back to the Country Park.

The other Barrow Hill: We can start at either Ashleworth village centre, or the *Boat Inn*. The destination is Barrow Hill, to which Ivor Gurney as a child was taken on walks by his father. A bridleway crosses the hill's lower slopes, which can be reached by footpaths either from the village, or from Ashleworth Court, where you can climb up the grassy slopes to the copse on the top. For the onward journey, I got back on the bridleway, down to Wickridge Street, then along the lane to the gates for Foscombe House. The Three Choirs Way follows the driveway behind the house and so eventually back to Ashleworth.

The hamlet of Brierley, where Winifred Foley grew up, is just off the main Coleford to Gloucester road. This being a Royal Forest, official footpaths are few and far between. As good a bet as any for exploring the countryside of Winifred Foley and Dennis Potter is to take the Beechenhurst Trail, an eight-mile circular walk which starts and finishes at the Beechenhurst visitor centre, and takes in both Lydbrook and the Speech House.

Viewpoints

There are any number from which to choose, including the two Barrow Hills, Crickley Hill and Chosen Hill above Churchdown, another of Gurney's favourite haunts.

Pubs

The Boat on Ashleworth Quay changed hands in the wake of the 2014 floods for the first time since Ivor Gurney came but in other respects is very much as he would have known it. The food is simple but good; the local beers and ciders first-rate; the setting by the Severn looking up to Barrow Hill the essence of Gloucestershire.

The Red Lion at Arlingham, which was saved from closure by the local community in 2013, is now a thriving concern specialising in locally produced food, beers and ciders.

In the Forest of Dean, the *Speech House* is worth visiting for its historical significance, even if it is now more of a restaurant and wedding venue than a pub.

The Boat at Ashleworth

Select Bibliography

Ivor Gurney   www.ivorgurneytrust.com
Collected Poems, edited by PJ Kavanagh (1982)
Michael Hurd: *The Ordeal of Ivor Gurney* (1978)
Pamela Blevins: *Ivor Gurney and Marion Scott – Song of Pain and Beauty* (2008)
Eleanor M Rawling: *Ivor Gurney's Gloucestershire* (2011)

Will Harvey   www.fwharveysociety.co.uk
Collected Poems 1912-1957 (1983)
Anthony Boden: *F.W. Harvey – Soldier, Poet* (1988)

Winifred Foley
A Child in the Forest (1974)

Dennis Potter   www.yorksj.ac.uk/potter
The Changing Forest – Life in the Forest of Dean Today (1962)
Pennies from Heaven (1978)
Blue Remembered Hills (1979)
The Singing Detective (1986)
Humphrey Carpenter: *Dennis Potter – The Authorised Biography* (1998)

Chapter Twelve

Last Thoughts

So, a literary journey which began on the Wiltshire Downs with Richard Jefferies, ends in the Forest of Dean with Dennis Potter. The contrasts, between both landscapes and writers, could hardly be starker. But what conclusions and thoughts arise from what we have seen, walked through and read?

First of all, that for all the changes wrought by urban development, agricultural technology, Dutch elm disease and the motor car, our seven counties remain an inspiring part of England. The views of Shropshire from the summit of the Wrekin, of the Severn winding its way to the sea from May Hill, of the Worcestershire Plain from Bredon Hill or the Malverns, of the Wiltshire Downs rolling southwards from their northern escarpment, of the ancient glory of the White Horse galloping along the slopes above its vale, of Oxford's dreaming spires from Boars Hill, and many more beside, are still such as to gladden any heart and fire any creative spirit. Much may have been lost from the fabric of our countryside over the past century or so, but much more still remains.

Something else which I find infinitely reassuring is the interest and enthusiasm which our cast of writers – not all of them household names, by any means – still inspire. Most of them have their own appreciation societies. Some, and not always the best known of them, have their own museums or exhibitions. Then there are the writers' walks: the four 'Mary Webb trails' to take you into deepest, darkest Shropshire, the 'Poets' Paths' which open up the countryside around Dymock (or at least will do, once they are cleared), the Laurie Lee Wildlife Trail and the Dreaming Spires walk on Boars Hill, to name but a few. It can only be a matter of time, surely, given the enthusiasm and ingenuity which is abroad, before we have a Jefferies jaunt on the Wiltshire Downs, a Flora Thompson trail to connect Lark Rise with Candleford and a combined Dennis Potter and Winifred Foley woodland walk through the Forest of Dean.

One other thing which strikes me is how many of the writers sought and found inspiration not just from knowing and loving a particular stretch of country, but by walking through it. For the poets especially – Housman not excepted – getting out into the countryside, to be in amongst the natural world, was an essential part of the creative process. A good brisk walk is also the ideal pace at which to combine enough time to smell the flowers along the way with a new scene around every corner, so that the mental stimulation is both constant and constantly changing. It is an experience which we all can share. Much of this book was written as I went along, walking in the writers' footsteps. I was on my own, left to my own thoughts, but there is absolutely no reason why the inspiration should not be even greater if it springs from an experience shared with kindred spirits. The moral is a simple one – if you want to discover your inner poet or novelist, go for a good long tramp through beautiful countryside. There is nothing quite like it for getting the creative juices to flow!

When Housman wrote of 'the coloured counties', he doubtless had in mind the palette of greens, browns, yellows and blues which the English countryside offers to the eye, when seen from Bredon Hill on a fine summer's day. But there is much more to landscape than vegetation or topography. What brings real colour to the scene are the human, historical and, yes, literary associations of the countryside we are looking at. Nowhere is this more true than in the countryside of England: so much has it witnessed in terms of human conflict and endeavour, and so much great writing has it inspired. The Grand Canyon may be a breathtaking sight, but it won't get you thinking to the same extent that Bredon Hill will, if you understand its history, are aware of its Shakespearean connection and have read your John Moore and Fred Archer. It is thanks as much as anything to their literary associations that our seven counties are so vividly, memorably, meaningfully coloured.

I hope that this book helps readers to a deeper appreciation of some beautiful landscapes, and a greater understanding of what inspired some of our finest writers. If it adds an extra dimension to your enjoyment of the countryside on the one hand, and of the writers on the other, then it will have done its job.

Sunset from Lyth Hill

Acknowledgements

The following are gratefully thanked for their help:

John Light and Mrs Elisabeth Skinner, for Laurie Lee and Frank Mansell;

John Price, Chairman of the Jefferies Society, for Richard Jefferies;

Jonathan Chatwin, for Bruce Chatwin;

Alan Brimson, Honorary Secretary of the Kilvert Trust, for Reverend Francis Kilvert;

Marie Fraser Griffiths of the FW Harvey Society, for Will Harvey;

Michael Christie, for John Drinkwater;

Richard Emeny, Chairman of the Edward Thomas Fellowship, for the Dymock poets;

Jim Smith, Secretary of the Browning Society, for Elizabeth Barrett Browning;

Dr Gladys Mary Coles, for Mary Webb;

Peter Sisley, Treasurer of the Housman Society, for AE Housman;

John Barton of the George Eliot Fellowship, for George Eliot;

Martin Greenwood, for Flora Thompson;

Margi Blunden, for Edmund Blunden;

Sharon Smith, former Curator of Tom Brown's School Museum, for Thomas Hughes;

Simon Lawton, Curator of the John Moore Museum, for John Moore;

Geoff Relph of the Fred Archer Trust, for Fred Archer.

Works are reproduced with the permission of the following copyright holders:

John Murray, an imprint of Hodder and Stoughton Ltd, for *To Stuart Piggott* and *Uffington*, from *Collected Poems* by John Betjeman;

Random House Group Ltd for *Putting in the Seed* and *Iris by Night*, from *The Collected Poems* by Robert Frost;

Peters Fraser and Dunlop Ltd for extracts from the *Brensham Trilogy* by John Moore;

David Higham Agents for extracts from *Village Sketches* by Edmund Blunden and *Edward Thomas – The Last Four Years* by Eleanor Farjeon;

Curtis Brown Group Ltd, for WH Auden and Laurie Lee;

Judy Greenway, for Wilfrid Gibson;

Elaine Jackson, on behalf of Mrs Eileen Griffiths, daughter of Will Harvey;

Elizabeth Swaffield, for Flora Thompson;

Aitken Alexander, for Bruce Chatwin;

Society of Authors, for John Masefield;

Ampersand Agency, for Winifred Foley;

Fred Archer Trust;

Estate of Dennis Potter.

Illustrations

The two maps, on pages 8 and 157, were created by Susanna Kendall.

The photographs of places have been taken by the author Anthony Gibson, with the exception of the Sheepscombe cricket ground, which appears by kind permission of Arunabha Sengupta.

Geoff Relph kindly supplied the photograph of Fred Archer.

The following portraits appear by permission of the National Portrait Gallery:
Richard Jefferies *(by William Strang, c. 1880-1902)*
Walter Scott *(by Edwin Landseer, 1824)*
Thomas Hughes *(by Julia Margaret Cameron, 1865)*
GK Chesterton *(by EH Mills, 1909)*
John Betjeman *(by Howard Coster, 1953)*
Thomas Hardy *(by William Strang, 1893)*
Matthew Arnold *(by GF Watts, 1880)*
Robert Bridges *(by Will Stroud, 1923)*
Edmund Blunden *(by Lady Ottoline Morrell, 1920)*
William Shakespeare *(oil painting, c. 1600-1610)*
George Eliot *(by London Stereoscopic and Photographic Company, undated)*
AE Housman *(by Francis Dodd, 1926)*
John Masefield *(by Elliott and Fry, 1910s)*
Elizabeth Barrett Browning *(by Michele Gordigliani, 1858)*
Lascelles Abercrombie *(by Walter Stoneman, 1937)*
Edward Thomas *(by FH Evans, 1904)*
John Drinkwater *(by William Rothenstein, 1918)*
Arthur Quiller-Couch *(Wills cigarette card, after Walter Benington, 1937)*

Index

WITH MAGIC IN MY EYES
West Country Literary Landscapes
Anthony Gibson
foreword by Michael Morpurgo

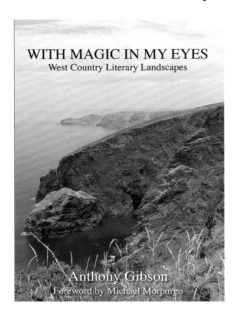

A wonderful book. A book of exploration. Here we can walk the landscapes of the West Country in the writers' footsteps. We don't just get to know this inspiring landscape anew; we get to feel it as the writers all did. **Michael Morpurgo**

A rare book and a glorious one.
Clive Aslet, *Country Life*

A fount of knowledge. I felt as if I was learning something on every page.
Thomas Hardy Society Journal

A splendid and proper book, elegantly designed, fluently written and brimming with fascinating content.
Dartmoor Online

The companion volume to *The Coloured Counties*, *With Magic in my Eyes* covers the four most westerly counties: Cornwall, Devon, Somerset and Dorset.

Among the featured writers are Thomas Hardy, Henry Williamson, Daphne du Maurier, Samuel Taylor Coleridge, John Fowles, Ted Hughes, John Betjeman, Charles Causley, John Cowper Powys, Arthur Conan Doyle, RD Blackmore, William Barnes, Jack Clemo and Virginia Woolf.

A 288-page hardback, with 100 colour photographs.

Available for **£20 post free** from:

Fairfield Books
17 George's Road, Bath BA1 6EY
tel: 01225-335813
www.fairfieldbooks.org.uk